The

JANUS VIEW

*from the American Academy
in Rome: Essays on the Janiculum*

Edited by
KATHERINE A. GEFFCKEN *and* NORMA W. GOLDMAN

THE AMERICAN ACADEMY IN ROME – 2007

ISBN 1-879549-15-8

Orders for the book may be sent only to the American Academy in Rome, 7 E. 60th Street, New York, NY 10022, or more directly via the Academy website: www. aarome.org under Publications. Along with all the Academy books, *The Janus View* is listed with instructions for ordering. Orders may also be sent to the Rome address: Via Angelo Masina 5; 00153 Rome, Italy.

Grateful acknowledgement is made to Academy Trustee William B. Hart and his wife Constance Eaton for their generous financial gift to the American Academy making the publication of this book possible.

Published by Mundus Media, 616 Rochester Road; Clawson, MI 48107; phone: 248-535-6134; mundus@comcast.net, but distributed by the American Academy in Rome using AAR addresses or via the direct order website: www. aarome.org

Mundus Media in Europe can be contacted at Mundus Verlag GmbH; Im Teelbruch 60; D 45219 Essen, Germany. Mundus Media is a global trademark listed in the ERC and the USA. It is an affiliate of Athenaion Press, Phaidon Press, and Magnus Press.

The Janus View was designed by Michael Savitski of Savitski Design at 102 Nickels Arcade; Ann Arbor, MI 48104. It was printed at Thomson-Shore, Inc.; 7300 W. Joy Road in Dexter, MI 48130.

Opposite the title page is the Janus-head seal located over the entrance to the Academy's McKim, Mead & White Main Building. The seal was designed by William Mitchell Kendall, an architect in the firm of McKim, Mead & White. It was executed by Gorham Phillips Stevens, head of the Academy's School of Fine Arts, in collaboration with Harry Thrasher, Fellow of the American Academy in Rome 1914. (C. Huemer, "Notes on the Janus-head Seal," unpublished ms. AAR, 2002).

INTRODUCTION

O n behalf of the American Academy in Rome, I would like to thank editors Katherine A. Geffcken and Norma Wynick Goldman for their tireless efforts in the creation of *The Janus View from the American Academy in Rome: Essays on the Janiculum*. Fellows, Residents, Trustees, Officers, staff members, and visitors to the American Academy quickly become aware that our ten-building, eleven-acre site occupies hallowed ground. Like any spot in Rome, it is accumulated layers of history — from ancient times to the present — all part of a continuous record that is fundamental to Western Civilization.

Geffcken and Goldman, students and ardent admirers of the Academy, have gathered an impressive group of essays that cover most aspects of the Janiculum's history. Although not one of the storied Seven Hills of Rome — it lies outside the boundaries of the ancient city — the Janiculum is the highest hill within the Papal walls of Rome and is named for the uniquely Roman god Janus, the Academy's patron deity.

Written by Academy hands of all ages and specializations, *The Janus View* conveys the most richly detailed history to date of our own buildings, walls, orchards, and gardens. It includes stories about the heroes of the 1849 battles on the Janiculum between the forces of Garibaldi and those of the French fighting to restore papal rule, some of whose names are carried on nearby streets: Masina, Medici, Garibaldi, and Manara. It contains stories about Scarpone (still the restaurant of choice for many of us on a Sunday night), the Acqua Paola, Trajan's aqueduct, the mills, the Syrian Sanctuary, the church of San Pietro in Montorio and Bramante's Tempietto (built on what was once thought to be the place of St. Peter's crucifixion), and many other sites on the Janiculum. The nineteenth and twentieth century history of the area is particularly welcome, as it is harder to come by.

We who have the good fortune to live at the Academy come to see that we are momentary stewards of a place that has been hospitable to human habitation for thousands of years. An important part of our stewardship involves understanding what has transpired in times past — in the words of Horace, "the smoke and wealth and din of Rome," — protecting our historic site from unnecessary change, and com-

municating and handing down our story to our successors. This book will help us to carry out these tasks.

Known as a god of passage, Janus is the patron symbol of the American Academy in Rome. Traditionally represented with two faces looking in opposite directions, the image of Janus perfectly captures the spirit of the American Academy community [fig. 1]. As artists and scholars working and living in Rome, we are nourished by the past while we work our way into the future. We salute Katherine A. Geffcken, FAAR '55, and Norma Wynick Goldman, CSAAR and Visiting Scholar off and on from '80 to '06, for helping us on that journey with this book.

— Adele Chatfield-Taylor, FAAR '84,
President, American Academy in Rome

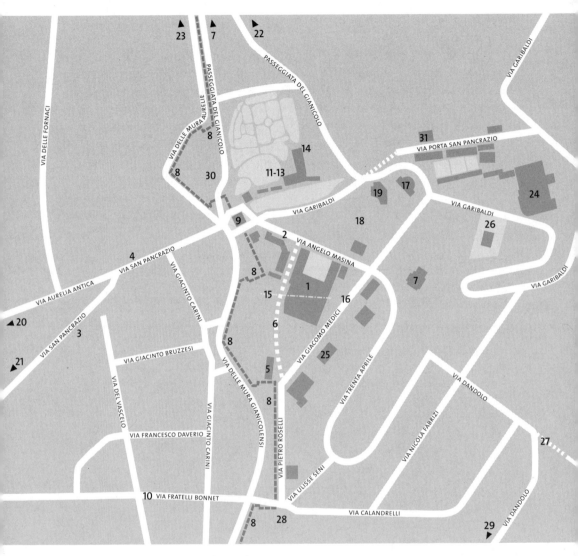

Fig. 2. Map of the Janiculum area. Numbers on the map are keyed to the Table of Contents.

N.B.: Several of the Chapters are beyond the extent of the map. They are indicated by an arrow in their direction.

TABLE OF CONTENTS

[keyed to the map opposite, fig. 2]

Preface

One need look no further than the American Academy in Rome Main Building with its impressive palazzo entrance, its serene cortile with the central Hercules fountain, and its secluded garden beyond the cortile with the historic Casa Rustica on the low hill above the ruins of the Casino Malvasia to experience the beauty of the Academy and its grounds. When one adds the Chiaraviglio and the private garden next to it across from the Academy gate, the Villa Aurelia, and the Villa Richardson, all visible from the balustraded roof terrace of the Main Building with its panoramic views of the entire city of Rome, one begins to appreciate the wealth of historic splendor encompassed in the Academy experience. In the interior of the Main Building, the Library alone is a treasure, its books and periodicals stored on four floors. The elegance of the Salone, the friendliness of the Pool Room, the social attraction of the Bar make the AAR memorable. The amiable staff assures that all activities within the AAR work smoothly; the staff members make coming to the Academy a delight and a privilege.

The following chapters have been written by those who return frequently to the Academy and who have learned about the history of the area from years of seeing and researching the sights along the Via Masina, the Via Medici, Pietro Roselli, and Fratelli Bonnet on the way to and from the 75 and 44 bus lines. Some chapters are revisions of articles that appeared in the *Newsletters* of the Classical Society of the American Academy in Rome (CSAAR). Many of the chapters represent study of previously unexplored areas. To all of the authors we owe our thanks for their insight and research.

We are indebted to President Adele Chatfield-Taylor for her enthusiastic support of our idea of collecting these essays and to Wayne Linker, former Executive Secretary of the AAR, for his unfailing help and good judgment. We are grateful to former Director Caroline Bruzelius for her support of our project and to former Director Lester Little for approving our efforts and recommending the forthcoming book to the new Fellows. We are especially grateful to Director Carmela Franklin and to Associate Director for External Affairs R. William Franklin for their enthusiastic interest in our project. We thank the staff of the Library and the Photographic

Archive at the American Academy in Rome: Christina Huemer, Denise Gavio, Antonio Palladino, and Lavinia Ciuffa for helping with research of books, articles, and photographs. In her many years of service in the Academy Library, former librarian Antonella Bucci was an unfailing source of information. We are indebted to Karl E. Longstreth, Head of the Map Library at the University of Michigan, for his aid in obtaining copies of maps. We thank Antonio Ortolan for his photographic skills and Jon Cooper for digitizing precious Academy photographs. To Gary Dwyer, photographer, we express our thanks for his superb color images, which we have translated into black and white. For his sensitive black and white photography, as well as his editorial skills, we thank Bernard M. Goldman. We are indebted to Architect Elisa Silva for her skill in preparing the new, up-to-date maps in the book. We also wish to thank Thomas Moeller for supervising the digitizing of the illustrations in the book, and we thank Armand Banooni for the careful digitizing of these illustrations.

For their hospitality at the Italian Institute of Germanic Studies in the Villa Sciarra-Wurts, we are most grateful to Head of Conferences Giuliana Todini and Librarian Bruno Berni. For similar hospitality, we thank Sandra Carraro for permission to photograph in the garden of the Bosco Parrasio. To the Sforza Cesarini family, we give special thanks for the tour of the Villa Sforza-Cesarini and for permission to photograph from the roof. We were delighted at the opportunity to enter through the door in the Michelangeo Façade so that we could view the works inside the Janiculum Reservoir, thanks to the kindness of Cristiano Franceschini, who generously shared his knowledge of the aqueduct system with us. We thank Daniela Scialanga of the Biblioteca Anglica for permission to have the professional photographer at their Library photograph the Botanical Garden from one of the rare books in that fine collection. We also thank Mike Vitale from the NY Office of the AAR for his help in locating and sending photographs.

We are especially grateful to Academy Trustee Willliam B. Hart and his wife Constance Eaton for the generous funding of this publication to see it successfully into print. Without their support the book would not become a reality.

We owe a special thanks to Christina Huemer, who provided computer liaison between the producer of the book in Ann Arbor, Michigan, and a printer at the AAR Library so that Kathy Geffcken could edit the text while she was in Rome. Christina also contributed her editing skills to the text. We also thank editor, author, and Fellow Dave King, my neighbor at the AAR, who took time from writing his second novel to help with editing the last twelve chapers.

We wish to express appreciation to Richard and Joanne Kinney for encouraging this project and for contributing their advice and expertise. We especially thank book designer Joanne Kinney for donating her services to the trial layout and design of the book. For their driving skills and generous donation of time to my work,

I thank my good friends Sally Rubiner and Sandra Sherman, who transported me and the manuscript many times to and from Ann Arbor so that I could consult with the book designer. We thank the talented and sensitive book designer Michael Savitski, for his expertise in the design of the present volume, and we thank him for his patience with all of our changes as he transformed a typed manuscript into a printed book. Finally, for his faith in our scholarship, we thank Walter Stender of Mundus Media for accepting the publication of our book.

— Norma Wynick Goldman, June 2007

While in Rome off and on from 1979 to 1992, I had the great fortune to live in a *superattico*, a modest roof-top dwelling, at Piazza San Pancrazio overlooking Villa Doria Pamphilj. The broad views I enjoyed from high up on that tall building led me to look widely around and wonder in fresh ways about the landscape stretching out below me. I watched sunsets behind Algardi's Belrespiro in the Villa, but nearer I saw Prince Doria Pamphilj's Arch of the Quattro Venti. And so began my interest in the history and buildings of the Janiculum, especially in the battles for the Roman Republic of 1849 that took place on terrain I walked daily from San Pancrazio to the grounds of the American Academy.

I am extremely grateful to Norma Goldman, then editor of the *Newsletter* of the Classical Society of the American Academy in Rome, for welcoming and publishing my first essays on the Janiculum, and for being the hardworking, driving force behind the present volume. To subsequent editors of the *Newsletters* I am also grateful, Brian Rose and Susan Wood, as well as to the officers and staff of the Academy who have encouraged our research. And to those who have contributed essays to this volume, many thanks. For the names of those who have especially helped and cheered me on, please see the Acknowledgements in the Appendix, p. 277.

In assembling this collection of essays, we have not aimed to cover every important spot. Nor have we tried to replace any of the standard guides. As will be evident in the references and endnotes following many chapters, we have ourselves frequently turned to the fascicles of the *Guide Rionali di Roma* that cover the Janiculum and also to the Associazione Montedoro's *Il Balcone di Rome: da Montedoro a Monteverde*. Instead, we have tried to bring together history, topography, buildings, and people, all presented through the eyes of observers ever eager to learn about our splendid Roman neighborhood.

— Katherine A. Geffcken, April, 2006

Aerial view of the top of the Janiculum Hill, ca. 1950.
Photograph, Photographic Archive of the AAR.

FOREWORD

Those who come to the American Academy in Rome on the Janiculum should know about the history of the grounds on which the Academy buildings and their neighbors are located and about the origin of the names of the streets surrounding the area. This book is intended to do just that. Most of the streets are named for Garibaldini, the soldiers who fought in the crucial battle of 1849 defending Rome against the French attacking the city. Some of the ruins from that battle are still visible.

Immediately one begins to ask questions about the area: What was the Casa Rustica originally? What existed here on the top of the Janiculum before the Academy was built in the first quarter of the twentieth century? How did the Academy come to have the Villa Aurelia as part of its property? Who built the walls encircling the garden? The answers to these questions lie in the present volume. We are supplying answers to the questions one would ask when coming to the Academy for the first time, or after many visits [fig. 2, numbers on the map are keyed to the Chapter numbers].

Those who have walked the parks nearby — the Janiculum Passeggiata with the statue of Garibaldi, the Villas Sciarra, and Doria Pamphilj — will want to know from what estates these parks have been created. They want to know about the walls visible from the back garden, along Pietro Roselli, and behind the Villa Sciarra. Who built them and when? What were they designed to enclose and keep out? What enemy did the Roman Emperor Aurelian fear? What invasion did Pope Urban VIII fear? We have given some historical background of the Janiculum, a name traditionally associated with the god Janus. We have recreated the traumatic times when Garibaldi and his troops defended the city. We have included the earlier history of the hill when the aqueducts, commissioned first by Augustus and later by Trajan, ran along the Via Aurelia and continued under the present Academy grounds. Water from these lines satisfied not only domestic need, but also supplied power for the mills at the top of the hill, one of which has been documented by recent excavations in Via Medici and on the Academy grounds. As restored by Pope Paul V, the Trajanic line today still fills the present Acqua Paola. The aqueduct waters of the Augustan Alsietina probably descended originally to fill the *naumachia*, an enormous artificial

Fig. 3. Bust of J. Pierpont Morgan by
Albin Polasek, FAAR 1913, in the Cortile of
the AAR. Photograph, K. A. Geffcken, 2005.

lake in the valley below where mock naval battles were held, a site as yet unidentified, but where today the Viale Trastevere runs its course, with its center possibly near the former Standa (now Oviesse) Department Store.

We have included chapters on the Villa Aurelia, which was given as a bequest in the will of its American owner, Mrs. Clara Jessup Heyland. That gift and the lure of the Janiculum moved John Pierpont Morgan [fig. 3] to acquire the adjacent land presently occupied by the Main Building, a grand *palazzo* designed by the architectural firm of McKim, Mead & White. A chapter on the Casa Rustica explains how it was built on the mound above the foundations of the original larger building, the Casino Malvasia. The Casino Malvasia was destroyed in the battle of 1849 when the French broke through the wall overcoming the forces of Garibaldi.

Outside the walls the *osteria* (inn) called Scarpone (now a restaurant) and the remains of the Vascello are described, as well as the role they played in efforts by

Fig. 4. Aerial view of the area at the top of the Janiculum, showing many of the sites described in the present book, dated Spring, 1925. Photograph, Photographic Archive of the AAR.

Italian defenders to hold French attackers at bay. A chapter on the Aurelian and Papal Walls is included, as well as a chapter on one of the most notable features at the top of the hill, the Porta San Pancrazio. There is also a chapter on the Church of San Pancrazio, for whom the Porta is named.

The four main properties of the American Academy in Rome, covering eleven acres of land, include the following structures: the Villa Aurelia; the Main Building with its gardens and the Villa Bellacci; the Chiaraviglio and its gardens; and the Villa Richardson with its adjacent garden. The last, guarded by *carabinieri*, is presently leased to the American Ambassador to the Vatican, whose gala 4th of July reception we all watch with interest. For all who walk the grounds of the Academy and the parks and streets in the adjacent areas, this book explains the background of what you are seeing firsthand [fig. 4].

— Norma Wynick Goldman, Editor

TOP

Fig. 1. 1. The Main Building. Photograph, Photographic Archive of the AAR, 1914.

ABOVE

Fig. 1. 2. The Main Building under construction. Photograph, Photographic Archive of the AAR, 1913.

CHAPTER 1

McKim, Mead & White
Academy Main Building

Steven Bedford

Addendum on the Library by Christina Huemer

The Main Building of the American Academy in Rome, designed by the architectural firm of McKim, Mead & White, is a grand *palazzo* housing the essential working spaces for the Academy [fig. 1. 1 & fig. 1. 2]. It contains the offices for the staff, both administrative and financial. It provides living and working rooms, study rooms, and studios for the Fellows who win the coveted Rome Prize – scholars, architects, landscape architects, painters, sculptors, composers of music, novelists, and poets. Surrounding the central *cortile* [fig. 1. 3] are the *salone* [fig. 1. 4], billiard room [fig. 1. 5], dining room [fig. 1. 6], the bar [fig. 1. 7], and kitchen. Most important, the Main Building contains the Academy Library [fig. 1. 8], with reading rooms on the ground floor and the books themselves on open shelves on floors above and below. Originally the Main Building contained also an archaeology study area, a cast collection of sculptures, and a costume storeroom.[1] Of these only the archaeology laboratory exists today, now in the Casa Rustica.

In 1991, the Main Building was 77 years old and in need of renovation. Its longstanding physical problems required immediate remedy to meet the European Economic Community mandates, which required a new standard of electrical service. ENEL (Ente Nazionale per l'Energia), the national utility, had set a timetable for compliance that forced the Academy to act. The Academy viewed these ENEL requirements as an opportunity to renovate the entire Main Building.

The first step in the renovation was the preparation of a Master Plan, a plan crucial in guiding work on the structure. To ensure that all voices were heard, the Plant and Planning Committee solicited suggestions for renovation from Academy Fellows, visiting scholars, and periodic guests. All comments and proposals were used to assist the Committee in deciding what was necessary to prepare the Main Building for its continued use. A Historic Structures Report (HSR), documenting the original design and assessing all the changes made to the building over time, was prepared as part of the renovation process. The work on the HSR has provided us with a history of the origins of the Main Building, the Academy property, and some of the many changes.

As planning proceeded, it was clear that the necessary construction would

TOP

Fig. 1. 3. The Cortile with the
Hercules fountain by Paul Manship.
Photograph, Photographic Archive of
the AAR, 1939.

ABOVE

Fig. 1. 4. The Salone. Photograph,
G. Dwyer, 2005.

require the closing of the building for the entire 1992-93 academic year and part of 1993-94, with preliminary work on the Library starting in August 1991. The Library reopened in November 1991, and it stayed open, accessed by a wooden tunnel walkway down the right side of the *cortile*, to serve scholars while the renovation of the building was in progress from fall 1992 until early 1994.

On May 5, 1911, the Academy acquired the deed of ownership to the Villa Aurelia, a property whose location matched the aspirations of the institution. The American owner, Mrs. Clara Jessup Heyland, had died on September 13, 1909, and bequeathed her Villa to the Academy. High upon the Janiculum, the Villa looked over the nearby Spanish Academy and faced, across Rome, the French Academy at Villa Medici. This symbolic position was one that the trustees certainly could not ignore, particularly considering the remote location of the Academy at that time, beyond Porta Pia in the Villa Mirafiori, which the Academy had purchased in 1906. Villa Aurelia, however, was too small to accommodate the needs of the Academy even as it was then constituted. Given the impending merger with the American School of Classical Studies, then with offices and library in rather tight quarters at Villa Bonghi, the need to create proper facilities for a newly expanded Academy reached almost crisis proportions.

As early as 1906, Frank Millet, a painter and one of the incorporators of the Academy, who served the Academy in a multiplicity of roles including trustee, executive secretary and chief administrative officer, had foreseen this problem and had urged Academy founder Charles McKim [fig. 1. 9] that the Academy:

Fig. 1. 6. The Dining Room with Gabriel Soare. Photograph, N. Goldman, 2004.

Fig. 1. 7. The Bar with Jean Davison at the table, Gabriel Soare behind the counter, and F. Thomas Luongo (FAAR 2006) at the bar. Photograph, N. Goldman, 2005.

build [its] own building and show . . . how . . . much better we have taken to heart the lessons of the past . . . , show . . . what we can do and how we can be modern and not forget the masters of the past.[2]

J. Pierpont Morgan shared Millet's goal and, once the Academy acquired full title to the Villa Aurelia in 1911, he quietly began investigating the purchase of property opposite the Villa. This would serve eventually as the site of the Main Building.

In May 1911, William Rutherford Mead, President of the Academy and the only surviving partner of the firm of McKim, Mead & White, fearing that Morgan would donate land but not the funds to develop the property, went to Paris (where Morgan was staying at the time) and asked Morgan what his intentions were. Morgan suggested that the Academy initiate plans with the understanding that he would partially underwrite the cost of any new construction.

Mead and his associate, William Mitchell Kendall, went to work designing a structure large enough to accommodate the Academy. A scheme worked out and presented to Morgan in 1911 earned ". . . his approval in every particular," and he reaffirmed his financial support for the project. Despite great trepidations over the financial health of the Academy, the trustees approved Mead's initial plan and accepted Morgan's offer. A watercolor rendering, which may be the original scheme, was found among the records donated to the Academy by the firm. It depicts a vast building with two courtyards, one of which butted up against the Villino Bellacci. Curiously, the building turned its back on the Villa Aurelia. The partially sloping northern façade, facing the Villa, was devoted to large windows for studios, while the drawings for the eastern and western façades were reminiscent of McKim, Mead & White's design for the Boston Public Library. The eastern façade was to serve as the main entrance.

The initial design was further refined by Mead, Millet, Jesse Benedict Carter (Director of the Classical School and after the merger Director of the Academy), and George S. Koyl, FAAR '14 in Architecture, in Rome between February and April, 1912. A member of the McKim, Mead & White staff, Gorham Phillips Stevens, was

Fig. 1. 8. The Library. Photograph, Photographic Archive of the AAR, 1925.

sent to Rome in December 1911, as Director of the Academy. He would supervise final plans on the spot. In order to deal with the Rome authorities and secure building permits, they engaged the services of an Italian architect, Filippo Galassi. Galassi believed that the imposing and massive scheme worked out in New York would not be approved because new construction on the Janiculum was limited to buildings conforming to the residential character of the area. Indeed, the Rome authorities turned down the plans. Accepting Galassi's view, Mead, Millet and Koyl (and Stevens) started a new scheme on March 24, 1912. An undated drawing by Koyl laid out the basic idea: the part with the courtyards was retained but reversed, now facing and responding to Villa Aurelia. The building's organization was quite simple, with the open forecourt of the entry flanked by the most public elements of the Academy – the classical library and museum. Adjoining these buildings, in separate pavilions, were architectural studios and an art library. Rising above this court was a broad, three-story block containing painting and sculpture studios. Appended to the south was a two-story residential court. This final scheme became, more or less, the building as constructed. Galassi immediately set to work preparing drawings and estimates. To speed the process, Gorham Stevens was recruited to make drawings for the new building. After more consultations with Morgan in Paris over the revised plans, construction contracts were put out to bid on June 10, 1912. Ground was broken on the Fourth of July, a particularly appropriate day, with the major contract calling for the building to be roofed by May 31, 1913 and totally completed by February 28, 1914.

Fig. 1. 9. Charles Follen McKim (1849-1909), of McKim, Mead & White, first President of the AAR. Photograph, Photographic Archive of the AAR.

During the summer of 1912, Mead, in New York, revised the elevations, requiring that Kendall travel to Rome in September of 1912 to change the drawings and, subsequently, to reapply for approval from the authorities. Once again, in order to complete the drawings, Gorham Stevens and the entire Rome-based leadership of the Academy were enlisted, provoking Stevens to complain that too much of his time had been employed in making drawings for the new building and that too little was left to spend with the Fellows. Stevens's dissatisfaction must have been somewhat allayed by J. Pierpont Morgan's decision to pay the entire cost of the new building when he visited Rome on his way to Naples, his health obviously failing, in January of 1913. The year before, Morgan had bought the Villa Chiaraviglio house and garden [fig. 1. 10] on January 2, 1912. Morgan had also proposed buying the adjacent Villino Bellacci [fig. 1. 11], which consisted of the main house, garden, and a tiny gardener's cottage next to it on Via Medici. Morgan directed that Carter offer a low price for the property. Carter found that the owner wanted 200,000 lire and also that the owner was "getting interested in a law suit, the favorite Italian pastime, . . . against the Academy to have us compelled to alter the shape of our building and to prevent us from erecting the studio which lies next to the villa." This threat resulted in the Academy's buying the Villino Bellacci for 192,500 lire, through the beneficence of Morgan.[3] Two weeks before the Academy acquired the property, this friend of the Academy had died. Morgan's son honored his father's pledge, and the Bellacci Villino thus became property of the AAR.

As happens with most similar projects, the Main Building was not completed on time. It was "roofed" by the specified date, but the interior work proceeded at a much more measured pace. Director Stevens was again pressed into service, preparing many of the drawings for the interior and supervising their execution. The typical construction practice of the period required that pieces of ornament and important architectural details be modeled in plaster and then, once approved by Stevens, be reproduced in the finished material. Stevens also ensured that the color scheme for the outside stucco, developed by Kendall in 1912, was carried out "as nearly as possible." Curiously, as the building went up, it became a local tourist attraction, bringing some 1,500 Roman sightseers to the top of the Janiculum.

Other problems threatened to delay further the opening of the building. Both 1913 and 1914 were years plagued by strikes of all trades, including a fifty-five-day strike by the travertine cutters. In the final months of construction, labor problems were exacerbated by Italy's general mobilization for World War I. While Kendall worked up to the last minute designing the shield over the main door, what worried the trustees was the new danger to transatlantic shipping, which was starting to delay the arrival of donated furniture and fittings, including a massive billiard

TOP

Fig. 1. 10. The Chiaraviglio. Photograph, Photographic Archive of the AAR, 1925.

ABOVE

Fig. 1. 11. The Villino Bellacci, acquired with funds from Morgan in 1913. Photograph, Photographic Archive of the AAR, 1930.

table from Paris. When the furnishings arrived to complete the interior, the new building finally opened on October 1, 1914, having cost $276,500 to build and another $12,000 to furnish.

The building, as finally completed, is organized around a series of courtyards. The first, flanked by four rusticated pavilions housing the sculptors' studios, serves as an entry court affording an excellent view of the main façade. The rustication and general organization bring to mind Villa Lante in Bagnaia, but the building also seems to rely on Roman precedents, although no identifiable structure can be cited. The idea of ascending a staircase inside the front door is not Roman at all, but is very much like the sixteenth century palaces, many designed by Galeazzo Alessi, in Genoa. McKim, Mead & White frequently drew upon designs illustrated in Letarouilly's *Édifices de Rome Moderne*, but a plate matching the building's façade cannot be found. The strong, rusticated ground floor supporting a stuccoed upper story enlivened by double height pilasters is very common in the work of Antonio Sangallo, the younger, especially in his Zecca in Rome, the present-day Palazzo del Banco di Santo Spirito. It is also evident on the base and façade of Palazzo Caffarelli-Vidoni in Rome and Sanmicheli's Palazzo Canossa in Verona. However, the corner juncture of the quoining and pilasters seems awkward and surprising in a building whose history indicates that adjustments were constantly being made to the design. This motif had been used with greater success by Vignola in the Palazzo Farnese in Caprarola. In examining the architectural treatment of this façade, one can see that the architects, in reducing the height of the building at the corners, were attempting to reduce the visible mass of the building and make the structure more acceptable to the Roman bureaucracy.

The west façade along the now de-mapped Via Paolo Narducci (part of which survives as the Vicolo Cieco) is much more successful. Articulated as a series of separate buildings, the treatment disguises the great depth and size of the building. Again the windows seem to refer to such great Renaissance models as the Palazzo Farnese in Rome, but do not appear to match any specific source.

As originally planned, the Academy's major public rooms were grouped around the ground floor of the court, whose decoration is typically Roman, clearly based on the Palazzo Altemps or the remarkably similar old University of Rome (La Sapienza), now housing the State Archives. One enters the court through a grand vestibule, which in the original design was intended to give access to the cast museum, archaeology museum and architects' library. The main library, facing the former Via Paolo Narducci, was inspired by the Piccolomini library in Siena, its walls intentionally left blank for decoration by future Fellows in mural painting. The exterior shape of the Main Building is sheared off at the right rear corner to accommodate the former road.

The upper floors of the building were clearly organized for an almost monastic lifestyle of study, work and sleep, reflecting the trustees' original intention that all male Fellows focus on their studies, virtually pledging celibacy. There were no provisions in the building for female Fellows or for Students of the Classical School.

Fig. 1. 12. The Cryptoporticus in the Sotterraneo of the Main Building. Photograph, B. Goldman, 2003.

Around the court small studies are separated, in the English manner, from the Fellows' bedrooms. Double-height architects' and painters' studios with bedrooms across the hall, create the mass above the entry to the building. The extra height of these rooms allowed the insertion of a mezzanine containing rooms for servants (now converted into apartments).[4]

Given the fact that the Main Building is an early twentieth century American vision of what a Roman villa should be, and that it was the collaborative effort of at least five architects and one patron, placing the building in some kind of critical context is rather daunting, especially when written from this side of the Atlantic. I think one can safely say that the structure is a competent example of its type, and considering the number of "cooks in the stew," a very successful joint effort. The building appears to rest easily among its more august neighbors, as it should, projecting a dignified image influenced by quiet confidence.

As the needs of the Academy have changed, the building has changed only slightly to accommodate new conditions. Gone are the architects' library, the cast sculpture and costume collections. The Library has gained by leaps and bounds, expanding into spaces which once held coal bins. Obviously the technological expectations of modern artists and scholars – and the comparable overhaul of modern mores – are issues very different from those that guided the original design of the New Building. The renovation of the 1990's, which addressed these contemporary needs, did so without rending the historic fabric of the McKim, Mead & White Main Building. In the individual bedrooms, the large closets were converted into baths with private showers and lavatory facilities, eliminating the need for communal bathrooms. Another result of this renovation was the clearing of the original cryptoporticus in the *sotterraneo* lit by glass panels in the *cortile* arcade above [fig. 1. 12]. This area can now can be used as an exhibition gallery and space for occasional concerts. In addition, a much needed and often used assembly hall has been installed in the area under the *salone*, providing an ideal space for lectures and small conferences.

◈ **NOTES**

1   In the original plans, the cast collection was to be arranged in a room as a museum, as was the costume collection. However, the cast sculpture pieces were, in fact, distributed throughout the Main Building (see Archives of American Art, AAR papers, microfilm reel #5756, Mead to Stevens, 26 May, 1914), and the museum as a separate space never materialized. The collection of costumes was stored in a room on the *primo piano*, and some of the costumes were taken from it for special events. Stevens refers to them in his diary, but finally he decreed that the costumes had become too fragile and were no longer to be used. Both the cast sculpture and the costume collection are no longer at the Academy. Their location, if they still exist, is unknown.

2   This chapter is the result of an investigation of all major American archives for information on the American Academy in Rome's New Building. Archives consulted included the Academy's own files in New York, the Archives of American Art, some Academy files in Rome, Avery Archives at Columbia University, University of Pennsylvania Architectural Archives, Museum of the City of New York, Amherst College, and the New York Historical Society. The only fruitful repositories were the Academy itself and its records at the Archives of American Art. The New York Historical Society appears to have more information on the building in its McKim, Mead & White Archives, but the files relating to the building have been lost or misplaced. That institution's continued closure has prevented extensive searching. An earlier version of this chapter appeared in AMACADMY, Summer, 1991.

3   Carter to Mead, Rome 29 January 1913, (Archives of American Art, AAR papers, microfilm reel #5754; also on #5754 see Carter to J. P. Morgan. Jr., 20 March, 1913). Purchase date was April 13, 1913. On Prince Torlonia and Cesarina Bellacci, see Addendum to Villa Sforza Cesarini, pp. 159-161.

4   After World War II, one female member of the staff continued to live on the mezzanine, but since the other rooms were then assigned to women Fellows, it became known for years as "the women's corridor."

◈ **ADDENDUM**

THE ACADEMY LIBRARY

Christina Huemer

T he Library retains many of the features of the original McKim, Mead & White design, although it has expanded far beyond the space originally allotted to it. The original entrance vestibule was in the northwest corner, where the Barbara Goldsmith Rare Book Room is now located. This room was also connected by a door to the collections of antiquities in the Museum (the present Exhibition Galleries). Readers entered the main reading room (now known as the Arthur Ross Reading Room), from the north end. The use of alcoves, which permits the housing of many books in a relatively small space, is typical of several libraries designed by the McKim, Mead & White firm, such as the library of the University Club in New York and the Avery Library at Columbia University. Indeed, the wooden furniture (in Italian walnut) is modeled on that of the Avery Library. With its high ceiling and walnut furnishings, the Library maintains the feeling of a university college or a gentlemen's club. The vault of the main reading room was inspired by that of the Piccolomini Library in Siena, as were the moldings and trim. The center of the room was occupied by a bronze candelabrum copied (by Gorham Phillips Stevens) from a fifteenth century candelabrum in the cathedral of Pistoia and fabricated by Galleria Sangiorgi in Rome. Bronze busts of Academy notables were added to the decoration beginning in 1917.

Early published plans show a separate Architects' Library adjacent to the Museum, but this seems not to have remained there for long. Instead, the art and architecture books from the Academy's library in Villa Mirafiori were soon integrated into the new classification system developed by Albert Van Buren, the Librarian at the time of the move.

The Catalogue Room, adjacent to the stairwell, which housed a series of wooden card-catalogue cabinets from 1928 to 2003, now hosts a bank of computer terminals.

The Linda Bettman Reference Room, on the southwest corner, first housed the Library's photograph collection and later became a periodical room. This room's irregular shape owes its origin to the fact that a road through the back garden of the Academy, the Via Narducci (see Chapter 6) continuing from Via Pietro Roselli to meet Via Angelo Masina, once cut off the corner of the building. The wooden shelves and balustrade in the Reference Room were not part of the original design, but were added in 1928/29.

It was not long before the collections expanded beyond the reading rooms and into the basement below. Stacks for lesser-used books were installed immediately on the two levels below, while a full mezzanine and a rare-book cage were added in the mid-1960's, and the Library eventually expanded into the west side of the cryptoporticus and north into the old coal bins. The collection, now ten times the size of the library that moved here in 1914, occupies the lower levels of the whole west side of the building, plus three rooms of compact shelving in the building next door (5B).

In the original plan, the Library was completed by a Librarian's office and a cataloguing room on the ground floor on the south side of the building. The entrance to the Library is now in this corner of the courtyard. In 1996, the Barbara Goldsmith Rare Book Room, designed by Michael Graves, took over the old entry vestibule (later the Fototeca Unione), re-establishing the original connection to the Arthur Ross Reading Room. The Academy's photographic collections and the Fototeca Unione are now united in the Photographic Archive, which occupies the rear building at Via Angelo Masina 5B.

A new renovation of the Library began in the late summer of 2006, scheduled to be completed in September of 2007. This project was designed to improve the use of space within the present boundaries of the Library and to provide for future growth. The plans called for a new reading room in the cryptoporticus, new folio shelving for large volumes, compact shelving for periodicals, increased seating throughout the Library, and a more logical order for the collections. The overall intent of the restoration is to help the Library to remain what it has always been: a place of discovery, communication, and contemplation at the heart of the Academy.

Fig. 2. 1. Via Angelo Masina, where the Academy is located, named for the cavalry colonel killed on June 3, 1849. Photograph, B. Goldman.

Fig. 2. 2. Angelo Masina. Bust in the Passeggiata del Gianicolo. 1889; artist unknown. Note the skull and crossbones on cap and baldric (symbol of the Lancieri della Morte). Photograph, N. W. Goldman.

JUNE 3, 1849 AND ANGELO MASINA

Katherine A. Geffcken

Sitting in the back garden of the Academy on a quiet summer after-noon, I find it hard to grasp the nightmares of war that swept across this graceful space in the late spring and early summer of 1849. At the rear of the Academy property rises Bastion Eight, the first bastion in the Papal Wall south of Porta San Pancrazio. From it for many weeks three pieces of Italian artillery fired at the attacking French outside the wall. Beginning on June 3, one of this battery's principal targets was the Villa Corsini dei Quattro Venti (the Villa Corsini of the Four Winds). On that day, the French captured the Villa Corsini, and from then on could fire their cannon from this high spot over the Roman defenses and down into the center of Rome itself. Among the many Italians who died in fatal attempts to regain the Villa of the Four Winds was Angelo Masina, whose name we recall every time we mention the Academy address [fig. 2. 1]. This essay will concentrate on the events of June 3, 1849, and the death of Masina. First, some background is appropriate, to set the scene for this confrontation of June 3.

On November 24, 1848, Pope Pius IX had fled from Rome to the protection of King Ferdinand II of Naples, and those Italians who dreamed of uniting the penin-sula in a republic swarmed to Rome. Among these republicans was Giuseppe Garibaldi, who arrived in December, 1848. It was only the second time in his life that Garibaldi had visited Rome, and he came for only a brief stay, accompanied by a new friend and fellow republican Angelo Masina [fig. 2. 2]. A prominent Bolognese, Masina was colonel of his own company of mounted lancers and a man already long involved in revolutionary causes.[1] In February 1849, Garibaldi was back in Rome again to participate in the proclamation of the Roman Republic. With the arrival of Giuseppe Mazzini a month later, the young republic began to take shape. As G.M. Trevelyan says in his epic account entitled *Garibaldi's Defence of the Roman Republic*, "Little as they (Garibaldi and Mazzini) liked one another, these two men between them turned a rather limp revolutionary movement . . . into one of the great scenes of history" (Trevelyan 92). The desperate battles to preserve this republic against the invading French took place primarily along the Janiculum stretch of the Papal Wall. Indeed, our whole *zona* is a memorial to Garibaldi's defense. Just call to mind the equestrian statue of Garibaldi in the Janiculum *passeggiata* and the portrait busts of

Fig. 2. 3. The Quattro Venti Arch, Prince Doria Pamphilj's arch (1859) on the site of the destroyed Quattro Venti. Architect: Andrea Busiri Vici. East Façade, photographed on June 3, 1989, just after the ceremony to commemorate the battle of June 3, 1849, by naming the area Piazzale dei Ragazzi del 1849 in memory of those who fought there. Photograph, K. A. Geffcken.

his followers around him in the park, as well as all the streets named for Garibaldini.

On April 25, 1849, a French army numbering about eight to ten thousand men landed at Civitavecchia and rapidly advanced on Rome to overturn the Republic and restore Papal authority. (By the end of the campaign, the French would number 30,000.) On April 30, Garibaldi, the commander of the Janiculum defenses, had only a little more than 2,000 men. He understood at once that he must not only prevent a breach in the Papal Wall at Porta San Pancrazio, but also hold the Quattro Venti outside the Wall because the villa stood on the highest point of the Janiculum. Should the French take it, they would hold the key to Rome. By incredible effort the Italians were successful on April 30, securing the Quattro Venti as well as all the important nearby structures. But shortly after midnight on June 3, the French broke a guarantee they had given not to attack until June 4. They stealthily seized the Villa Pamphilj to the west, and then the Quattro Venti. Throughout June 3, the Italians by means of suicide missions repeatedly regained control of the Quattro Venti, but also repeatedly could not hold on to it in the face of superior French forces. The carnage was incredible. Garibaldi himself wrote, "I have seen very terrible fights . . . but I have never seen anything to equal the butchery of the Villa Corsini." (Garibaldi 252).

The contrast between the elegant pleasure house of the Quattro Venti and the terrible scene that unfolded there on June 3 is a theme that appeals to writers recounting the day's events. Now when you enter the Villa Doria Pamphilj by the main gate, you see on the rise ahead an arch with allegorical statues of the four winds on its four corners [fig. 2. 3]. It stands on the site of the Villa Corsini. The inscription on the attic of the arch states that Prince Filippo Andrea Doria Pamphilj built this *aditus* in 1859 after he had purchased the ruined Villa Corsini. In 1856, shortly before the Prince bought the Corsini property for 19,000 *scudi* and added it to his own Villa Pamphilj just to the west, his architect Andrea Busiri Vici, who subsequently designed the arch, drew up a description and plans of the shattered villa. Besides these floor plans, there survive views of the villa when intact and then in ruins after June 1849 [figs. 2. 4 & 2. 5].

The Quattro Venti was an imposing showpiece, tall in its design to emphasize the high point of its site. It was built on property acquired in 1662-1663 by Cardinal Neri Corsini, who commissioned Carlo Fontana to draw up plans for improving his investment. But the Quattro Venti itself seems not to have been started until 1687, when Neri's nephew Lorenzo Corsini, the future Pope Clement XII, initiated construction under the supervision of Simone Salvi (Eleuteri 29-31). In the course of building, the architectural plans were modified more than once. When, in the eighteenth century, later members of the Corsini family acquired properties extending up the Janiculum from the Via della Lungara, the Quattro Venti became the most westward element in a superb chain of Corsini buildings, gardens, and *vigne*.

Like the Algardi casino in Villa Pamphilj, the Quattro Venti was designed for entertaining, not daily living. On the ground level, it had four large entrances, oriented to the cardinal points and suggesting the four winds. The central room above on the *piano nobile* was decorated with wall painting and eight marble busts of gods and the seasons on pedestals. The painting in the vault above depicted Aurora preceding the chariot of the Sun. An extraordinary total of twelve doors opened into this central *sala* (Eleuteri 31-32). Outside, on the eastern side, a monumental double staircase led up to a grand belvedere or terrace surrounding the building. Below and around in its gardens were flowers, vegetables, vineyards, and a *pineta,* a pine grove which still survives. Altogether, the Quattro Venti provided a splendid retreat for enjoying cool breezes and distant views — until June 3, 1849.

The fate of the young Republic hung on recapturing the Quattro Venti from the French. Garibaldi wrote, "At any cost, therefore, it must be taken; for Rome it was a question of life or death" (Garibaldi 248-49). He describes six successive assaults on the house that day, June 3. The first, second, and fifth were successful, but at shocking human price. The French each time soon retook the house. Out of his now 4,000 men, Garibaldi lost approximately 1,000, including many of his leading officers. For the Italian troops to reach the Quattro Venti it was necessary to enter by the villa gate (where now stands the rusticated entrance to the Villa Pamphilj, built in 1860) and to proceed up the straight lane lined on either side by high boxwood hedges. This driveway (we still walk up it when we enter the Villa Pamphilj, though the boxwood hedge is long gone) became a narrow lane of death. The French, protected inside the Quattro Venti and behind every potted orange tree in the garden, fired a rain of ammunition into this approach. Meanwhile, during pauses between attacks, the Roman batteries on the Papal Wall blasted away the elegant façade of the Quattro Venti in an effort to dislodge the French.

Fig. 2. 4. View of the Via Aurelia immediately outside Porta San Pancrazio; the Villa Corsini dei Quattro Venti, in the distance; and to the right, the Vascello. By Giuseppe Vasi, from his *Le Magnificenze* (1760). Photograph, A. Ortolan from the volume in the Library of the American Academy in Rome.

Fig. 2. 5. The Quattro Venti in July 1849. Print by Carlo Werner, property of the Villa Aurelia. Photograph, A. Ortolan.

19

Fig. 2. 6. Flag and flowers placed on June 3, 1989, approximately where Angelo Masina's body lay in 1849. The occasion was the hundred and fortieth anniversary of the battle of the Quattro Venti. Photograph, K. A. Geffcken.

Colonel Angelo Masina figures in two of the assaults. In the first attack of the morning when Masina was one of those leading the charge, he was wounded in the arm, but undeterred "... raised his bleeding arm aloft and cried: '*Avanti!*'" (Garibaldi 249). When the attack proved, if only briefly, successful, Garibaldi ordered Masina to report for treatment at the field hospital set up in S. Pietro in Montorio. But Masina was not one to rest under these circumstances. With his arm bandaged, he returned to take part in the fifth assault in the afternoon. Mounted and leading his Cavalieri della Morte (Cavalry of Death), Masina managed to reach the grand staircase on the front of the Quattro Venti. Here is Garibaldi's description:

> I beheld something that I should have deemed incredible achieved
> before my very eyes. Masina, followed by his Lancers, was at the head
> of the column. The intrepid horseman simply flew across the ground, cleared
> the terrace and reached the foot of the staircase. Then, putting spurs to his
> horse, he made him gallop up the stairs, with the result that, though only
> for a moment, he appeared on the landing leading to the grand salon, like an
> equestrian statue. The apotheosis was only of an instant's duration. A shower of
> bullets, fired at close range, brought down the rider, and his horse fell on top of
> him pierced by nine balls (Garibaldi 252).

Floods of infantry, Roman citizens, and students, seized with fervor at the sight of Masina's extraordinary ride, charged into the villa gardens, falling over piles of human bodies and dead horses, undaunted by flames rising from the burning interior of the villa. When the retreat was finally, and inevitably, sounded, Masina's body was somehow left behind on the sloping driveway about halfway down from the house. It lay there in full view, between the opposing forces, in no-man's land, under the hot summer sun [fig. 2. 6]. Finally, on July 5, after Rome had surrendered to the French and Garibaldi had departed with his remaining forces, Masina's corpse was collected for burial.[2]

▣ REFERENCES

Ai Caduti per Roma: MDCCCXLIX-MDCCCLXX (Rome, 1941). See 176-77 for Masina.

Belli Barsali, Isa. *Ville di Roma: Lazio I* (Milan, 1970).

Benocci, Carla. *Le Ville Storiche di Via Aurelia Antica* (Rome, 1995).

Benocci, Carla. *Villa Doria Pamphilj* (Rome, 1996), 230-35.

Costa, Giovanni (Nino). *Quel Che Vidi e Quel Che Intesi,* ed. Giorgia Guerrazzi Costa (1927), excerpted in *Scrittori Garibaldini,* ed. Gaetano Trombatore (Turin, 1979), Vol. 1, 9-31.

Eleuteri, Francesco. "Il Casino dei Quattro Venti" in *Fondare la Nazione: i Repubblicani del 1849 e la Difesa del Gianicolo,* ed. Lauro Rossi (Rome, 2001), 28-36.

Garibaldi, Giuseppe. *Memoirs,* ed. Alexandre Dumas, trans. R. S. Garnett (London, 1931). This edition incorrectly calls Masina "Marina."

Hoffman, Paola. *Villa Doria Pamphilj* (Rome, 1976).

Schiavo, Armando. *Villa Doria Pamphilj* (Rome, 1942).

Trevelyan, G. M. *Garibaldi's Defence of the Roman Republic,* 3rd ed. (London, 1912).

▣ NOTES

1   Angelo de Masini, usually called Masina, was born November 14, 1815, of an ancient and wealthy Bolognese family. When only a boy he fought valiantly against Carlist forces in Spain. Back in Italy, he was arrested several times for political conspiracy and was jailed in Castel Sant'Angelo. He gained his freedom under the amnesty of Pius IX. In 1848, he fought brilliantly for republican causes in northern Italy. In autumn, 1848, he recruited his own company of forty-two Bolognese Lancers (the Cavalieri della Morte). On November 23, 1848, he joined Garibaldi, and his Lancers served thereafter as the cavalry for Garibaldi's Italian Legion. The Lancers were colorful in their red pants, blue jackets, and red fezzes; Masina himself wore a visored red helmet with a black plume. The insignia of the Lancieri della Morte was, not surprisingly, a skull and bones.

2   The artist Giovanni (Nino) Costa left a vivid description of fighting at the Quattro Venti in his memoir *Quel Che Vidi e Quel Che Intesi.* Costa says that, by the afternoon of June 3, the *pianterreno* of the Quattro Venti was completely filled with bodies of dead Italians, which the French stacked up as barricades and which then were blown into ghastly, bloody pieces by Italian shelling (p. 18). He heard the sound of Masina's horse mounting the stairs to the *primo piano* above. When Masina had fallen dying, Costa watched a friend loosen Masina's foot from the stirrup and kiss it (p. 19).

TOP

Fig. 3. 1. Ristorante Scarpone, as it appears today. Photograph, K. A. Geffcken.

ABOVE, LEFT

Fig. 3. 2. The old carriage door of Scarpone, on Via di San Pancrazio. Photograph, K. A. Geffcken.

ABOVE, RIGHT

Fig. 3. 3. Scarpone from the west, showing surviving wall of the southwest wing (Casa Bruciata). Photograph, K. A. Geffcken.

CHAPTER 3

SCARPONE

Katherine A. Geffcken

The Ristorante Scarpone is proud today of both its abundant menu and its historic past. Owned since 1816 by the same family, the Adducci, this eighteenth century *casale* and its surrounding property rank among Rome's oldest surviving country *osterie*. It was also the scene of desperate Italian defense in June, 1849. As we walk west on Via di San Pancrazio (dodging with difficulty the hurtling traffic), the tall, slender *casale* appears soon on the left, fronting directly on the road [fig. 3. 1]. Recently repainted, it glows with a bright golden color, its windows simply but elegantly framed in soft cream. A large carriage door in the façade shows how visitors used to enter from the road [fig. 3. 2]. Now, guests of the restaurant enter to the side from a modern parking lot and sit at tables spread under cool arbors or near fireplaces in modern annexes. But the old stable, now a storeroom, still abuts on the northeast end of the house, and the wall surviving from the southwest wing, which burned in 1849, now forms a high barrier along the road [fig. 3. 3]. Threatened in 1936 by proposed widening of Via di San Pancrazio, the house was saved through efforts of citizens, especially the association of the Garibaldini. As the most advanced outpost of the Roman defense in 1849, the house was declared a monument and placed under the protection of an official *vincolo*.[1]

In Risorgimento literature, Scarpone is usually cited as "Casa Giacometti," a name deriving from an owner before the Adducci family. Tradition says that the name Scarpone originated with Garibaldi in 1849, that the General often stopped by for refreshment, tied up his horse to a tree,[2] and chatted with the host Antonio Adducci. To greet the General, Adducci tramped in from his adjoining *vigna* wearing large shoes *(scarponi)* caked with mud. As the big, dirty shoes were distinctive, Garibaldi called the host "Scarpone." If this tale contains some element of truth, these visits must have taken place before the battle of April 30, or between May 1 and 3, or on June 1 or 2. On May 4, Garibaldi left Rome for his campaign against the Neapolitans at Palestrina and Velletri. Between his return to Rome on May 31 and the dreadful battle of June 3, there were two quiet days when Garibaldi probably inspected the Italian outposts at the nearby Villa of the Quattro Venti. From June 3, Casa Giacometti came under unrelenting fire. It was hardly a tranquil place to sit for a glass of wine. In any case, the tale is one among many demonstrating how people especially remembered Garibaldi's visits around the battlefield.

On the morning of June 3, when the French had stealthily gained control of the Villa Pamphilj, the Corsini Villa of the Quattro Venti, and the Villa Valentini, they also threatened other outlying buildings including Casa Giacometti. Therefore, Garibaldi sent forward a company of the Lombard *bersaglieri* to take and hold the Giacometti and drive back the French.[3] From the upper windows of the house, the Italian riflemen could fire down into the street below and over into the Villa Corsini. The Italians somehow managed to hold the Giacometti until the night of June 23-24, when defending the house was no longer practical. By the night of June 20, the French had extended their trench all the way from the Quattro Venti to the southern edge of the Giacometti. Then, on June 24, the French successfully extended trenches on the south and east sides of the *casale,* thus encircling the Giacometti.[4] As Trevelyan described the house, it was ". . . closely netted by the enemy's trenches and riddled by his fire." (204) Under cover of darkness on the night of June 23-24, the Italian defenders withdrew from the Giacometti through their own trench that linked them, for replacements and supplies, to the Vascello. Military historians observe that defending the Giacometti, the most exposed of all the Italian outposts, for twenty days, postponed the fall of Rome about a month.

Previously, in the night of June 20-21, the Italians had almost lost the Giacometti. Although by then 35 men of the *Unione* Regiment guarded the house, in fact everyone that night expected the French to attack through the new breaches in the Papal Wall around Villa Barberini (Sciarra). And so, at Casa Giacometti, all were asleep except one sentry. When he heard the enemy creeping through the vineyard outside (150 French in all), he awakened his fellow soldiers, who reacted with heavy fire at close range. There followed intense combat with bayonets on both sides, all in the dark and all terrifying. The Italians prevailed, with one dead and one wounded; the French withdrew, having lost four dead, many wounded, and four taken prisoner. The next day, after the Giacometti had held firm, Garibaldi boasted of this small success in a letter to his wife Anita (text of letter: Trevelyan 205).

A member of Giacomo Medici's legion, Giovanni Cadolini, narrates in his memoirs an event at Casa Giacometti that explains why the house is sometimes called "Casa Bruciata" (burned house). He places the episode on the evening of June 25, an unlikely date, since the Italian garrison abandoned the Giacometti almost two days earlier. In any case, he remembered that Giacomo Medici came through the Italian trench from the Vascello and ordered the men to pile up a mound of combustible objects on the ground floor. Medici thought it might become prudent to burn the house rather than leave it for the French to fortify. Somehow, probably by someone's carelessness, the mound caught fire and flames spread fast, engulfing the floors above. At once, the men thought of their comrades' bodies still lying in the upper rooms. They raced upstairs to bring down the dead and save them for decent burial. Then they hurried to beat back the fast-spreading fire, by then almost up to the roof. Their vigorous efforts saved the basic structure, but the southwest wing, that part closest to the French batteries, was so damaged that today only the wall with two grated windows facing on the road survives [fig. 3. 3].[5] Cadolini proudly recalls how honorable it was that he and his comrades thought of their fellows' burial in the midst of intense flames (Cadolini, quoted in Bosi 84-85).

We cannot now know if in fact these bodies were the human remains found in January of 1940, when the commission for the *mausoleo ossario gianicolense* (monumental tomb for the bones of the Risorgimento dead) entered the *cantina* at Scarpone. This *cantina* is actually an ancient underground burial complex that may have connected originally with catacombs under the church of San Pancrazio. In addition to ancient bones, the commission discovered skeletons of ten men, identified later by experts as belonging to the nineteenth century. It has been suggested that these skeletons were collected from shallow burials on the battlefield and then brought down into the *ipogeo* (underground tomb) (Bosi 85-86). But it has also been suggested that they were defenders of the house, killed at their posts and buried quickly and silently in the nearest underground space (*Ai Caduti* 46). Today the entrance to the Ipogeo Scarpone lies down a flight of steps outside the east end of the stable.

The most memorable scene, however, at Casa Giacometti took place back in the late afternoon of that first day Italian troops took control of the house, on June 3. There, in the stable, Emilio Dandolo finally located the body of his older brother Enrico. Just short of 22 years old, Enrico Dandolo was captain of the second company of Luciano Manara's Lombard *bersaglieri*.[6] The younger Emilio was at that time a member of the fourth company. The brothers last saw one another that morning as they sat near Porta San Pancrazio sharing a bit of bread and awaiting orders to proceed into battle. Then Garibaldi decided to send forward the first and second companies of Lombards. In their trim, dark uniforms and plumed hats, the *bersaglieri* advanced in military precision with their characteristic jog, to the sound of their trumpeters (four trumpets to a company).[7] As French bullets hailed on them, Dandolo led his company off to the south side of the Quattro Venti. Then a strange and deadly thing occurred.

Suddenly a French company emerged from the southern side of the Quattro Venti, headed by an officer who gave a friendly sign and cried in Italian *"Siamo amici!"* So strong was Italian faith in French honor that Enrico ordered his troops to cease fire. When the French had approached to within 30 feet, the officer deftly moved aside, and his men immediately fired at close range. The *bersaglieri* were decimated, Enrico falling with a bullet straight through his chest.[8] Those still standing retreated except Emilio Morosini, who remained beside Dandolo, himself a target for enemy sharpshooters, but amazingly untouched. Finally, covered by renewed Italian firing, two soldiers reached them and carried the dying Dandolo from the villa garden and eventually across the road to the stable at Casa Giacometti [fig. 3. 4].

All this while, Emilio Dandolo was just inside Porta San Pancrazio awaiting orders for his own company and wracked with anxiety about his brother. When a procession of litters carrying wounded and dead appeared at Porta San Pancrazio, Emilio sensed doom from survivors of his brother's company. But he could only pace

Fig. 3. 4. Stable door at Ristorante Scarpone where Enrico Dandolo's body was brought. Photograph, K. A. Geffcken.

back and forth, gnawing on his pistol handle, until he was sent in the afternoon with twenty men to try once more to push the French out of the Quattro Venti. Of his twenty soldiers, only six made it back to the Vascello, Emilio himself wounded in the thigh. His vivid description of the day conveys the total carnage, the horrific sounds, and desperate courage of the Italians (Dandolo 189-192).

After treatment at a first aid station, Emilio limped for two hours about the battlefield, looking frantically at every dead and wounded man. At one point he came within a few steps of his brother, but a friend, probably Morosini, hid the body from him. He sent soldiers off to infirmaries to search, but everyone he met either avoided Emilio or told him his brother was only slightly wounded and safely carried away to a farmhouse. Near the end of his physical and emotional strength, Emilio approached Casa Giacometti and saw Colonel Manara in the window beckoning him to enter. There, as Emilio arrived, all others but Manara quietly moved away. The colonel took Dandolo's hand and said, *"Non correre a cercar tuo fratello, non sei più in tempo: ti farò io da fratello."* (Don't run to search for your brother, you are not any longer in time: for you I will serve as a brother). And Emilio fainted away from grief and loss of blood (Dandolo 194-5).

Casa Giacometti appears first on Nolli's map (1748), with its vineyard and garden extending in a wedge southeast from the old Via Vitellia. This ancient road is attested in Suetonius (*Vitellius 1*), but later it was often called "Vicolo della Nocetta." Today the stretch as far as Piazza San Pancrazio has become Via di San Pancrazio. Nolli shows the Giacometti property divided into sections, with a long, straight driveway dividing the land to northeast and southwest. Unfortunately, he does not name the holding. The property to the west he labels "Vigna Grassi," that to the south "Vigna Briganti," to the southeast "Vigna Berngardi,"and to the east "Vigna del Collegio Propaganda."

Today on its façade the Scarpone building has four windows, regularly spaced, on the *secondo piano* and two to the side on the *primo piano*. Over the large carriage entrance is an *edicola* (image sculpted or painted, set in a frame and affixed to a building) containing a fresco, much effaced. The owner of Scarpone does not know the identity of the human figure in the fresco. To me, what remains in shadowy form is a frontal figure standing on a mound and holding objects in each hand. Above, between the frame of the fresco and the small gabled roof of the *edicola* is a six-pointed star in relief, now freshly painted bright golden. It is tempting to associate this star with the crest of the Briganti family (see fig. 3. 2), which includes such six-pointed stars. (*Enc.* II. 185) But the significance of this *edicola* awaits further research.

Within the vaulted carriage entrance, an ancient funeral inscription is set into the wall. Probably from a nearby tomb, it honors the memory of twin sisters who died at 16 within a short time of one another, Lucia Licinia Urbana and Marcia Tarria Plotina (*CIL* VI. 31730).[9]

Scarpone has been celebrated in music and verse. Cesare Pascucci wrote an operetta '*Na vignata da Scarpone* (A wine drinking party at Scarpone); Ettore Petrolini included it in his *L'Ottobrata* (October country party/excursion); and Trilussa refers to it in his poem *Il Ratto delle Sabine* (The Rape of the Sabine Women). In the early twentieth century, Hans Barth described afternoons relaxing under Scarpone's protecting pergola and watching flirtatious Trasteverine with their enormous pendant earrings and their amazing capacity for the abundant local wine. The *Ottobrata* outings may have disappeared, but we can still consume varieties of abundance at Scarpone.[10]

⊞ REFERENCES

I wish to thank the late owner of Scarpone, Signora Maria Luisa Adducci, for her patient and helpful responses to my queries about her property. Signora Adducci was the fifth generation of the Adducci to own Scarpone. She was the daughter of Giuseppe Adducci, who was born in 1892. Now in charge at Scarpone is Signora Adducci's son, who long assisted his mother in managing the *ristorante*. My other sources were:

Ai Caduti per Roma MDCCCXLIX-MDCCCLXX (Rome, 1941).
Bosi, Mario. "Casa Giacometti, Ultima Testimone della Gloriosa Epopea della Repubblica Romana," *Lunario Romano* (Rome, 1973), 69-90.
Dandolo, Emilio. *I Volontari ed I Bersaglieri Lombardi* (Milan, 1849/50, reprint Milan, Rome, Naples, 1917). A valuable and moving eyewitness account.

DeSantis, Leonella, and Francesco Del Canuto. *Le Osterie Romane* (Rome, 1997).

Enciclopedia Storico-Nobiliare Italiana II (Milan, 1929).

Fiocchi Nicolai, Vincenzo. "L'Ipogeo detto di 'Scarpone' presso Porta S. Pancrazio." *Rivista di Archeologia Cristiana* 58 (1982), 7-28.

Garibaldi, Giuseppe. *The Memoirs of Garibaldi*, ed. A. Dumas, trans. R. S. Garnett (London, 1931).

Trevelyan, G. M. *Garibaldi's Defence of the Roman Republic* (London, 1912).

▥ NOTES

1 Legally bound property, frozen in status quo.

2 A brochure handed out at Scarpone (no author stated) says that the trunk of the tree, "half-destroyed by a thunderbolt, can still be identified nowadays." De Santis and Del Canuto identify the tree as a eucalyptus (54).

3 In his memoirs (251), Garibaldi recalled that he sent Gustav von Hofstetter and 50 men from the Students' Corps to hold the Giacometti, but Garibaldi's own bulletin for June 3, quoted verbatim by Dandolo (184), specifies that Manara's *bersaglieri* were dispatched to the house on June 3. Later, from his post at the Vascello, Giacomo Medici also commanded the Giacometti, and men from the *Unione* Regiment garrisoned the house.

4 For the location of the French and Italian trenches, I depend on the map of General Federico Torre. Another map, by Guglielmo Cenni, contains many interesting details, but strangely reverses the *osteria* (i.e. the Giacometti) with Casa Torlonia, labeling the Giacometti as Casa Torlonia and Torlonia property west of the Vascello as *osteria*.

5 Contemporary views of the battlefield and the surviving wall show that this southwest wing was only about half the height of the house itself.

6 Enrico Dandolo was born June 26, 1827, at Varese, a town northwest of Milan. His father, Count Tullio Dandolo (1801-70), was a historian and a descendant of the great Dandolo family of the Veneto. Enrico and his younger brother Emilio (1831-59) grew up nurtured in Italian patriotism. They joined Luciano Manara on the barricades at Milan during the *Cinque Giornate* (1848) and later accompanied Manara when he reconstituted the Lombard *bersaglieri* as the sixth battalion of the Piemontese army (October 1848). When the Austrians defeated the Italians at Novara on March 23, 1849, Manara embarked with his battalion for Civitavecchia, to join the defenders of the new Roman Republic.

After Enrico Dandolo's death on June 3, his body was eventually moved from Casa Giacometti to the Cento Preti (see p. 45 on Morosini's body). Following the Italian surrender, his coffin, Manara's, and Morosini's were transported by sea back to Lombardia for burial in family property. Emilio Dandolo lived on for ten sad years, traveling in the Orient and then hoping to serve again in the Piemontese army. But the Austrians forced him to return home, where his health declined. Though he deeply mourned the loss of his young compatriots, he still hoped for Italian freedom. His funeral at Milan became a political demonstration that the Austrian authorities dared not prohibit (*Ai Caduti* 161, introduction to Dandolo viii). In Rome, tree-lined Via Dandolo winding up from Trastevere to Via Fabrizi honors the brothers. For color reproductions of portraits of Emilio and Enrico Dandolo, see *Fondare la Nazione: I Repubblicani del 1849 e la Difesa del Gianicolo*, ed. Lauro Rossi (Rome, 2001), 134, 136.

7 Dandolo (181) recalls that on the morning of June 3, when the Lombard Corps trotted eagerly across Rome to the Janiculum, they kept perfect ranks all the way to the notes of their trumpets, and the people cheered them on with *frenetici applausi*.

8 Trevelyan (179, note 2) urges caution in accepting this tale of French treachery, but Dandolo, who tells it (190), could easily have heard it firsthand from his good friend Emilio Morosini.

9 The owner of Scarpone reported to me that another antiquity, a relief that was located above the fountain on the rear house wall, was stolen in the 1970s.

10 Trevelyan (182) writes a brief, evocative description of Scarpone in 1906, conveying the remoteness of this spot before Roman expansion overtook the area: "It [Scarpone] still stands, an unnoticed memorial of that calamitous day [June 3, 1849], in an isolated position by the roadside, with a pleasant court behind opening on to the vineyards, where, under an arbour, carters take a glass of wine before they enter the walls of Rome; several ancient stones and inscriptions are built into the fine old archway at the entrance." And in note 1 on p. 182, Trevelyan adds: "Present-day visitors to Rome (1906) can identify it by the word *Scarpone* written large on its walls."

Fig. 4. 1. The Vascello as it appears
today. Photograph, K. A. Geffcken.

CHAPTER 4

THE VASCELLO AND GIACOMO MEDICI

Katherine A. Geffcken

Among all buildings, walls, and gates honored as memorials of the brief 1849 Republic, the first rank unquestionably belongs to the Vascello, now numbered 6 and 8 on Via di S. Pancrazio [fig. 4.1].[1] In the years after the French army defeated the Italian patriots, other damaged structures were either demolished or rebuilt, but the Vascello was left a ruin, a symbol of determination and courage. While every other structure outside Porta San Pancrazio fell to the French, the Vascello was never captured. From June 3, 1849, when it became headquarters for the Italian advanced line, until early morning hours of June 30, Giacomo Medici[2] and his men held the house against numerous French infantry attacks and constant shelling from the Villa dei Quattro Venti to the west, which the French had captured on June 3. From there, about 250 yards away, more than 400 cannon balls, besides shells and sharpshooters' bullets, rained on the Vascello. As day approached on June 30, after the ultimate night of devastating French advance, Garibaldi ordered Medici to withdraw into Rome because the enemy had circled around the Vascello and taken the Porta San Pancrazio.

Traffic today is so frenetic on Via di San Pancrazio that it is almost suicidal to stop along the road to look at what remains of the Vascello. Fronting directly on this stretch of the old Via Aurelia is the wall of the property, in which the portion that is part of the house itself still shows the rusticated façade of the *pianterreno*, with square windows flanked by oval windows, stucco decoration, and crenellations above [fig. 4. 1]. To the left at an angle opens the carriage entrance. Just above the central *portone* of the house, it is still possible to see the curve of the *piano nobile*. In the eastern section, parts of the *primo piano* rise above the crenellations.

Immediately after the 1849 conflict, more of the eastern wall survived, up to the attic, as Werner's view of the building shows [fig. 4. 2]. But as this wall was dangerously unsupported, it must have either fallen or been removed. To understand the design of this large, complex villa before its destruction, we can turn to seventeenth century drawings, Nolli's map of 1748, Vasi's *veduta* of 1760 (see Chapter 2, Masina, fig. 2.4), a painting by an anonymous eighteenth century artist, and various descriptions. The house was shaped like an inverted "T," with the horizontal bar fronting on the road and the vertical trunk stretching into the park. On both east and west sides of the vertical bar at *pianterreno* level, there were porticos. Facing the road, the bay of the *piano nobile* had large windows; above, on the *secondo piano*, there was a terrace with a belvedere, over which rose two round towers. The other, interior end of the house had a balancing pair of towers. The villa was so tall (above the *secondo piano*, there were a *mezzanino* and two attic floors) that views from the top over the countryside must have been magnificent. The long shape of the building and the prow-like bay looming over the rusticated wall caused observers to remark that this structure resembled a ship above a craggy rock. Hence the nickname *Il Vascello*.

As shown by John Varriano, the original designer of this remarkable building was Plautilla Bricci (1616 – ca. 1690 to 1700), the earliest female architect with work still extant. She was said to be a friend of Suor Maria Eufrasia della Croce, the sister of Abbate Elpidio Benedetti, Cardinal Mazarin's agent at Rome and later the representative of the French Crown. It was Benedetti who commissioned Plautilla to design his villa just outside Porta San Pancrazio as well as the chapel of San Luigi in San Luigi dei Francesi.[3] Varriano demonstrates that the Villa Benedetti (the Vascello), as it emerged ca. 1667, retained Plautilla's basic ground-plan of 1663 but was much more elaborate. Given Benedetti's known involvement with temporary French displays (*apparati*) at Rome, Varriano attributes the additional embellishments to Benedetti himself.[4]

The interior was extremely splendid and busy, with mirrors, pavements of black and white majolica, frescoes, and aphorisms inscribed everywhere.[5] On the *piano nobile*, there were three galleries, in the most important of which Pietro da Cortona painted the ceiling fresco, an Aurora. Plautilla also executed a fresco, *Felicità* surrounded by allegorical figures, as well as the altar panel in the chapel, an Assumption. Other artists who worked in the building include F. Allegrini, G. F. Grimaldi, and G. B. Carlone. Altogether, the Vascello was an opulent, highly decorated, rather bizarre structure with a strong French touch. The chapel Plautilla designed in San Luigi dei Francesi shows, on a small scale, what kind of ambiance visitors might have found at the Vascello. Swirling stucco angels, a large gilded metal crown, and paintings, all framed by immense, dramatic curtains of plaster painted blue with gold fleurs-de-lis, combine to make an ornate, almost overwhelming space.

In Werner's engraving of the Vascello in ruin, the entrance doors and the beginning of barrel vaulting in two of the three galleries on the *piano nobile* still survive. Timbers from upper parts of the building hang at crazy angles over the remains. In the foreground, the west garden that had been laid out in terraces and allées with a central circular fountain appears tossed up into mountains of earth from the impact of shells. A small, irregular lake, probably caused by destruction of the fountain and its pipes, floods part of the garden. Margaret Fuller's description, written after the Italians surrendered, complements Werner's *veduta* [fig. 4. 3]:

> July 10. . . . Yesterday I went over the scene of conflict. It was fearful even to
> *see* the Casinos Quattro Venti and Vascello, where the French and Romans

Fig. 4. 2. The Vascello and surrounding area, viewed eastward from the grounds of Villa Corsini dei Quattro Venti. Engraving by Carlo Werner, July, 1849. Property of the Villa Aurelia, American Academy in Rome. Photograph. A. Ortolan.

In the foreground is the gate to the Villa Corsini, opening into the long driveway leading up to the Quattro Venti (out of sight beyond the left hand corner). In the middle distance on the left of Via Aurelia is the Vascello in ruins. To the right is Porta San Pancrazio, and behind it to the left is the Villa Aurelia.

had been several days so near one another, all shattered to pieces, with fragments of rich stucco and painting still sticking to rafters between the great
holes made by the cannonade, and think that men had stayed and fought in
them when only a mass of ruins (Fuller 420).

The steadfast Italian commander of the Vascello, Giacomo Medici, was well
prepared and selected for his hazardous post. His family was originally from Castello
di Annone in the Piemonte, but he was born in Milan on January 15, 1817. When he
was twelve, his father, a merchant, went into political exile at Lisbon, and Giacomo
accompanied him. In 1836 Giacomo enrolled in campaigns against the Carlists in
Spain, gaining his first military experience. But about 1840 he was forced to leave the
Spanish peninsula. Next, at London, he entered the commercial world, and most
important, met Mazzini. Medici was tall, attractive in looks and personality, and
apparently sturdy, but the British climate affected his health. Because his father had
joined other Italian exiles in South America, at Montevideo, Giacomo sailed from
England to Uruguay. There he met Garibaldi and became a "red shirt" in Garibaldi's
Italian Legion. Thus began one of the longest-lasting teams in Risorgimento history
– Garibaldi, the fearless, patriotic guerrilla general, and ten years younger, his equal-
ly fearless, more politically astute comrade Medici. In early 1848 when Garibaldi was
planning his return to Italy, he sent Medici ahead to prepare an uprising in Tuscany.
Within the year, Medici fought in campaigns against the Austrians in the north, at
Como, Varese, and Lugano, then escaped to Tuscany, where in winter 1849 he raised
the "Medici Legion," about 300 men mostly from Lombardy. When news reached
Medici that republican forces were gathering at Rome, he marched to Bologna, then
to the Marche, and finally entered Rome through Porta S. Giovanni on May 16, 1849.

During the 28 days he defended the Vascello, Medici saw about 300 of his
men killed and many more wounded. Since he had arrived with approximately 300
soldiers, it is clear that, as his men fell, replacements were sent out to the Vascello
from other units. About twenty of his men were buried alive when a large part of the
Vascello ". . . fell with a roar, amid a cloud of darkness, like a bursting volcano"
(Trevelyan 213). The French not only pulverized the Vascello, especially the exposed
western side, with cannon fire from the six guns placed in front of the Quattro Venti,
but attacked it in hand-to-hand bayonet charges from their intricate labyrinth of
trenches. These trenches the French dug ever closer after the night of June 23-24,
when the small Italian garrison was withdrawn from the even more exposed Casa
Giacometti (today the restaurant Scarpone) back to the Vascello. As for the Vascello,
however, Medici was able each morning to send Garibaldi word that he and his men
still held the villa — or what was left of it. Indeed, it has been suggested that Italian
control of the Vascello postponed the fall of Rome more than three weeks and compelled the French to breach the city wall to the south at Villa Sciarra and later, at the
end, right behind Casino Malvasia (where the Casa Rustica now stands).

Medici was a tough survivor who commanded his men with gusto and even
humor. At eight on the morning of June 22, Sergeant Luigi Magni, a 22 year old

Fig. 4.3. The Vascello in ruins after the siege, July, 1849. Engraving by Carlo Werner, property of the Villa Aurelia, American Academy in Rome. Photograph, A. Ortolan.

Milanese, fired his carbine with accurate aim and hit a high-ranking French officer (the Vascello garrison and men in the advanced French trenches were engaged in constant sharpshooting). Medici was standing behind Magni watching the action with a telescope, and seeing the French reacting tumultuously to the fall of their leader, he said, *"Bravo! Un altro colpo simile e pago una bottiglia di Champagne!"* ("Bravo! Another shot like that one, and I pay a bottle of Champagne!"). *"Accettato!"* "Agreed!"), answered the young sergeant, and raised his rifle to aim. At that moment, he was hit by a French bullet between his nose and right eye, and fell dead (*Ai Caduti*, 174, quoting Vittorio Ottolini). What Medici said then is not reported, but at some other time he marveled at the building he was defending and said "I wish that I had a daguerreotype of these ruins." (Trevelyan 213, quoting Hoffstetter).[6]

On June 30 when, on Garibaldi's orders, the still unconquered Medici withdrew from the Vascello, he was promoted from major to lieutenant colonel (later in his long career he would become General Medici). He chose not to accompany Garibaldi on the long retreat across Italy, but instead went to London, where many sympathized with the Italian republican cause. He was soon back in Italy, however, at Genoa. He subsequently fought in many campaigns of the Risorgimento, for instance commanding a brigade of the Cacciatori delle Alpi (1859) and leading the second wave in the Sicilian invasion of June, 1860. He headed a division in Sicily, served as commander of Messina, and finally, in 1866, of all Sicily. Apparently he accepted the Piemontese monarchy more readily than many other republicans, for in 1874 he became King Victor Emanuel's first aide-de-camp and was awarded a gold and a silver medal [fig. 4. 4]. In December 1876 he was given the title Marchese del Vascello, and as he had no children, laws were later passed to establish inheritance of the title among his brother's descendants.[7]

Fig. 4. 4. Bust of Giacomo Medici in his later years, Passeggiata del Gianicolo. Sculptor: Ettore Ferrari (1883). Photograph, K. A. Geffcken.

G. MEDICI

He and his heirs were also given the Vascello and its garden in perpetuity.[8] A branch of the family married into the Pallavicini, and these Medici del Vascello Pallavicini created a house amid the rubble. Most descendants are reported to live now in Milan or Turin, although in 1995 the family was still listed in the Rome telephone book. The western portion of the park with the carriage gate (#8) is used by the Masons, the Grande Oriente d'Italia di Palazzo Giustiniani, historically appropriate since Freemasonry was deeply involved in the nineteenth century republican movement.

Between Abbate Benedetti and Giacomo Medici, the Vascello had many owners. It passed first to the Dukes of Nevers; on Nolli's map (1748) it is labeled

"Giard. Muti cosi detto il Vascello di Francia."[9] It later became Giraud property; then in 1824 it belonged to Cardinal Guerrieri, by 1850 to Cardinal Belisario Cristaldi, afterwards to Cavaliere Primoli, and to Conte De Angelis. Today the garden includes the triangle inscribed "Vig. Dell'Eredità Bonaventura"[10] on Nolli's plan, so that the property wall along the road extends for a greater length than in 1748.

What is it like to live in a ruin? In a national monument? So I had often asked myself, but since the Vascello is a private residence, its doors do not open readily to the curious. Then, in June 1994 with the help of luck, a winning plea from Signor Latini of the Museo Garibaldino and the generous hospitality of the residents, an Academy group visited the house and garden. Living in the villa at that time were a leading figure in international sports, Primo Nebiolo, and his wife Signora Nebiolo.[11] The elegant long *salone* on the *pianterreno*, just a few steps above ground level, has a glass roof with canopies to cut the glare. Remaining parts of the *pianterreno* contain the dining area, terraces at different levels, and a handsome library. Outside, the gardens are exquisitely maintained. Trees, shrubs, roses and lush grass combine to ensure a tranquil retreat, far from nightmarish memories of cannon balls and desperate defense, and from the modern fury of traffic outside the protecting wall.

Even in his last years Giacomo Medici remained an impressive man. In the funeral procession of King Victor Emanuel (January, 1878), he caught the eye of the English travel writer Frances Minto Elliot. Before Medici, up the Corso marched troops, deputies, senators, judges, ambassadors, foreign royalty, civil dignitaries, and knights. Next came " . . . a single figure on horseback, General Marchese Medici, then an aged man, in splendid uniform, gray and wrinkled, with a look of deep sorrow in his face, bearing the dead Sovereign's sword, drawn in so many battlefields in the cause of Italy." Then walked, behind the mounted Medici, the new king and the royal princes, followed by the King's funeral car and finally his war horse (Elliot 161). Medici himself would live four years more, dying on March 9, 1882, three months before Garibaldi (June 7, 1882). On the wall of the Albergo Quirinale on Via Nazionale is a plaque:

Il IX Marzo MDCCCLXXXII
morì in quest'albergo
Il Generale Giacomo Medici
difensore del Vascello
nel MDCCCXLIX
primo aiutante in campo
dei due primi Re d'Italia
dal MDCCCLXIX al MDCCCLXXXII
SPQR
IX Marzo MDCCCLXXXIII.
(On the 9th of March, 1882 General Giacomo Medici, defender of the Vascello in 1849, died in this hotel. He was the first aide-de-camp of the two first Kings of Italy from 1869 to 1882. The Senate and the Roman People, March 9, 1883, [have placed this inscription].)

▨ REFERENCES

Ai Caduti per Roma MDCCCXLIX-MDCCCLXX (Rome, 1941).

Belli Barsali, Isa. *Ville di Roma: Lazio I* (Milan, 1970), 408-09.

Benocci, Carla. *Villa il Vascello* (Rome, 2003).

Elliot, Frances Minto. *Roman Gossip* (Leipzig, 1896).

Fuller, Margaret. *At Home and Abroad,* ed. A.B. Fuller (Boston, 1856).

Kieven, Elisabeth. "Anonimo: inizio del XIX secolo: prospetti e piante della Villa Benedetti Giraud, detto il Vascello," *Architettura del Settecento a Roma* (Rome, 1991), 125-28.

"Medici del Vascello," *Enciclopedia storico-nobiliare Italiana* IV (1931), 529.

Medici, Giacomo in Giuseppe Garibaldi. *The Memoirs of Garibaldi.* ed. A. Dumas, trans. R. S. Garnett (London, 1931), 200-13 (Medici's memoir covering events up to Rome, 1849.)

Menghini, Mario. "Giacomo Medici del Vascello," *Enciclopedia Italiana* XXII (1934), 703.

Michel, O. "Bricci, Plautilla," *Dizionario Biografico degli Italiani* 14 (1972), 223-24.

Ranaldi, Antonella. "Il Vascello," in *Fondare la Nazione: I Repubblicani del 1849 e la Difesa del Gianicolo,* ed. Lauro Rossi (Rome, 2001), 37-43.

Trevelyan, G. M. *Garibaldi's Defence of the Roman Republic* (London, 1907).

Trevelyan, G. M. *Garibaldi and the Making of Italy* (London, 1914).

Varriano, John. "Plautilla Bricci 'Architettrice' and the Villa Benedetti in Rome," *An Architectural Progress in the Renaissance and Baroque: Sojourns in and out of Italy,* eds. H. A. Millon and S. S. Munshower, *Papers in Art History from the Pennsylvania State University, 8.1 (1992), 266-279.*

▨ NOTES

1 Help from many persons made this essay possible. I am grateful to the late Dr. Primo Nebiolo and Signora Nebiolo for their hospitality at the Vascello; to Signor Latini of the Museo Garibaldino; to Antonella Bucci for Werner's *veduta* of the Vascello; to Christina Huemer for calling my attention to Varriano's article; to Professor Joseph Connors for reminding me of Plautilla Bricci's chapel in S. Luigi dei Francesi; to Professor Malcolm Bell for noting the plaque about Medici on the Albergo Quirinale; and to Marina Lella for all sorts of help.

2 Most Academy residents know the name Giacomo Medici from the street running between the main Academy building and the Villa Richardson.

3 Plautilla Bricci was born August 13, 1616, at Rome, a daughter of Giovanni Bricci and Chiara Recupita. Her paternal grandfather was Genoese; her father moved in Roman artistic circles and was a painter, musician, and writer of plays. Her mother, a Neapolitan, bore eight children, three of whom survived to adult life. Her father's talents and connections provided an encouraging atmosphere for gifted Plautilla. She became a painter and architect, and a member of the Accademia di San Luca. Her work for Abbate Benedetti extended from 1663 (first stone of the Vascello) to 1680 (inauguration of the chapel of San Luigi in San Luigi dei Francesi). In 1677 Benedetti gave her a house in Trastevere for life. She died about 1700, or a little before, in a convent, but there is no evidence that she entered an order.

4 Under the name Matteo Mayer, Benedetti published an account of his villa, *La Villa Benedetti descritta* (1677), in which he names Plautilla's younger brother Basilio as architect, with help from his sister, but in fact documents of October 5, 1663, and February 12, 1665, list Plautilla as *architettrice*.

5 For a more detailed description of the Vascello, see Ranaldi 37-49.

6 On the front wall of the Vascello is the following inscription: "Pochi contro moltissimi / senza speranza di vincere/ duce però Garibaldi / I non degeneri figli / di Roma e d'Italia / quì pugnarono / un intero mese costanti / esempio ai venturi / come non conti i nemici / chi combatte / per la libertà e per la patria / assedio di Roma 1849 / ad iniziativa dei non elettori del V. Collegio / anno 1875. ("Few against very many / without hope of conquering / with Garibaldi however as leader / the non-degenerate sons of Rome and of Italy / here fought / an entire month, steadfast / an example for those to come / like the enemy unknown / [the heroic example] who fights for liberty and the fatherland / siege of Rome 1849 / on the initiative of the non-voting [members] of the V. College / year 1875.)

7 Though Medici had no children, Elliot states that he did not lack female companionship: "many good things had fallen to his lot, and last, not least, the hand of a wealthy English lady, devoted to him as long as he lived . . . " (166-67).

8 Ranaldi (42-43) states that in 1877 Medici bought the property for 10,000 *scudi*, and that in 2001 the house became the property of Rizzoli. A plaque with the name "Medici del Vascello" can still be seen on the building at the corner of Piazzale Aurelio and Via Aurelia.

9 Muti Garden, the so-called Vascello of France.

10 Vineyard of the Bonaventura Estate, or hereditary property.

11 Now deceased, Primo Nebiolo was president of the International Amateur Athletic Federation, also of the International University Sport Federation and of the Association of Summer Olympics International Federations, and a member of the International Olympic Committee.

Fig. 5. 1. The Casa Rustica in 2004 with a rise in earth covering the foundation of the Casino Malvasia. Photograph, B. Goldman.

CHAPTER 5

THE CASA RUSTICA; JUNE 29–30, 1849, MOROSINI AND THE CASINO MALVASIA

Katherine A. Geffcken

Addendum by Susan Wood

The Casa Rustica, now a principal feature of the Academy garden [fig. 5. 1], was built in the later nineteenth century on the ruins of the Casino Malvasia. But we have to imagine the original casino a story taller and almost twice as wide as the Casa Rustica. Indeed, the Malvasia towered above the Papal Wall, an outpost essential to the Italian defense.

As each day of June 1849 passed, French artillery outside the walls of Rome increasingly shelled Italian defenses on the Janiculum and even the center of the city. Entrenched in their high position at the Villa dei Quattro Venti, which they had captured on June 3, the French fired on and over Porta San Pancrazio. From spots to the south, their batteries pounded the Villa Sciarra and Trastevere below. Meanwhile the weather had turned extremely hot and sultry. During the day, Romans inside the city labored feverishly to erect barricades in the streets. Exhausted, they no sooner fell asleep about midnight when the French opened fire. On June 23, the American journalist Margaret Fuller described the scene she watched nightly from the balcony of her room at Piazza Barberini, " . . . t'is pretty, though terrible, to see the bombs, fiery meteors, springing from the horizon line upon their bright path, to do their wicked message" (Fuller 409). When morning came, the daily count of dead and wounded among soldiers and citizens soared.

On the Janiculum, the French crept ever closer to the city wall through the honeycomb of trenches they dug in a zigzag pattern. On the night of June 21-22, their guns breached the Papal Wall in three areas around the Villa Sciarra. Then, with troops installed just inside the wall, they mounted batteries capable of pouring a lateral rain of fire on the Villa Spada, on S. Pietro in Montorio, and on the principal Roman artillery nearby (now the park containing the mausoleum of the Caduti). Garibaldi and his troops worked breathlessly to fortify his second, inner line of defense south of Porta San Pancrazio, the Aurelian Wall, which old photographs show standing sometimes as high as fifteen feet, sometimes lying in a mound of rubble. Its course led southeast from the Porta San Pancrazio down the Janiculum, passing approximately under the front of the present Academy *cortile*. In the wedge of land between the Papal Wall and the Aurelian Wall stood the Casino Malvasia, a *palazzina* built probably in the last quarter of the sixteenth century, originally isolated

41

Fig. 5. 2. Repairs in the wall behind the Casa Rustica, showing where the breach of June 29 occurred, appear in lighter stonework. Photograph, B. Goldman, 2004.

on its high point of land, afterwards crowded on its southern side by the Papal Wall of the 1640's.

By late June, Italian soldiers and Roman citizens alike sensed that the final hour of the young Roman Republic was fast approaching. Margaret Fuller remarked, ". . . this state of suspense is agonizing" (Fuller 409). The fatal night came on June 29-30, after the French had bombed open a fourth breach in the Papal Wall, this time right behind the Casino Malvasia [fig. 5. 2]. Some of the French shells also hit the Malvasia, shattering its southern wall. If the French succeeded in entering the breach and securing the house, they could take the Porta San Pancrazio and nearby bastions from the rear and sweep the Aurelian Wall barricades with fire.

June 29 was, of course, that most characteristic Roman *festa*, San Pietro. The evening hours were a time of incredible contrasts. In downtown Rome, despite pressures of the siege, citizens were celebrating the holiday with candles in windows and fireworks in the streets. The dome of St. Peter's was illuminated. But on the Janiculum, while French cannons roared away, enemy infantry waited quietly in their trenches. Especially silent were those French hidden in the trenches leading up to the breach at the Malvasia. Behind battered defenses, the Italian survivors crouched and listened. All the Italian artillerymen had long been killed; the infantrymen who replaced them had been decimated. With frightening brevity, Garibaldi states that the last Roman cannon still on its carriage was dismounted on the evening of the 29th (Garibaldi 274). In fact, the Roman line was so inadequately manned that remnants of Masina's cavalry left their horses behind, and now prepared to fight on foot using their lances as long bayonets. Late in the evening a fearsome *temporale* crashed about the city and deluged the battlefield. To both invaders and defenders, their struggle seemed magnified to a cosmic scale. Garibaldi describes the scene vividly:

> Night enveloped Rome on the 29th like a winding-sheet. To prevent our
> attempting to repair the breaches the French artillery continued to pound
> away all night. It was a night of terror. The tempest of the heavens mingled

with the tempest on earth. The thunder crashed; the lightning flashes coun-
tered those from the flaming guns; thunderbolts fell in two or three places,
as though to point the sacredness of the city. In spite of the anniversary of
the festival of St. Peter, the two armies continued their duel to the death
(Garibaldi 274-75).

Under this natural and man-made rain, a detachment of Lombard *bersaglieri*
was sent forward to hold the Casino Malvasia and the breach behind it [fig. 5. 3]. The
bersagliere Emilio Dandolo recalled, "'The poor riflemen, buried to their knees in
mud, struck down by the frequent and fatal descent of the bombs, took the perilous
places assigned to them in silent discouragement.'"[1] We imagine these *bersaglieri*
slogging up what is now the Via Medici, which roughly follows the route of an old
allée in the Vigna Malvasia.

At midnight the storm ceased, and the cannons also fell silent. There followed two hours of eerie stillness, while the sentries, stretched thinly on the walls
from Porta San Pancrazio to Porta Portese, watched. Then, at two o'clock, the

Fig. 5. 3. Sculptural group by
Emilio Gallori of the *Bersaglieri*
in Defense of Rome, 1849, on the
base of the Garibaldi Monument
on the Janiculum. Photograph,
N. W. Goldman, 2005.

French cannon again sounded, and the French infantry poured up through the breach behind the Malvasia, surrounding and assaulting the building. From inside the battered house, the *bersaglieri* trained their disciplined fire on the attackers, but though gallant and determined, they were dreadfully outnumbered. The French overpowered them, taking the house, room by room. When the threat of Italian sniper-fire from the Malvasia ceased, a second line of French marched from another breach to the south in the Villa Sciarra grounds to seize the defenses of both the Porta San Pancrazio and the Aurelian Wall. For most of June 30, the Italians would struggle on, in hand to hand combat, around the Villa Savorelli (the Villa Aurelia), the Villa Spada, and San Pietro in Montorio. But Garibaldi knew, as he rushed into battle in the early hours of the 30th, that the definitive engagement was beginning, *"Orsù! Questa è l'ultima prova !"* (Trevelyan 221) ("Come on! This is the last test!")

In command of *bersaglieri* detached to hold the Casino Malvasia was a young Milanese lieutenant, who had just turned eighteen on June 26. From his childhood, Emilio Morosini had come under patriotic Italian influences in his family upbringing and education. In 1848, at Milan he joined Luciano Manara in the Five Days' battle on the barricades against the Austrians (*Le Cinque Giornate Milanesi*). Later, after the Austrians reasserted control in Lombardy, he followed Manara and other Lombard volunteers into Piedmont, where he helped Manara reorganize a battalion of *bersaglieri*, henceforth known as the Lombard *bersaglieri*. A proud, able outfit of rifle-men containing many Italians who had learned military skills as conscripts in the Austrian army, the Lombard *bersaglieri* were left a battalion without a country after Austria defeated the Piemontese at Novara. Hearing of the new Republic at Rome, they sailed down the Italian coast, and entered Rome on April 29, 1849. Their striking dress set them apart: dark blue uniforms with red and gold trim, and wide-brimmed hats with green-black cock feathers on the side.[2]

Emilio Morosini [fig. 5. 4] had an amazing effect upon those around him, even on battleworn veterans. His fellow *bersagliere* Emilio Dandolo describes "'his attractive, his angelic goodness'" and "'the unswerving rectitude of his principles.'" (Dandolo in Trevelyan 218; Dandolo 215) In the struggle at the Casino Malvasia, Morosini was slightly wounded in his head and left hand, more seriously in the chest.[3] Four of his men put him on a litter and set out for the *bersaglieri* headquarters just on the eastern side of the Aurelian Wall at Villa Spada. Unfortunately, in the darkness they ran into the second French column on its way from the Villa Sciarra breaches to attack the Aurelian Wall barricades. Surrounded, the four *bersaglieri* put down the litter and attempted to protect themselves and Morosini from certain death. But Morosini somehow managed to stand and pick up his sword, which lay with him on the litter. The old French sergeant in command of the enemy contingent ordered him to surrender, but Morosini replied, "Mai!" ("Never!"). Seeing that the Italian lieutenant was only a boy, the sergeant tried to intimidate him by pointing his bayonet at Morosini's chest, and he forbade his men to fire. Morosini, however, was determined to sacrifice his life "in the name of Italy" (Note! not Rome — the Lombard *bersaglieri* were primarily loyal to the concept of a united Italy).

Fig. 5. 4. Emilio Morosini
(Museo Storico dei Bersaglieri
at Porta Pia, Rome). Photograph,
B. Goldman.

As he was raising his sword to strike, a French soldier shot
him in the abdomen. This was Morosini's fourth and mortal
wound.[4] At dawn the French took him to one of their medical stations outside the walls, where a Corsican surgeon
treated him tenderly. He lived for thirty hours, praying and
speaking of his family, and died quietly on the morning of July 1
(Dandolo 215).

Emilio Dandolo's efforts to retrieve Morosini's body show
the special affection in which he was held. On July 1, Dandolo hurried from
office to office in downtown Rome to obtain permission to leave the city. With the
document finally in hand, he reached the French line and persuaded a sympathetic
Frenchman to let him search the nearest first aid station. But Morosini was already
dead, and his body had been removed to a distant cemetery for burial. An unsympa-
thetic superior officer arrested the sympathetic soldier and ordered Dandolo to
return to Rome. But Dandolo did not give up; he wrote immediately to the French
high command. The next morning, before he left for Colonel Manara's funeral, the
French permission arrived. And so, after the funeral, Dandolo walked back beyond
Porta San Pancrazio to the French lines. Still weak from wounds in leg and arm, he
was led blindfolded, under a scorching sun, for more than two hours, to a ditch,
where his eyes were uncovered, and he was made to watch the exhumation of
Morosini's body. Then he sadly followed the coffin as it was carried back into Rome,
to San Francesco dei Mendicanti, a church attached to the convent of the Cento Preti
at Ponte Sisto.[5]

There at S. Francesco, the Milanese military surgeon, Dr. Agostino Bertani,
got permission to see the body, and later wrote a graphic account of locating it in a
dark corner of the deserted church. Holding a lamp in one hand, Dr. Bertani untied
the shroud and examined the body. He saw the handsome but now disfigured face,
"paler than the shroud which had covered it." (Bertani in Garibaldi 283). Though
hardened by experience among the wounded and dying, Bertani was unexpectedly
moved by this one corpse. He cut a lock of Morosini's hair, said his farewell, then left
the church, trembling with shock. The body was later transported to Genoa, then to
Milan for burial. He is remembered at Rome in the unpretentious Via Morosini,
where buses cross Viale Trastevere to reach the Janiculum ascent on Via Dandolo.

According to Dr. Bertani, Morosini carried, in his belt, two pistols which the
Polish patriot Kosciuszko had given to Morosini's grandfather. Despite all efforts to
recover them, and also Morosini's sword, Bertani learned that the French sergeant
who had taken them would not part with them at any price (Bertani in Garibaldi
285).

Though now reduced by French shells to almost complete wreckage, the Vigna Malvasia had had a long and distinguished history. In his 1984 article, Paolo Mancini traced the owners of this *vigna* in which the back garden of the Academy now lies. The most important proprietors were Monsignor Innocenzo Malvasia (1553-1612), Cardinal Antonio Barberini (1607-1671), and Maffeo Barberini Colonna di Sciarra, usually called Maffeo Sciarra (1850-1925).[6]

In 1575, Malvasia bought the *vigna* from the Massaruzi family and, in the years following, built the casino called after him, on the highest point of the property, a spot sometimes referred to as Montagnolo. Drawings made in June [fig. 5. 5] and July of 1849 show that the Casino Malvasia had a wide façade facing east, with loggias on the *piano nobile* and the floor above looking out on splendid views of the Alban Hills. Indeed, Joseph Connors first pointed out to me that in 1611 from the Casino Malvasia Galileo demonstrated the amazing capacities of his telescope to see distant objects (see pp. 52).

In 1653, however, when Cardinal Antonio Barberini bought the casino and its *vigna*, he seems to have found the house a little confining for his princely status. But fortunately in a marriage settlement, the adjoining property to the south had come into the hands of Barberini's cousin Domenico Vaini. We know the nucleus of this property today as the Villa Sciarra. In 1654, Vaini gave his *vigna* and its more pretentious house to Antonio Barberini for the latter's lifetime. Thus began a long association between the Barberini and what was to become the Academy's part of the Janiculum. When Antonio's heir, Cardinal Carlo Barberini, bought the Vaini property in 1688, the Casino Malvasia became an integral part of a large, active agricultural holding.

The Nolli map of 1748 [fig. 5. 6] shows the Casino Malvasia hemmed in by the Papal Wall on its south side, with semicircular landscaping before its eastern façade and a network of allées and patterns of orchards all around. Although Nolli labels the *vigna* Villa Ottoboni, the property had already passed at auction back into Barberini hands in 1746 (financial constraints had forced the Barberini to sell the Malvasia in 1710). The buyers in 1746 were Cornelia Costanza Barberini and her husband Giulio Cesare Colonna di Sciarra. In the 1880's their great grandson Maffeo Sciarra entered into various business arrangements leading to real estate development on much of his Villa Sciarra property. Hence, the old Malvasia *vigna* became available for Academy acquisition in the twentieth century.

Drawings made after June, 1849, show the Casino Malvasia standing precariously on its northern and eastern sides, its southern wall completely blown away and its floors fallen [fig. 5. 7]. At some unknown time in the later nineteenth century, the Casa Rustica was constructed over much of its foundations and *cantina*. Olive and fig trees were planted on the table-like rise of earth covering the remaining northern portion of its *cantina* [fig. 5.8]. Today, the extensive basement is still there, cut in part out of living tufa and containing bearing walls for the original floors above. A *pozzo* (well) opens down to a large cistern below, and a staircase leads down to this lower, cistern level.

Fig. 5. 5. View toward the Janiculum from the Capitoline Hill, June 1849, by C. Andrese. Engraved by Pulini and sold at Spithover, Piazza di Spagna. To draw this view, Andrese stood at a window in the Palazzo Caffarelli on the Capitoline (or possibly on a high terrace or on the roof). He probably used a telescope.

1. Casino Malvasia, seen here from the front. Note the breach in the Papal Wall just to the left of the Casino. This detail shows that Andrese made his drawing at the end of June.

2. Villa Spada, seen from its back southeastern corner.

3. S. Pietro in Montorio. The clouds of smoke immediately around the Villa Spada and behind S. Pietro come from the Roman battery in the area called Il Pino.

4. Acqua Paola (the Fontanone).

5. Porta San Pancrazio.

6. Villa Aurelia.

7. Casino Farnese.

Information on engraving and publication of this view comes from G. M. Trevelyan, *Garibaldi's Defence of Rome* (London, 1919). 372.

47

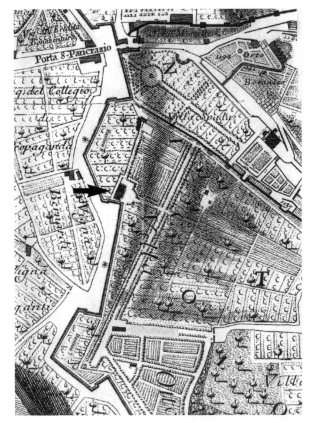

Fig. 5. 6. Portion of the map by Nolli (1748) showing the Casino Malvasia as indicated by the arrow on grounds identified as Villa Otto[boni].

Fig. 5. 7. Casino Malvasia and the breach in the Papal Wall, July 1849. Print by Carlo Werner. Property of the Villa Aurelia, AAR. Photograph, A. Ortolan.

Some confusion about the house's name seems to have arisen. In 1849, Professor de Cuppis labeled the building "Cas. Malvasia" on his map of the battle-field, but some sources call it Casa Merluzzo or Cascina ("dairy") Merluzzetti. By the early years of the twentieth century it was known simply as the *"Trattoria."* Professor Lawrence Richardson reports that when Tatiana Warscher came to Rome (for the first time about 1912), she knew the building as a *taverna*, "where people who made the excursion to the Janiculum to see the view over Rome could find refreshment . . ." [fig. 5. 9] (Richardson 2).

Even after the Academy was installed in the Main Building, years passed before the lot on which the Casa Rustica stands could be purchased and even longer before the "noisy," "undesirable" tenants could be evicted. The land development company which sold lots from the old Sciarra and Spada holdings had installed a street, Via Narducci, leading from Via Masina diagonally across the present Academy property to the turn in the Papal Wall where Via Medici becomes Via Roselli. The Academy owned the eastern plot, but not the northwest section towards the wall enclosing the Casa Rustica. As early as February 1913 Director Jesse Benedict Carter urged purchase of the so-called Lot #2; he was eager to see a dormitory for women built on this lot. But World War I intervened. Finally, in 1921 the Academy bought the lot for $23,053.38. Then a legal struggle ensued between the land development company, which owned the street, and Monsignor Ubaid, owner of the property between the Academy and Porta San Pancrazio. At last, in May 1927, the land company won the suit, and in October 1927, the Academy acquired the street, uniting Lot #2 with the main plot, leaving as a paved street only the portion between Ubaid's

Fig. 5. 8. The Casa Rustica in 1989 with a clearly marked rise in earth covering the foundation and the cantina of the Casino Malvasia. (In recent reworkings of the garden, earth has been shift-ed to make the rise less evident). Photograph, K. A. Geffcken.

TOP

Fig. 5. 9. The Casa Rustica as an *osteria*, in a photograph taken before 1927, when the tenants finally departed. The fence to the right encloses the Academy's Lot #1, on which the Main Building sits. This view shows the three-way intersection of Via Roselli from the left, Via Narducci leading off right behind the fence, and the beginning of Via Medici in the immediate right foreground. Photograph, Academy archives, New York.

BELOW

Fig. 5. 10. The Casa Rustica when the trattoria and tenants used the building. Photograph, Photographic Archive of the AAR, before eviction in 1927.

property and the Academy. The 35 obnoxious Casa Rustica tenants had finally departed in 1927 [fig. 5. 10]; the building then was renovated as housing for Academy employees.[7] Three years later the Casa Rustica became really rustic when the wealthy American Henrietta Tower Wurts, last private owner of the Villa Sciarra, gave the Academy 172 hens, 3 ducks, and 11 pigeons, which were then installed behind the *"Trattoria."* Mrs. Wurts's generosity not only reaffirmed the historical link between the Villa Barberini-Sciarra and the Casino Malvasia, but also revived, on a small scale, the old *azienda agricola* (large-scale farm) that so long existed on the Janiculum.

REFERENCES

I am indebted to Giovanni Cimoroni of the Academy staff for taking me on a tour of the *cantina* under the Casa Rustica and for his observations on the structures there; to the *Colonello Direttore* of the Museo Storico dei Bersaglieri at Porta Pia for talking with me about the record of the Lombard battalion in the 1849 war and for allowing me to photograph a small portrait of Morosini; and to Professor Connors for telling me about Galileo's visit to our part of the Janiculum.

Ai Caduti per Roma MDCCCXLIX-MDCCCLXX (Rome, 1941). On Morosini, 179; on the Lombard *Bersaglieri*, 93 and Plate opposite 88.
Annual Report of the American Academy in Rome, 1913, 1914, 1916-17, 1918-22, 1924-25, 1926-30.
Dandolo, Emilio. *I Volontari ed I Bersaglieri Lombardi* (1849-50; repr. Milan, Rome, Naples, 1917).
Fuller Ossoli, Margaret. *At Home and Abroad,* ed. Arthur B. Fuller (Boston, London 1856).
Garibaldi, Giuseppe. *Memoirs,* ed. Alexandre Dumas, trans. R. S. Garnett (London, 1931). For Dr. Agostino Bertani's account of Emilio Morosini's death, see 281-85.
Mancini, Paolo. "Villa Sciarra," *Alma Roma* 25 (1984), 1-31.
Richardson, Lawrence, jr on the Liszt piano, *AMACADMY* 2 (1979), 2.
Stevens, Gorham Phillips. Diary 1911-1932. Unpublished notebooks. Library of the AAR.
Trevelyan, G. M. *Garibaldi's Defence of the Roman Republic* (London, New York, Toronto 1908, 1949).
Trevelyan often cites the English trans. of Emilio Dandolo's work: *The Italian Volunteers and Lombard Rifle Brigade (1851).*

NOTES

1 Trevelyan 218, quoting the English edition of Dandolo. In the Italian edition, 212, Emilio Dandolo accompanied his *povero amico* Morosini and other *bersaglieri* up to the Casino Malvasia, but about eleven o'clock felt compelled to return to his duties as aide to Colonel Manara at the Villa Spada (Dandolo 211-15).

2 For more on the Lombard *Bersaglieri* and their Colonel Manara, see "Scarpone," pp. 23-29 and the "Death of Manara," pp. 72-73.

3 In my account, I have followed details recorded by Dr. Agostino Bertani, who examined the body of Morosini (Bertani in Garibaldi 281-85). See also Dandolo 213-14.

4 At the Museum of Modern Art, Rome, there is a small bronze by Ettore Ferrari (1848-1929), Inventory Number 8349, showing Morosini on the litter, raising himself up and fiercely challenging an unseen enemy. His plumed hat lies under the front of the stretcher. The placard gives his first name incorrectly as "Antonio": "La morte di Antonio Morosini." I thank several members of the 2003 NEH Summer Seminar at the American Academy in Rome, a seminar on the Risorgimento, for telling me about this piece.

5 In 1835, the Convent of the Cento Preti at Ponte Sisto had become a military hospital, and by July 2 the French had taken it over. The church of S. Francesco dei Mendicanti was demolished in 1879 to make way for the Tiber retaining walls and Lungotevere.

51

6 For a detailed chronology of Malvasia owners, see pp. 54.

7 The families of many employees grew up in the Casa Rustica. In 1966 the Academy began redoing the building as studios for Fellows, and employees moved out to housing they rented elsewhere. A few years later the carpenter's shop was also removed from the Casa Rustica. At present it houses the Archaeology laboratory and several studios for Fellows of the AAR.

 ADDENDUM

A NOTE ON THE CASINO MALVASIA AND GALILEO

Katherine A. Geffcken

In summer 1989, when I was preparing my essay on Morosini and the Casino Malvasia, I stopped to exchange a word with Professor Joseph Connors, then Director of the Academy. It was one of those felicitous moments that happen so often around the Academy. I mentioned that I had just been down in the *sotterraneo* of the Casa Rustica to see what remained there of the late sixteenth century Casino Malvasia, which I had been reading about in Paolo Mancini's article on the Villa Sciarra. Professor Connors said, "Oh! That's where Galileo demonstrated his telescope." Then he mentioned the dinner party organized by Federico Cesi at the Malvasia on April 14, 1611. Eight years before, Cesi and three others had founded the learned society of the Lincei (lynxes) to foster a penetrating study of nature. Thus, when Cesi assembled his scientific circle in 1611 to learn about Galileo's new instrument, the Malvasia with its high location on the Janiculum was an ideal spot from which to view remote objects.

Thanks to Professor Connors and many other interested scholars, the site of our Casino Malvasia / Casa Rustica has now become well known for that celebrated scientific event and dinner party, an important moment in history of science. On April 14, 1997, the Academy and the Accademia Nazionale dei Lincei observed the anniversary of that occasion with an important conference *"Giornata Lincea per celebrare le dimostrazioni astronomiche di Galileo Galilei (14 aprile 1611)."*

REFERENCES

Bucci, Antonella, James M. (Jim) Lattis, and Cristina Puglisi. "Casa Rustica reopens with a Ghost of Galileo," *Society of Fellows Newsletter* (Fall/Winter, 1997), 22-27.

Lattis, James M. (Jim). "Galileo celebrated: a night with the stars," *ibid.*, 28.

Lattis, James M. *Between Copernicus and Galileo: Christoph Clavius and the Collapse of Ptolemaic Cosmology* (Chicago and London, 1994).

Orbaan, J. A. F. *Documenti sul Barocco in Roma* (1920). The entry dated "1611, aprile 16" describes the demonstration, names the guests, and identifies the site as " . . . the vineyard of Monsignor Malvasia outside Porta San Pancrazio, on a high and open place."

RENOVATING THE CASA RUSTICA

Susan Wood

In 1993, as part of Italy's commitment to the EEC, the Italian government enacted new regulations for all building owners, demanding a report from a structural engineer on the state of all buildings in use. The Casa Rustica was found to be structurally unsound: some of the antique wooden beams were rotten; the electrical system was below code; and the boiler room failed to conform to safety requirements.

In 1996, the Academy remedied all of these deficiencies under the direction of Cristina Puglisi, Assistant Director for Academy properties, without sacrificing the rich history of the structure [fig. 5. 11]. The renovation was nearing completion when Cristina Puglisi gave me a tour of the Casa Rustica. The rotten beams had been replaced, and in some places, smaller steel beams had been added for additional support alongside the wooden ones, so that the steel beams became the load-bearing members. In other instances, only the ends of the beams had deteriorated, where they were exposed to rain and weather on exterior walls. These supporting beams were replaced, but the rest of the beam, if perfectly sound, was trimmed for reuse elsewhere. All of the roof and most of the floor tiles are original. The workmen had to remove them to reach parts needing repair, but when the structural restoration was completed, the original tiles were reinstalled. The result is an accurate, pleasant, and safe restoration of the historical building, comfortable and utilitarian.

Fig. 5. 11. Composite photograph of the Casa Rustica in 1998. The word VINO discovered during restoration on the façade is faintly visible today. Photograph, K. A. Geffcken.

CHRONOLOGY OF THE MALVASIA PROPERTY

Katherine A. Geffcken

Because Paolo Mancini's thoroughly documented article on the Villa Sciarra (and Malvasia) is not easy to locate, I am including a chronology drawn from Mancini's research ("Villa Sciarra," *Alma Roma* 25 [1984], 1-31). Although the Malvasia property had many owners through the years, I will use only the name Malvasia for clarity.

JUNE 2, 1549: Raffaele Massaruzi purchases the Malvasia *vigna* from the Church and Chapter of S. Maria ad Martyres (the Pantheon).

1575: Monsignor Innocenzo Malvasia (1553-1612) purchases the *vigna* and builds a *palatium* (the *Casino*).

SEPTEMBER 26, 1614: Gaspare Rivaldi buys the property from Malvasia's heirs. After Rivaldi's death, the R. Camera Apostolica confiscates the property for debts.

APRIL 4, 1641: Giulio Ornano buys it at auction.

NOVEMBER 29, 1653: Cardinal Antonio Barberini (1607-1671) purchases it. Cardinal Barberini's cousin Domenico Vaini lends him, for life, the villa nearby, the core of which is now the Villa Sciarra. At Barberini's death, the Vaini property reverts to the owners.

AUGUST 25, 1674: Antonio Barberini's heir and nephew Cardinal Carlo Barberini acquires a small vineyard (de Blanchis) to be added to the Malvasia, between the Malvasia piece and the Vaini property.

MARCH 16, 1685: Marchese Bernardino Spada rents the Malvasia property. Inventory shows the Casino is in poor condition – but there are 130 paintings.

JANUARY 29, 1687: Marchese Spada buys the Malvasia.

OCTOBER 18, 1687: When the Vaini family objects to the Spada purchase, Cardinal Carlo Barberini reacquires the Malvasia.

OCTOBER 2, 1688: Carlo and other Barberini relatives win the right to purchase Villa Vaini, which the Vaini family had sold to Pietro Gabrielli (January 19, 1688). Thus, the large property enjoyed by Antonio Barberini (Malvasia + Vaini) was reunited.

SEPTEMBER 23, 1710: Carlo Barberini's heir, Cardinal Francesco Barberini, sells the Malvasia and Vaini to Cardinal Pietro Ottoboni.

1740: On Ottoboni's death, his heir consigns the property to creditors for Cardinal Ottoboni's debts.

DECEMBER 6, 1746: Cornelia Costanza Barberini and her husband purchase the Malvasia and Vaini property at auction.

1811: Their grandson Maffeo Colonna di Sciarra (1771-1849) is assigned the Janiculum property after his legal actions against his family. His posthumous son Maffeo Barberini Colonna di Sciarra (1850-1925), called Maffeo Sciarra, inherits the Janiculum property.

1886, 1889: Keeping the immediate core of the Villa Vaini/Sciarra intact, the Compagnia Fondiaria Italiana draws up plans to sell off most of Villa Vaini/Sciarra, all of the Malvasia, and most of the Spada in residential lots. Maffeo Sciarra is a partner.

1896-97: Land speculation collapses. The land partnership is dissolved. Sciarra is ruined. The lands are ceded to the Bank of Italy.

1905: The Bank of Italy cedes all land lots to the Società Anonima Gianicolo (President: Marchese Luigi Medici del Vascello). These lots were sold. AAR property now rests on several of these lots.

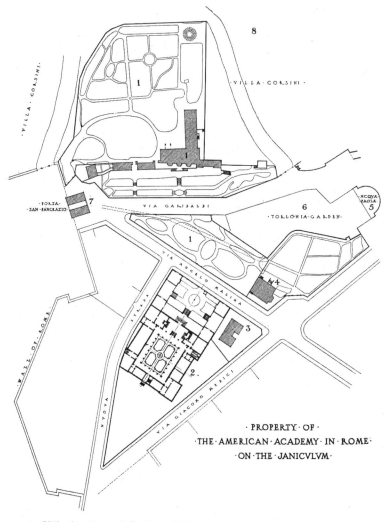

1. Villa Aurelia and Gardens (Administrative Offices, Lecture Room and Residence of Director).
2. New Building (Library, Studios, and Fellows' Quarters).
3. Villa Bellacci (Property of the Academy).
4. Villa Chiaraviglio (Property of the Academy).
5. Acqua Paola.
6. Torlonia Garden.
7. Porta San Pancrazio.
8. Corsini Gardens.

Fig. 6. 1. Map prepared in 1914 to show the Academy and its immediate neighborhood. Through the Heyland bequest and the generosity of J. Pierpont Morgan, the Academy then owned properties numbered 1–4. The street labelled NVOVA STRADA, known as Via Paolo Narducci on city maps, separates the Main Building ("New Building") from Abate Ubaid's plot on Via Masina and, below it, so-called Lot #2 (not yet in 1914 Academy property). Ubaid and the Collegio di S. Isaia later, in 1937, built 5B facing Via Masina and the "Nuova Strada." Behind it stood the oldest structure on his property, now rebuilt and leased as the Photographic Archive of the Academy. This map appeared in the 1914 Annual Report of the Academy. Note how the Nuova Strada (Via Narducci) caused the curve at the back corner of the New (Main) Building.

CHAPTER 6

THE VICOLO CIECO, PAOLO NARDUCCI, AND VIA ANGELO MASINA 5B

Katherine A. Geffcken

The Academy's recent long-term lease of Via Angelo Masina 5B and the little building behind it has focused our attention on the short street often known as the *vicolo cieco* (blind alley) between the main Academy building and 5B. Closed at both ends with gates, it served in the past as an often untidy parking lot. Though rarely used, the principal entrance of 5B opened on it, and the street once extended from Via Masina through the Academy's back garden. It intersected with Via Roselli and Via Medici in front of the Casa Rustica. After the Academy, in October 1927, finally purchased this street from the liquidator of the Società Anonimo Gianicolo (a land development company), the Academy could unite the two parts of the back garden, removing all of the street except the short stretch we see today. This stretch was left intact so that the Maronite Abate Luigi Ubaid, owner of the lot between the street and Porta San Pancrazio, could have access to his property (Abate Ubaid had, in fact, carried on long litigation with the land company about the street. See also p. 49.) Today, even though much of the former street has given way to lush gardens and grass in the Academy's back property, its line can still be imagined. For instance, it caused the curving of the Library's back corner wall [fig. 6. 1] and determined the placement of the Academy's back gate.

The *vicolo cieco* and its vanished extension were named Via Paolo Narducci, honoring, like all streets in the neighborhood, a figure in the conflict of 1849. Indeed, the nineteen-year-old Narducci was especially noteworthy because tradition says that he was the first man to die in defense of Rome, on April 30, 1849, a kind of Protesilaos in Risorgimento lore. This report is not entirely accurate, since Narducci, though fatally wounded in the chest on April 30, lingered among the injured at Ospedale Santo Spirito until 2:30 A.M. on May 2. But he was a native Roman, and it must have seemed appropriate for the first casualty for Rome to be a Roman.

Paolo Narducci was born in Rome on June 8, 1829, the son of Francesco Narducci and Teresa Maciucchi. The family lived near Aracoeli, where in their *salone* they frequently entertained liberal political thinkers. Their visitors caught the attention of the Papal police, who then kept the building under almost constant surveillance. And in fact, after the Italians surrendered to the French, Paolo's mother was twice arrested and his father once imprisoned. An able student, Paolo was pursuing philosophy and mathematics at the Accademia di San Luca when in March, 1848, the war for independence broke out in northern Italy. He longed to participate, but his parents refused to let him go north.

Instead, the next October, he took examinations for the artillery, emerging the leading candidate. By the end of December, 1848, he was *tenente in seconda* (lieutenant) in a local Roman unit. When the French landed at Civitavecchia and marched toward Rome, Narducci asked to be sent to the Italian front line. He was first posted with his artillery at Porta Angelica at the Vatican, and then near the southwestern corner of the Vatican defenses, the bastion of Santa Marta above Porta Pertusa. An observant officer, he quickly pointed out to his superiors that his two cannons were not sufficient to guard the approaches from the Via Aurelia Nuova and that another road, circling south from Monte Mario, was completely unprotected.

On the morning of April 30, 1849, the French army arrived, intending to assault Porta Pertusa, not realizing that this gate was walled up.[1] Narducci's cannon hit the French with all the ammunition his unit could fire. But the experienced French troops quickly returned shot. So many of the Italian artillery men fell, including *sottotenente* (second lieutenant) Enrico Pallini of Ancona, that Narducci had to load and fire the cannon himself. Then, he was himself struck with a rifle bullet. Mortally wounded, he was taken to the nearest hospital, Santo Spirito. To his younger brother Pietro, who stayed close by his side, he said, *"Bacia Mamma per me."* After his death, his portrait was cherished by the patriotic young Castellani sisters, who kept fresh flowers before it. In response, the Papal police sequestered the painting.[2]

Today, in the Janiculum *passeggiata* not far from Villa Lante stands Narducci's bust, decreed in 1920 and sculpted by Publio Morbiducci [fig. 6. 2]. The portrait suggests a more mature man than the young real Narducci. Unfortunately, vandals have slightly disfigured the piece.

Via Narducci on the Janiculum was part of an elaborate plan for breaking up and selling off tracts of Villa Sciarra and Villa Spada (1883-1889). The street was to run beyond Via Masina, down to Via Garibaldi. Another street, Via Gustavo Spada, was to run just inside the Papal wall, ending at Porta San Pancrazio. Furthermore, yet another street, Via Andrea il Moro, was to begin behind the Chiaraviglio and end behind the Acqua Paola, right across from the entrance to the Janiculum *passeggiata* (di Vico Fallani 263). Had all these streets been realized, the Academy's neighborhood would now contain densely packed buildings on small plots. But these plans were never fully carried out because the early purchasers bought large tracts. For instance, to ensure her view from the Villa Aurelia, Mrs. Heyland acquired land on the northeast side of Via Masina and made it into a small park, now part of Academy property. Nevertheless, the heroes in whose honor streets were planned or even paved, but later eliminated, like Via Narducci, were not forgotten. When allées in Villa Sciarra were named, one became Viale Paolo Narducci, and another, Viale Gustavo Spada. And elsewhere in Monteverde Vecchio, stairs leading down from Via Fratelli Bandiera were named for Andrea Aguyar, Garibaldi's devoted South American *moro* ("moor" or dark-skinned man), who was killed on June 30, 1849.

Fig. 6. 2. Paolo Narducci: bust in the Janiculum *Passeggiata.* Sculptor: Publio Morbiducci, 1920. Photograph, K. A. Geffcken.

The area belonging to the Maronites, extending from Via Narducci up to Porta San Pancrazio, was originally part of the Spada *vigna* and became available for development in the land speculation schemes of the late nineteenth century (see p. 55). By 1913, photographs of the new Academy building under construction show, next door, Abate Luigi Ubaid's land intersected with narrow allées, a fountain in the middle, and a small *villino* at the back, where the "Bishop's Palace," as it has been nicknamed, now stands.

In 1929 Abate Ubaid donated his property to the Collegio di S. Isaia for Maronite missions.[3] The document of donation describes three buildings: a *villino* with twelve rooms (presumably the Maronite house close to Porta San Pancrazio), a new building with thirty rooms (no doubt the large structure with a tower fronting directly on Via Masina, often in the past known as Scala A), and the gardener's house with five rooms (either the *villino* seen in the 1913 photograph or the later so-called "Bishop's Palace"). Scala B (that is, 5B) had not yet been built. In 1937 the Collegio di S. Isaia erected 5B and planned to build a church between it and Scala A. But when the Academy objected to the church, only the front section was left, with its large archway and three arched windows above, serving as a link between Scala A and

59

Fig. 6. 3. The arched entrance between Scala A and Scala B (5B), façade of the church never completed. Photograph, K. A. Geffcken.

Fig. 6. 4. The Vicolo Cieco and Building 5B. Those who come to consult the Archive usually enter through the courtyard of 5B. Photograph, K. A. Geffcken, 2001.

Scala B [fig. 6. 3]. Middle Eastern influences everywhere in the structures reflect the Maronites' Lebanese origins.

Over the years the Collegio di S. Isaia housed many occupants. For a while Lebanese nuns lived in parts of Scala A. But the Collegio itself moved to Via Boccea, and the buildings entered an incertain period, eventually becoming rental property. Many Academy people and friends of the Academy were tenants of the Padri Maroniti, such as Berthe Marti FAAR '51, RAAR '62, the archaeologist Baldo Conticello, and a long series of Professors-in-Charge of the Intercollegiate Center for Classical Studies. Several families of Cape Verdians grew up in the basement, and ground-level units near the gate were occupied by furniture makers and auto mechanics. Meanwhile upkeep of the buildings suffered.

The Maronites developed several projects for their property: for instance, a hostel for families with sick children in nearby Hospital Bambin Gesù and a hotel for the Jubilee. But their tenacious tenants desperately filed suit after suit fighting eviction from our lovely neighborhood, a struggle that evolved through almost ten years. In the end, the Maronites' plans were too long delayed, the costs too high, and the Padri were open to other possibilities. The Academy had first urgently negotiated for purchase of the property from Ubaid in 1919-24, and again, from the Maronites in the early 1960's. But many conferences with Ubaid proved futile, and later persuasion

Fig. 6. 5. Photographic Archive, AAR in rear of 5B. Photograph, K. A. Geffcken, 2001.

Fig. 6. 6. The main study room in the Photographic Archive of the American Academy in Rome. Photograph, K. A. Geffcken.

could never move the Maronites from their price (lire 500,000,000 = $800,000 in 1962). Finally at the end of the century, the Academy signed the long-term lease on 5B and the little "palace." As for Scala A, the Padri have renovated that building and leased it out for offices and apartments.

On June 19, 2000, work began on consolidating and adapting the "Bishop's Palace" as the Academy's new Photographic Archive (the "Fototeca"). Used not only as a gardener's house, but also as a garage, and then cut up into small flats, this structure had been condemned because of serious cracks. And indeed, it turned out to lack real foundations and had to be substantially strengthened [fig. 6. 5]. Meanwhile, Academy staff cleared abandoned furniture, stoves, and other rubbish from empty 5B, in preparation for a year of renovation. By summer 2001, the Fototeca had moved into its bright, clean quarters, fragrant with the wood of new shelves and furniture [fig. 6. 6]. And by late summer, 5B was ready for Fellows with families, its walls freshly plastered and its colored floor tiles carefully conserved.

Outside, the former Via Narducci for just a moment looked eerily empty. A property boundary line in the past, the *vicolo* was now an Academy passageway. But it will perhaps remain a bit *misterioso*, as Giovanni Cimoroni described it to me in summer 2000. Norma Goldman has compared it to roads leading out of the Forum but ending abruptly under later construction.[4]

REFERENCES

American Academy in Rome: Report 1968-73, 27-28.

Cozza, Lucos. "Mura Aureliane, 1: Trastevere, il braccio meridionale: dal Tevere a Porta Aurelia-San Pancrazio." *Bull.Com.* 92 (1987-88), 137-174, especially the plans reproduced on 159.

de Vico Fallani, Massimo. *Storia dei Giardini Pubblici di Roma nell'Ottocento* (Rome, 1992), particularly 263, fig. 236, which includes a plan, proposed and dated 1888, with the tight configuration of the streets I have mentioned.

Lizzani, Mario. "Salotti Romani dell'Ottocento." *Studi Romani* 3.4 (1955), 435-46, especially 441-42.

Marino, Antonio. *Il Gianicolo Illustrato* (Rome, 1922), 115-16.

Reggiani, A. "Paolo Narducci." in *Ai Caduti per Roma MDCCCXLIX-MDCCCLXX* (Rome, 1941), 127-30.

Stevens, Gorham Phillips. Diary 1911-1932. Unpublished notebooks. Library of the American Academy in Rome.

 NOTES

1   According to A. Reggiani, however, documents in the Archivio Narducci show that the French knew from informers that Porta Pertusa was blocked (Reggiani in *Ai Caduti* 128).

2   Members of the Castellani family were noted goldsmiths and collectors of jewelry in nineteenth century Rome. See the Castellani collection at the Museo Etrusco di Villa Giulia. The head of the family, Fortunato Pio Castellani (1799-1865) and his wife Carolina Baccani had five daughters and three sons. The family was liberal in its patriotic outlook. In particular, the son Alessandro was deeply involved for years in the Risorgimento cause. In November 1849 two daughters, Augusta and Francesca, were arrested for profaning a service for the military dead with references to the Republic. (Reggiani in *Ai Caduti* 129-130).

3   I am extremely grateful to Cristina Puglisi for information about 5B, the Maronites' property, and especially for photocopies of the Academy's purchase of the *vicolo* and of Abate Ubaid's donation to the Collegio of S. Isaia. I thank Wayne Linker for explaining that the Maronites began construction on a church but, owing to Academy opposition, completed only the façade.

4   For other references to Via Narducci, see pp. 10, 49.

 ADDENDUM

ACADEMY HISTORY RECORDED

· *Norma Wynick Goldman*

We who have benefited from the collaborative effort of five architects and J. P. Morgan, the generous patron, in the production of the Main Building are fascinated by the archival reporting by Steven Bedford in Chapter 1 of the present volume about the details of how the Academy structure became what it is today. The arresting illustrations (figs. 1. 1 and 1. 2) show the site during and after the building of the Academy and its studios. Notice the road to the right of the main building, the Vicolo Cieco described by Kathy Geffcken (pp. 56-62), which caused the curved corner of the Academy Main Building. Today the road which we have all climbed from the bus or the Centro, Via Pietro Roselli, ends at the top of the hill where it meets the Via Medici. Via Pietro Roselli then became the Via Narducci, named for the young Roman member of the *Garibaldini*, who died so tragically, one of the earliest to fall in the battle of April 1849 (See Geffcken's description of his mortal wound and death, p. 58). Off the Via Angelo Masina, this road had become for several years a narrow rectangular parking bay between the Academy and the structure to the right, closed off from Via Masina by a locked gate. Presently it is still locked from public access from Via Masina, but has been become part of Academy grounds. In the Roman Forum we have seen how roads leading out of the Forum have disappeared under later construction. Now we can see the same phenomenon in the Academy site, as the Via Narducci became an inconspicuous parking bay off the Via Masina, and now is the *Vicolo Cieco* (blind alley) between the Academy Main Building and the recently installed Photographic Archive.

Bedford's chapter gives the basic structure of the Main Building as finally realized. Evident today in the entrance courtyard is the addition of the central fountain surrounded by gravel walkways, and jasmine has been planted against the wall along each side of the stairway leading up to the interior entrance hall. And for all who come and go at the Academy, one of the most Roman aspects of Academy life is the friendly but discerning hospitality of the *portieri* (gatekeepers) in their cubicle at the front gate.

Bedford's chapter continues with a description of the ascending staircases "not Roman at all" and the main rooms emerging from the grand scale vestibule grouped around an open courtyard of typical Roman design. As Bedford predicted, the new renovations of 1991 and 1992-94 did not alter "the historic fabric of the McKim, Mead & White Building."

ABOVE

Fig. 7. 1. Villa Spada to which Garibaldi moved after the Villa Savorelli (Aurelia) was bombed, NW side. The eagles on the façade derive from the crest of the Nobili family. Photograph, K. A. Geffcken.

RIGHT

Fig. 7. 2. Section of the Nolli map (1748) showing the Villa Spada extending southeast from Porta San Pancrazio, bounded on the southwest by the Aurelian Wall and Vigna Malvasia, on the north by the Giardino Farnese (Savorelli/Aurelia), on the east by the Orto Botanico and the Acqua Paola.

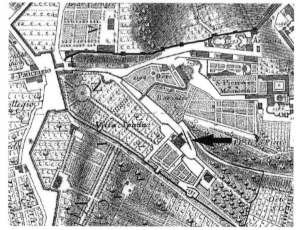

June 26, 1849, Anita Garibaldi and the Villa Spada

Katherine A. Geffcken

By June 21, 1849, the Villa Savorelli (Aurelia), where Garibaldi had established his headquarters, was so pulverized from French cannon balls flying eastward over Porta San Pancrazio that even Garibaldi conceded the building was no longer usable (see Chapter 11 of the present volume). Since June 3 he had conferred with his officers, eaten, and slept in the Villa, apparently unconcerned for his own safety. But reluctantly on the evening of June 21, Garibaldi evacuated the Villa Savorelli and moved a little downhill to the Villa Spada, just inside the line of the Aurelian Wall [fig. 7. 1].

The Spada *vigna* was a long narrow strip extending from the Via di Porta San Pancrazio (now Via Garibaldi) to a few feet beyond the modern Via Nicola Fabrizi. On the west, the Aurelian Wall separated it from the Malvasia and Sciarra properties [fig. 7. 2]. Although the western side of the house was badly damaged by increasingly intense French bombardment, the structure remained intact enough to be restored after the 1849 war. It now stands in the central core of its grounds, across Via Medici from the Villa Chiaraviglio. All the front portion of the Academy's Main Building and entrance, the Villino Bellacci, the Villa Chiaraviglio, and the Academy garden on the east side of Via Angelo Masina lie within the original Spada boundaries.

Headquartered in the Villa Spada between June 21 and June 30, Garibaldi and his staff used all their remaining resources to hold a line of defense, first at the Papal city wall, then behind the Aurelian Wall. On the morning of June 26, as Garibaldi and three colleagues were eating breakfast in a third floor room of the Spada, Anita Garibaldi unexpectedly arrived from Nice (known then by its Italian name Nizza).

Anna Maria Ribeiro da Silva, Garibaldi's first wife, was born about 1821 in the southern Brazilian state of Santa Caterina [fig. 7. 3]. Of Portuguese and Indian descent, Anna or Anita, as she was usually called, was about five feet tall, small-boned but sturdy, and endowed with vivid coloring. Observers commented on her interesting but not beautiful features, on her full figure, on a hint of masculinity in her stance, and on her splendid long black hair. In 1835 she had married Manuel Duarte de Aguiar and settled with her husband in a house overlooking the harbor at Laguna on the Brazilian coast. How Garibaldi first saw and claimed her, in August,

Fig. 7. 3. Anita Garibaldi. Under this miniature, the Garibaldi's younger son Ricciotti noted that his father commissioned it from the painter Gallino in Montevideo in 1845 and that it was the only true likeness of his mother. From Jesse White Mario, *The Birth of Modern Italy* (London, 1909).

1839, sounds like the script of an old swashbuckling movie. He was then a political exile from Italy, serving the young Republic of Rio Grande do Sul as commander of its small navy against imperialist Brazil. Shipwrecked off Laguna, he swam ashore, and with his surviving companions, captured not only the town but also the Brazilian fleet in the harbor. Yet he was so depressed over losing his fellow Italian exiles at sea and in battle that he needed new companionship. According to his own account, he stood on the deck of his captured flagship and turned his telescope to view the town. One young woman doing chores near her house especially caught his attention. He dropped the telescope, went ashore, and found the place where he had spotted her. A man whom he had noticed in the town invited him inside, and when Garibaldi saw the woman, he said, *"Tu devi esser mia!"* ("You must be mine!"). As he later remarked, "By these words I had created a bond which death alone could break." (Garibaldi 88-89).

In his *Memoirs*, Garibaldi romanticized the legend of Anita, probably both in its dramatic opening and in their later extraordinary life at sea and in the South American swamps. Nevertheless, it is certain that on October 23, 1839, Anita left her home forever and joined Garibaldi (whom she called José or Peppino) on his ship, and they sailed away to guerrilla battles, capture, torture, and fantastic escapes [fig. 7. 4]. Indeed, Garibaldi called Anita his "Brazilian Amazon" (Garibaldi 91). In 1841 they settled in Montevideo, and in 1842 they were married, when the couple had reason to believe that Anita's first husband was dead. By the time revolutionary activities in Italy called them back to Europe, Anita had borne two boys (the first in 1840) and subsequently two girls (one of whom survived). After she and the children had sailed to Garibaldi's home city of Nizza (Nice), he took ship for Italy in April of 1848 with sixty-three members of the Italian Legion he had formed from among fellow exiles in Montevideo.

For the remaining short time of her life, Anita moved back and forth between her children and her husband. She spent a few weeks in autumn 1848 with him in Tuscany, then in February 1849 joined him at Rieti, where the Italian Legion was quartered. But in April when Garibaldi, astride his magnificent white horse, and with his "wild-looking warriors" (Trevelyan 111, quoting Gibson) left for Rome, he persuaded Anita to return to Nice. By then she was pregnant and not well.

On June 21, as he was preparing to abandon the Villa Savorelli, Garibaldi wrote Anita a letter. It begins and ends with affection and concern for his family. In between, his words show his anticlerical stance, his association of the 1849 Republic with Rome's ancient greatness, and his pride in a small victory over the French at Casa Giacometti (Osteria Scarpone) (text of the letter in Trevelyan 205). Anita never

Fig. 7. 4. Bronze equestrian statue of Anita Garibaldi atop her tomb on the Passeggiata del Gianicolo. Sculptor, Mario Rutelli, 1932. Rutelli shows Anita during her days as a Latin American guerrilla with a raised pistol in her right hand and holding a baby in her left arm. Photograph, B. Goldman.

received the letter because she was already on her way to Rome. When the news of desperate fighting on the Janiculum arrived at Nice, she had determined to join her husband. She was now in her fifth month of pregnancy and subject to fainting spells (Montanelli / Nozza 224). Trevelyan sums up her decision: "She left posterity no record of her motives, and no apology for her choice, but her silent, set, immutable purpose to remain at his side until the end – whatever that end might be – pleads for her with more eloquence than words" (Trevelyan 206).

In his *Memoirs* Garibaldi describes the morning in late June when he and his colleagues Sacchi, Bueno, and Corcelli were sitting in their shirtsleeves upstairs in the Spada "taking *dejeuner.*" He himself was in an extremely somber mood because he had just sentenced to death an officer who, having been seized with panic in the night, had deserted his post:

> Suddenly we heard footsteps coming along the corridor. The door opened. I uttered an exclamation. It was Anita who had come to join me again. She was escorted by Orrigoni. The gentlemen with me, recognising my wife, put on their things and left me.
>
> "Do you know, General, how she has been amusing herself on the way here as she went along the Via della Carrozza?" asked Orrigoni.
>
> "No."
>
> "In stopping all the way along San Pietro in Montorio to look at the French batteries. Just look at how we both are covered with dust caused by their bullets striking against the wall. And when I said: 'Come along! Do come along! It is of no use getting killed here,' she replied, 'My dear, what do you think of the way in which the French, as Catholics, set out their churches?'"
>
> Dear Anita! I clasped her to my heart. It now seemed to me as though everything would go well. My guardian angel had returned to my side. (Garibaldi 267-68)

This scene can best be imagined as taking place in a room at the rear of the Villa Spada, where the terrain falls away and the *piano nobile* becomes a third floor [fig. 7. 5]. The rooms there on the southeast corner and in the center rear survived

Fig. 7. 5. The southeast façade of the Villa Spada, with the *portone* that opened on the old entrance road from Trastevere. Garibaldi was eating breakfast possibly in the room on the upper right when Anita arrived. Photograph, K. A. Geffcken.

Fig. 7. 6. Anita ill, being carried, on the base of the monument in the Janiculum *passeggiata*. Sculptor, Mario Rutelli. Photograph, N. W. Goldman.

the French bombardment well enough to possess even today their seventeenth-century frescoed ceilings.

Garibaldi offers no details about Anita's trip from Nice to Rome. Presumably she came by ship to Civitavecchia, and from there by coach. Orrigoni's reference to the "Via della Carrozza" [sic] shows that she had first gone to the modest hotel at Via delle Carrozze 59, near Piazza di Spagna, where Garibaldi had taken a room on his arrival in Rome. Not finding him there, she had made her way across the Tiber and up the Janiculum. Garibaldi recalls Orrigoni's words about her walking past San Pietro in Montorio because they show her disdain of danger and scorn for the French attackers. Since they passed so near San Pietro that dust from bullets hitting the wall covered them, they must have approached the Villa Spada from the Via di Porta San Pancrazio and walked down the long driveway to the northwest façade of the house. This route was much more exposed and dangerous than the old road to the back of the house, down in its ravine below San Pietro. By June 26, so many fruit trees and vineyards had been destroyed by shellfire that apparently Anita could see the French batteries above in the Villa Sciarra.

Garibaldi himself does not mention Anita's participation in the next days of fighting. He had earlier thought of her when he described the death of Colomba Antonietti who, fighting alongside her husband Count Luigi Porzi, was struck by a French bullet near Porta San Pancrazio on June 13 (see pp. 92–93): "It reminded me of poor Anita, who also was so calm under fire" (Garibaldi 264). One later nineteenth-century account, perhaps exaggerated, states that "Anita never left him through those hot battle days, but stood loading one musket after the other on that hard-fought Janiculum hill . . . ." (Elliot 181)

When the Roman Republic finally surrendered to the French on June 30, Garibaldi began to arrange his departure for the day before the French were to enter Rome. He wished only volunteers to join him in the weaving, zigzag march he planned in his best guerrilla style, north through Italy to the young republic at Venice. On July 2 about four thousand infantry and five hundred cavalry assembled in Piazza San Giovanni in Laterano, and Anita was among the first to arrive, dressed in a uniform of the Italian Legion and riding horseback.[1] Garibaldi had tried to persuade her not to accompany him, for her sake and that of the child she carried, but she insisted. In fact, his accurate prediction of the danger and privation they would endure as they struggled to elude French, Neapolitan, Spanish, and finally Austrian forces, only challenged even more la coraggiosa donna (Garibaldi, quoted in Trevelyan 230). As darkness fell, the column filed eastward out of Porta San Giovanni, with a wagon train and one small cannon. Garibaldi remembered, "My heart was sad as death." (Garibaldi 278).

The story of this long retreat across Italy, of sailing up the Adriatic coast pursued by Austrian boats, of Anita critically ill with "malignant fever," convulsions, and agonizing premature labor pains, of rescue by Gioacchino Bonnet on a beach north of Ravenna – all this story deserves an essay of its own. In the end, Anita fell into unconsciousness and died on August 4 in a farmhouse near the marshes between Ravenna and Comacchio [fig. 7. 6]. Garibaldi saw her death as vengeance from her first husband. He believed that there was a link between the beginning and end of his role in Anita's life: "I had come upon forbidden treasure . . . . But she is dead, and he is avenged. When did I recognize the greatness of the fault? There at the mouth of the Eridan (Po), on the day when, hoping to dispute with death, I pressed her pulse convulsively . . . ."(Garibaldi 89).

Anita's body was barely cold when Garibaldi, now accompanied by one companion, slipped into the pine forest to escape the Austrians, and eventually made his way to Tangier and to New York. For the farmers on the property where Anita died, immediate removal of her corpse was imperative. In their haste they buried her in such a shallow, sandy grave that an animal soon dug out and gnawed her hand and arm. A young shepherdess Pasqua Dal Pozzo happened on the protuding arm, and when the police were summoned by the terrified girl's father, the autopsy report led them to believe that the woman had been strangled — eyes and tongue protruded, and her trachea was severed. The farmers were arrested, and though they were released five days later, Garibaldi's enemies long spread the rumor that Garibaldi himself had murdered her in his anxiety to escape the Austrians. Anita's body was reburied at a church near the farm where she died. Later it was moved to Nice, and finally in 1932, it was enclosed in the base of the monument to her in the Janiculum Park, beneath her statue on horseback.

The driveway that Anita walked down to reach the northwest façade of the Villa Spada ran parallel to the route of the modern Via Angelo Masina and through the garden across from the Academy where presently Academy children play. It continued across the site where the Chiaraviglio now stands and ended before the double staircase, in front of the Villa Spada façade, at a fountain with two reclining statues. The house consists of a central block with wings on either side that wrap around the block to form the southeastern façade. Here the *portone* opens on sloping lawns where the old entrance road curved down to the Via della Paglia behind Santa Maria in Trastevere and San Cosimato. The first known owners of the Spada property were the Nobili family [fig. 7. 1]. On the northwestern façade, Vincenzo de Nobili placed an inscription in 1639 to celebrate his construction of the villa amidst the remains of an aqueduct. He thought it was the Aqua Alsietina; we know now that it was the Aqua Traiana. To design his house, Nobili employed the architect Francesco Baratta.

The Spada family was interested in this area of the Janiculum by March 1685, when Marchese Bernardino Spada Veralli rented the Casino Malvasia from Cardinal Carlo Barberini, and then in January 1687 purchased it. Less than a year later, however, Cardinal Barberini repurchased the Malvasia. In agreeing to sell the Malvasia back to Barberini, Spada cited obligations owed the Barberini family by the Spada. This Spada was a great-nephew of the well-known Bernardino Spada, whom Urban VIII Barberini had made Cardinal in 1626 (Mancini 8-9). Then, just a few months later, on March 7, 1689, Marchese Spada Veralli bought the Villa de Nobili for 9,200 *scudi* from Marchese Roberto de Nobili (Neppi 292).

After the 1849 conflict ended, not only were sections of the Spada's western wall destroyed, but parts of the roof had fallen in, and the shutters hung crazily at the windows. But since the main structure remained miraculously standing, the Spada owners soon repaired the Villa. When, however, real estate development began on the Janiculum in the 1880's, the *vigna* was broken into lots, in the same schemes as the Villa Sciarra. The house was left with only a small circle of surrounding park.

The Villa Spada's later history is best summarized from information gathered by Gearoid O'Broin, who in the 1990's lived in the Villa as Irish Ambassador to the Holy See:

NOVEMBER 9, 1874: Maffeo Barberini Colonna di Sciarra rented Villa Spada and the *vigna*. (On Sciarra, see "Morosini," pp. 46, 55 and "Villa Sciarra," p. 235).

NOVEMBER 17, 1878: Federico Spada Veralli sold the Villa and *vigna* to Roberto Wedekind. Sciarra continued to rent.

JANUARY 11, 1885: Paolo Wedekind sold the property to Maffeo Sciarra, who divided most of the Spada into lots for real estate development.

NOVEMBER 17, 1888: Sciarra leased the house and its immediate garden to the Missionary Franciscan Sisters of the Immaculate Conception.

1895: The Sisters moved elsewhere.

No Date Given: Banca Nazionale went to court against Sciarra, who owed the Bank more than 1,000,000 *lire*. The property eventually passed to the Bank of Italy.

August 10, 1903: Federico Spada Veralli repurchased the house and garden.

1925: On the death of Federico Spada Veralli, the Villa passed to his nephew Lodovico Spada Veralli Potenziani.

July 7, 1925: Contessa Nora Khuen (née Lutzow) bought the Villa.

January 15 (no year): Contessa Khuen sold the Villa to Valentina Amelia Fernanda Esmond (née Deutsch de la Meurthe).

March 2, 1937: Esmond gave the Villa to her daughter Sybil Yvonne Uzielli (née Esmond).

While property of Uzielli, the Villa was rented to the following: the Argentine Embassy; the American Ambassador (residence); then to a member of the Swiss Legation, who sublet it to members of the Agnelli family. (Chronology above by O'Broin 3-4)

After the Second World War, in 1946, the Republic of Ireland purchased the property, and ever since, the Irish ambassador to the Holy See has presided there, making every March 17 an especially festive day at the corner of Giacomo Medici and XXX Aprile.

I first visited the Villa Spada in the summer of 1990 when Patrick Power was Irish Ambassador to the Holy See. I talked at that time with the Chancellor Dr. Lamponi, and I was grateful for permission to see and photograph the house. In 1991 Gearoid O'Broin replaced Ambassador Power, and in his years at the Villa Spada Ambassador O'Broin developed a passionate interest in the Villa and the Nobili family. In his spare moments he came over to the Academy Library to do research and to chat about his discoveries. He and Mrs. O'Broin were also wonderfully hospitable at the Villa. I remember several fine visits there, with Mac Bell, Helen North, and others. We have missed the O'Broins since they left for another post.

▨ REFERENCES

Ascenzi, P. "Antonietti, Colomba, in Porzi." *Ai Caduti per Roma* MDCCCXLIX-MDCCCLXX (Rome, 1941), 152-53.
Ashby, Thomas. *The Aqueducts of Ancient Rome* (Oxford, 1935), 306.
Belli Barsali, Isa. *Ville di Roma: Lazio I* (Milan, 1970), 451.
Cozza, Lucos. "Mura Aureliane, 2." *Bull. Com.* 92 (1987-88), 137-74.
Curatulo, Emilio. *Anita Garibaldi* (Milan & Rome, 1932).
Elliot, Frances Minto. *Roman Gossip* (Leipzig, 1896). Elliot, 170 on Garibaldi's magnetism for women.

Garibaldi, Giuseppe. *Memoirs of Garibaldi*. ed. A. Dumas, trans. R. S. Garnett (London, 1931).

Hibbert, Christopher. *Garibaldi and his Enemies* (London, 1965, 1987).

Mancini, Paolo. "Villa Sciarra." *Alma Roma* 25 (1984), 1-31.

Mario, Jesse White. *The Birth of Modern Italy* (London, 1909), photograph of Anita Garibaldi.

Menghini, M. "Anita Garibaldi." *Enc. It.*, XVI (Milan, 1932), 389-90.

Montanelli, Indro and Marco Nozza. *Garibaldi* (Milan, 1962).

Neppi, Lionello. *Palazzo Spada* (Rome, 1975).[2]

O'Broin, Gearoid. "Historical Note on the Villa Spada." ms. I have not yet been able to see O'Broin's published version entitled "Villa Spada. A Historical Note," *Passageways* (1995), 19-31.

Trevelyan, G. M. *Garibaldi's Defence of the Roman Republic* (London, 1912).

MORE ABOUT THE VILLA SPADA – AND LUCIANO MANARA

Katherine A. Geffcken

The Villa Spada was also the house in which Luciano Manara, the idolized colonel of the Lombard *bersaglieri*, received his fatal wound. Adored by his men for his gallantry, leadership, and tact, the twenty-four year old Manara had survived numerous battles in the north of Italy and the excruciating dangers of the Roman campaign.

As he saw his battalion fall around him, he had comforted the dying and the bereaved. After becoming chief of staff on June 4, 1849, he also deftly dissuaded the impetuous Garibaldi from unwise reactions to often irrational orders arriving on the Janiculum from the Republican leadership downtown.

When, on June 30, 1849, morning light revealed vast carnage on the battle-field, the surviving *bersaglieri* had been driven back to the Villa Spada, surrounded by French troops. Emilio Dandolo, Manara's aide, described the horrible scene inside the barricaded house. Unremitting bullets and cannon balls rained on the house, pen-etrating windows no longer protected by shutters, now unhinged, and panes, now shattered. The noise of shells, ricocheting bullets, and agonized cries of the wound-ed in their pain were deafening. The air was impenetrable with smoke and dust, the pavement slippery with blood. The whole house swayed with the increasing crash of the cannonade.

For two hours, Manara circulated through the house, encouraging his men, with Dandolo in his wake. Then, a rebounding bullet struck Dandolo in the right arm (his second wound – he had been hit in the thigh on June 3). Manara exclaimed, *"Perdio! Hai sempre da esser tu il ferito? Io non devo portar via nulla da Roma?"* ("For God's sake! Are you always the one who has to get wounded? Must I carry nothing away from Rome?")With these questions Manara would certainly seem to have tempted fate. A few moments later, as he stood in a window looking through his telescope at French soldiers positioning a cannon, a rifle bullet pierced his stomach and passed through his body.[3] He took three steps, and then as he fell, face forward, said to

Fig. 7. 7. Santa Maria della Scala in Trastevere, to which Manara was taken and where he died. Photograph, K. A. Geffcken.

Dandolo, *"Son morto . . . ti raccomando i miei figli."* ("I am dead . . . to you I entrust my sons."). He had, at home in Milan, three young sons and a wife, Carmelita Fé, who shared his patriotic ideals.

In a brief respite of firing, Manara was placed on a stretcher and lowered through a broken window. His men then carried him down the winding way to S. Maria della Scala in Trastevere [fig. 7. 7], where the most gravely wounded were taken. At Manara's insistence, Dandolo accompanied the stretcher and stood nearby at S. Maria, as Manara asked to be left alone to receive the last rites and to die rapidly. Blood streamed from his wound, and his extremities became cold. As death approached, convulsions began. He complained only once of his terrible agony; instead he comforted the sobbing Dandolo, to whom he gave his ring. About noon on June 30, he died, and his body in his uniform was placed in a room to the right of the high altar.[4]

On July 2 all the *bersaglieri* who still stood or could rise from their hospital beds marched ahead of a military band and Manara's funeral bier to S. Lorenzo in Lucina, where Padre Ugo Bassi delivered the eulogy. Remembering the spectacle of that day, wrote Dandolo, would forever make him shiver.

That sorrowful procession contrasted starkly with the festive entry of the *bersaglieri* into Rome on April 29, moving briskly in their characteristic jog to the rhythm of their trumpets, cheered by the Roman population. Indeed, Manara's death and funeral symbolized to many the end of the brief Republic: *Con lui si estinse la romana repubblica* (With him died the Roman Republic, lit. [the flame] was extinguished) (Marino 109). Manara had seen his cause as repeating patterns of ancient history: he equated his men and himself with Coriolanus, Scaevola, and the Horatii.[5] Ironically, Manara had not arrived in Rome a Republican. He had taken an oath of loyalty to the monarchy of Piemonte, and he and his men wore the cross of Savoy on their belts.

As the weeks of summer 1849 passed by, Manara's body was transported back to Genoa and then to Milan, along with those of Enrico Dandolo and Emilio Morosini. In September he was buried in the family chapel at Barzanò. His bust, sculpted by A. Ilarioli, was dedicated in 1886, among the first portraits placed in the new Janiculum Park [fig. 7. 8].

Fig. 7. 8. Bust of Manara from the Janiculum passeggiata. Photograph, K. A.Geffcken.

Fig. 7. 9. Villa Spada from the SW. As the Werner print [fig. 7. 10] shows, this side of the villa was badly damaged in 1849, but in the subsequent restoration, the original design was carefully preserved. Photograph, K. A. Geffcken.

Fig. 7. 10. Villa Spada in July 1849. Print by Carlo Werner. Property of the Villa Aurelia, AAR. Photograph, A. Ortolan. Luciano Manara was standing in one of the windows on this southwest side when he was shot.

The window at the Villa Spada in which Manara took his fatal sighting must have been one of three on the *primo piano* facing southwest, on the side toward the principal French attack [fig. 7. 9]. Werner's view of the Spada shows grave damage to this part of the house, to both windows and roof [fig. 7. 10]. In fact, Dr. Agostino Bertani recounts that when he visited the Cento Preti at Ponte Sisto to see Morosini's body, he encountered a French captain who pointed out near-by the soldier who had shot Manara:

This soldier, who happened to be near him [the French captain] in the attack on the Villa Spada, had remarked to him just when Manara approached the window with his field-glass: "Note that officer carefully: he is doomed." The soldier fired as he spoke. The bullet reached its billet. He saw Manara fall (Bertani, in Garibaldi 282).

🔶 **REFERENCES**

Bertani, Dr. Agostino, in Giuseppe Garibaldi. *Memoirs*, ed. A. Dumas, trans. R. S. Garnett (London, 1931), 279-85.

Dandolo, Emilio. *I Volontari ed I Bersaglieri Lombardi* (Milan, 1849-50; rep. Milan, Rome, Naples, 1917), especially 216-20, 223-24.

Marino, Antonio. *Il Gianicolo Illustrato* (Rome, 1922).

Montini, Renzo U. "Luciano Manara." *Capitolium* 24 (1949), 337-46.

Trevelyan, G. M. *Garibaldi's Defence of the Roman Republic* (London, 1912). See 119 ff. and note 2 on 119 pointing out that in George Meredith's novel *Vittoria*, the character Luciano Romara was based on Manara.

🔶 **NOTES**

1   Curatulo (154) describes Anita's clothing: "la giubba della Legione, ma più lunga, calzoni maschili entro stivali alti, cappello floscio con piuma ed a tracollo una fascia tricolore" ("the jacket of the Legion, but longer, men's trousers [tucked] into high boots, soft hat with feather, and on her shoulder a tricolor band / sash"). On the road, Anita soon had her hair cut (155), and changed to a two-piece black brocade dress given her by the women of Cetona (159, and photograph of the dress itself, opposite 112).

2   I thank former Director Joseph Connors for the hint that led me to the note in this book on the date Marchese Bernardino Spada Veralli purchased the Villa Nobilia.

3   Dr. Agostino Bertani states that Manara had removed his sword and belt, which latter item would have protected him from the bullet in the stomach (Bertani in Garibaldi 279).

4   Two depictions of Manara on his deathbed exist: one a sketch by Andrea Belloli made on that June 30, 1849, and the other a painting by Eleuterio Pagliano.

5   Montini 343, and see Manara's letter dated June 29, 1849, quoted in Marino 109.

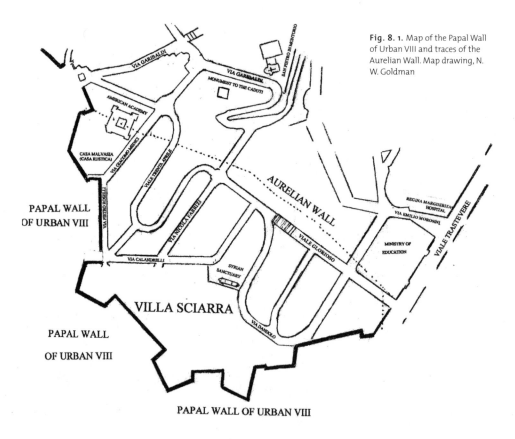

Fig. 8. 1. Map of the Papal Wall of Urban VIII and traces of the Aurelian Wall. Map drawing, N. W. Goldman

CHAPTER 8

THE WALLS: AURELIAN AND PAPAL

Ingrid D. Rowland

The wall that cradles the American Academy marks a stretch of the Janiculum Hill that has been a battleground for much of its history: Etruscans, Visigoths, Normans, seventeenth-century Roman barons, and nineteenth-century Garibaldini and French troops have looked down on Rome from its commanding heights across the river Tiber [fig. 8. 1]. In the earliest days of ancient Rome, the Janiculum marked the southernmost bastion of Etruscan territory, and from its slopes, in 509 B.C., the Etruscan warlord Lars Porsenna mounted his siege of the city he would have called "Ruma." In a series of vivid anecdotes, the Roman historian Livy told his readers how Roman bravery successfully beat back Porsenna's Etruscan hordes, but other ancient sources show that Porsenna actually took Rome and held it with his son Arnth (Latinized as Arruns) for the next thirty years.

As yet, however, the Janiculum had no fortifications; the "Servian" walls of early Rome were all built on the opposite side of the Tiber, and then, for centuries, Rome needed no walls at all, for it had subdued every nation around it. In the declining years of the Roman Empire, however, the Emperor Aurelian (271-275), finally fortified the huge city, which by this time contained a million inhabitants and extended to both sides of the river. As the Empire's borders came under increasing pressure from restive subjects and foreign attackers, even the capital itself no longer seemed secure; remarkably, Aurelian completed this massive defensive project in only four years. The Aurelian Wall also helped to protect the aqueducts that provided the city with water for homes, fountains, mills, and the immense public baths that played so central a role in Roman social life. One of these watercourses still runs along the Via Aurelia: the Aqua Traiana, built by Trajan in 109 A.D. and extensively repaired by Pope Paul V in 1612. Because third-century Rome occupied both sides of the Tiber, Aurelian's fortification wall enclosed both the Janiculum and the thriving neighborhood "Trans Tiberim" (across the Tiber), from the Porta Septimiana on the north to the Porta Portuensis on the south. A long extension of the wall climbed the slope of the Janiculum to flank the initial stretch of the Via Aurelia and the Aqua Traiana up to the plateau of the ancient Porta Aurelia, the present-day Porta San Pancrazio. A surviving part of this Aurelian wall [fig. 9.4] and one of its watchtowers have been incorporated into the lower levels of the Academy's Villa Aurelia.

The Aurelian Wall was built to withstand attack by ancient artillery, specifically the stone shot or metal bolts launched by ancient catapults, war machines specifically designed to bring down city walls (the Romans in the movie "Gladiator" waste good war machinery and precious shot by ranging their catapults against a German forest!). Attackers also built multistoried siege towers that carried rams, catapults, and archers on their various levels, and portable bridges that allowed troops to scale city walls as soon as the tower drew alongside them. An ancient defensive wall thus had to be thick enough to withstand pounding by catapults and stand tall enough to deter siege engines. Towers, built at intervals determined by the length of an ancient bowshot, afforded defenders a better view of their attackers and the opportunity for snipers to pick them off. The defensive tower incorporated into the Villa Aurelia has a projecting parapet, but this feature was added much later in the tower's history.

As we now see them, however, the walls around the American Academy were designed in an entirely different age, to protect different areas of the city, and to withstand guns rather than catapults. Most of the marble plaques set into the wall at regular intervals among the cascading caper plants bear a coat of arms with three bees, surrounded by the papal tiara and the keys of St. Peter that permit the Pope to do and undo the affairs of Heaven and earth [fig. 8. 2]. These are the arms of Pope Urban VIII (reigned 1623-1644), the former Maffeo Barberini, a vain, witty Florentine who changed his family coat of arms from three horseflies when he realized how far his ambitions might take him.

Pope Urban VIII was an inspired patron of the arts and sciences whose reign was marred by two tremendous mistakes. The first of these was the prosecution of his onetime friend, Galileo Galilei, for heresy in 1633. The last page of Galileo's *Dialogue on the Two Chief World Systems* of 1632 made fun of an argument the Pope had presented in conversation with his learned friend, and it turned out to be a move as unfortunate as the Pope's response to it. Urban's considerable pride was stung beyond forgiveness. He denounced Galileo to the Inquisition, presiding personally over every stage of the great scientist's subsequent trial, conviction, and sentencing to life imprisonment (later commuted to house arrest). It was not a popular decision: three of the ten cardinals assigned to Galileo's trial refused to sign the document ratifying Galileo's sentence, including the Pope's nephew, Cardinal Francesco Barberini, and in many ways, Urban never recovered from the blow. Neither, of course, did the seventy-year-old Galileo, confined for the rest of his life to the grounds of his little villa in Arcetri above Florence, forbidden ever to write again about the cosmos.

The second great mistake of Urban VIII was what led him to fortify the Janiculum with a wall that boasted all the latest features of modern military technology, and encompass, at tremendous expense, the Vatican as well as the Janiculum and Trastevere. The enemy against which he built this huge, expensive circuit from 1641 onward (the stretches around the Academy were completed in 1643) was no longer a barbarian horde, but a noble family with a far better claim to Roman citizenship

than the Pope himself: the Farnese, Dukes of Parma, Piacenza, and Castro, venerable Roman barons who boasted a Pope of their own: Paul III (1534-1549), whose lavish bronze

Fig. 8. 2. Wall of Urban VIII with Urban's coat of arms and slits through which defending rifle-men could fire on attackers. Note also caper plants. Photograph, K. A. Geffcken, 2002.

tomb, ironically, faces that of Urban VIII in the apse of St. Peter's Basilica. In 1639, on a visit to Rome, Odoardo Farnese, Duke of Parma and Piacenza, had tangled over questions of etiquette with the Pope's touchy, arrogant nephew Taddeo, whose title, Prefect of Rome, gave him a royal sense of entitlement, matched in his day only by the Farnese and the French ambassador, with whom Taddeo had picked a famous fight over rights of way on a Roman street. Ever protective of his family, Pope Urban VIII cut off Odoardo Farnese's right to import grain into the city from his immense fief of Castro, causing Farnese to default on payments to Roman creditors, who complained to the Pope in 1641. When the Pope occupied Castro with the excuse that he was exacting payment for Farnese's debts, most Romans assumed, rightly, that he was really planning to carve out a Barberini stronghold in Farnese territory. Then he excommunicated the delinquent Duke. From Parma, meanwhile, Odoardo Farnese, backed by Tuscany, Modena, and Venice, declared war on papal Rome, marching south in 1642 at the head of some 3000 horsemen and several thousand footsoldiers. These troops routed Pope Urban's army near Orvieto, leading to pro-longed negotiations, renewed hostilities, and an eventual treaty signed in 1644, short-ly before the Pope's death, in which the Farnese retrieved both their right to the sacraments and their properties. It was a humiliating defeat for the papacy. Furthermore, the huge, costly walls on the Janiculum were never used; all the fighting occurred well north of Rome. When the Farnese, however, continued their agitations against Urban's tough old successor, Innocent X, this new pope razed Castro to the ground.

Yet Urban's wall, if put to the test, would probably have performed far better than his pitiful troops. Its sloping courses of brick, crowned by a sturdy half-round marble molding, are especially designed to ward off cannonballs, and there are openings within the walls that allow ample range for defensive artillery as well as narrower slits for snipers (See fig. 8. 2). The wall's tortuous course follows the contours of the Janiculum, but it also offers defensive gunners a wide range of vantages from which to spot and shoot the enemy. Along the wall are bastions, projections arranged to give a wider firing range [fig. 3, showing the bastions with numbers indicated along the ridge of the Janiculum]. Seen from above, Bastions 8 and 9 on either side of the Porta San Pancrazio have a leaf shape; the curved stretches nearest the curtain walls are harder to pull apart with cannonballs or picks, and if the sharp points at the end of the bastions make them more vulnerable to demolition, they compensate by offering a wider range to the gunnery once housed within them. Now the walls offer more innocuous shelter to pigeons, rats, snapdragons and beautiful cascades of caper plants.

Not every marble plaque in the Janiculum wall bears the Barberini bees. Some of the coats of arms quarter rampant lions with diagonal blazes. These are the arms of Giovanni Maria Mastai Ferretti, Pope Pius IX (reigned 1846-1879), known to Romans by the euphonious "Pio Nono," and they commemorate the fact that slightly over two hundred years after the disastrous War of Castro, in 1849, the walls of the Janiculum finally saw some real action. This time the defenders inside the walls were Italians under the field command of Giuseppe Garibaldi; the attackers were French troops led by General Charles Oudinot. The cause of hostilities was, however, profoundly different from the siege Urban had feared when he constructed his wall on the Janiculum. In 1849 many regiments and battalions of Italian patriots gathered at Rome to defend the new Roman Republic, hoping thus to further their dream of a unified Italy.

The year before, in 1848, a critical series of events had paved the way for the republican government in Rome. On November 15, 1848, the Pope's hated chief minister, Count Pellegrino Rossi, had been surrounded by a crowd and murdered as he arrived at the Cancelleria to address the Council of Deputies. The next day, the Roman Civic guard and other citizens attacked the Quirinal Palace, the Pope's residence. Secretly, on November 24, 1848, Pio Nono slipped out from Rome, disguised as a monk, and took refuge at the fortified port of Gaeta in the Kingdom of Naples. In February 1849, the new Roman Republic was proclaimed, and on March 5, Giuseppe Mazzini arrived to head the government, in a triumvirate composed of himself, Carlo Armellini, and Aurelio Saffi.

From his exile at Gaeta, Pio Nono appealed for help from France, Spain, and Naples. All of these obliged him but most obliging were the French, who sent, under Oudinot, units from their highly trained professional army. With his first contingent

Fig. 8. 3. Map of the wall along the Janiculum
showing the bastions on the Falda map of 1676
from A. P. Frutaz, *Le Piante di Roma* III (Rome, 1962).
Bastion numbers have been added.

of troops, Oudinot landed at Civitavecchia on April 25 and headed to Rome on the
Via Aurelia.

Meanwhile, with Garibaldi appointed as field commander, the republicans at
Rome began strengthening the city's fortifications, especially on the Janiculum and
around the Vatican, where Oudinot and his troops would inevitably arrive. They
piled up sand bags and gabions and every possible kind of barricade. Just inside the
walls they mounted artillery, in particular around the most important, and the most
vulnerable gate, the Porta San Pancrazio. On the first day of conflict, April 30, the
Italians defeated the attacking French. Fighting centered near the Vatican, where the
fortifications held firm, and around Villas Valentini and Doria Pamphilj, outside
Porta San Pancrazio. The wall and gate on the Janiculum had yet to be truly tested.

81

Fig. 8. 4. Bastion 7 along the Via delle Mura Gianicolensi. Small white marble insets show the area where the wall was breached. Photograph, K. A. Geffcken, 2005.

Oudinot soon realized that he required more units and military resources than the approximately 6,000 men and light artillery he had initially led to Rome. By the end of May, he had been reinforced with about 12,000 more troops, heavy artillery, sappers, and engineers (in addition 10,000 more French troops would arrive in June). From June 3 on, when Oudinot's forces captured the high ground of the Villa dei Quattro Venti, French artillery, soon installed there, relentlessly bombarded Urban's wall and Porta San Pancrazio, while sappers dug trenches through vineyards ever closer to the wall.

The French military engineers shrewdly selected the spots where they would make their breaches. In particular, beginning about June 18, they aimed their cannon balls on the wall surrounding Villa Sciarra because the ground level was highest there and, once taken, would provide a commanding location for artillery firing down on the Italians. Today white marble inserts wedged into the wall's brick masonry along the Viale delle Mura Gianicolensi outline the places where French artillery finally pounded through the wall, and the repaired stretches are a slightly different color [fig. 8. 4]. Military engineers have assigned numbers to the bastions that support the high terracing of the Villa Sciarra, counting from south to north: 4, 5, 6, and 7. The French penetrated the wall at the last three of these bastions, and also the straight wall extending between Bastions 6 and 7. The breaches at Bastions 5 and 6 gave access close to the rear of Casa Barberini, which became a French outpost upon its capture. To increase the effectiveness of their nineteenth-century cannon,

Fig. 8. 5. Plaque in the Papal Wall along the Viale delle Mura Gianicolensi, showing the SPQR below the Papal insignia. Photograph, K. A. Geffcken, 2004.

the French focused their fire on the sides of the leaf-shaped seventeenth-century bastions and on the inside corners. Eventually the old masonry, designed for an older technology, crumbled away.

On the night of June 29 the French broke through the wall directly behind the Casino Malvasia. Repaired by Pio Nono, this stretch today extends along the back garden of the American Academy just inside the back gate [see p. 42, fig. 5. 2 for the repaired breach]. In 1849, however, the French infantry poured through this breach to attack Porta San Pancrazio from inside the walls.

Cleverly, the French never threw their infantry directly against the bristling defenses of Porta San Pancrazio; instead they shelled the gate relentlessly until they could penetrate the wall's weaker stretches. Even the finest work of seventeenth-century military architecture would have been no match for nineteenth-century artillery, and Urban's wall had been put up in haste. After a desperate defense, the Italians finally surrendered on June 30. Garibaldi and a portion of his followers left Rome on July 2. The French entered the city the next day.

On April 12, 1850, Pio Nono returned to Rome. Quickly he reinforced Urban's battered walls against further attack, attaching marble plaques of various size and elaboration to proclaim his repossession of the city and the Papal State [fig. 8. 5]. In 1854 he engaged the Roman architect Count Virginio Vespignani (1808-1882) to reconstruct the Porta San Pancrazio, which had been virtually destroyed in the bombardments of 1849; Vespignani completed his commission in 1857, one of many contributions this highly successful architect would make to the distinctive

Fig. 8. 6. Memorial plaque placed by the city of Rome, on the Wall skirting the Villa Sciarra, between Bastions 6 and 7. Photograph, K. A. Geffcken, 2004.

Fig. 8. 7. The Papal Wall along Pietro Roselli with hanging berry vines. Inside is Postal Code 00153; outside the Code is 00152. Photograph, N. W. Goldman, 2005.

Neoclassical style of nineteenth-century Rome. The gate's inscriptions, newly cleaned for the Jubilee Year of 2000, proclaim Pio Nono's invincible authority with all the bravado that art and architecture can muster; the gate's rusticated quoins and boasting inscriptions display Vespignani's careful study of ancient Roman gates like the Porta Maggiore (see the chapter on Porta San Pancrazio following, pp. 85–94).

Pio Nono's recovered power would last only until 1870, the year in which Italy finally became a unified nation-state and transformed this long-lived Pope into the proverbial "prisoner of the Vatican." A large plaque set into the part of Urban's wall that skirts the park of Villa Sciarra on the Viale delle Mura Gianicolensi bears the coat of arms of the city of Rome, with the initials SPQR [fig. 8. 6], celebrating the fact that by the end of the nineteenth century, and under Pio Nono's outraged gaze, the city once again boasted a republican government. In the same spirit, the gate itself has long hosted a small museum of Garibaldi memorabilia in its upper level.

The wall itself has been cut repeatedly to accommodate modern automobile traffic in the greatly expanded city, but it still marks some significant boundaries: between two postal codes, for example: 00153 inside its circuit (including the American Academy), and 00152 outside [fig. 8. 7]. As it approaches the Vatican, Pope Urban's wall also marks the border between Vatican property (including the Vatican gas station) and the Italian state. Its durable masonry still serves as a retaining wall for the splendid Passeggiata del Gianicolo, lined with busts of the Garibaldini who fought so bravely for an Italian Republic.

CHAPTER 9

PORTA SAN PANCRAZIO . . .
AND AN ERRANT FRENCH CANNON BALL

Katherine A. Geffcken

To a traveler about to leave Rome at the top of the Janiculum, the approach up Via Garibaldi to Via Aurelia focuses ahead on the Porta San Pancrazio, a massive squared arch surrounded by swirling traffic [fig. 9. 1]. Because the arch stands detached by modern openings from the Papal Wall, it seems less a gate in Rome's defenses and more a triumphal monument. Indeed, this structure was built to commemorate the triumphant restoration of Pope Pius IX to his throne after the French defeated the Italians in 1849, and it specifically celebrates the Pope's restoration of Rome's fortifications.[1] Pius commissioned his favorite architect Virginio Vespignani to design and construct it in 1854, as replacement for the badly damaged Porta San Pancrazio of Pope Urban VIII's defenses. (On Vespignani, see Richardson, p. 106). In this imposing, classicizing gate, Vespignani included space for guards and for officers who collected customs fees from those entering Rome.

Fig. 9. 1. The present Porta San Pancrazio, east façade, seen from the Via Garibaldi. Photograph, K. A. Geffcken, 2005.

Ironically, the gate today houses not papal offices but memorabilia of the Italian defenders defeated in 1849. Under the arch is a door and then a staircase leading up to the Museo Garibaldino, which contains portraits, flags, uniforms, newspaper articles, and other objects belonging to Garibaldi and his colleagues. This collection was assembled by Garibaldi's second son Ricciotti, whose daughters Rosa and Italia Anita donated it to the Associazione Nazionale Veterani e Reduci Garibaldini. The Garibaldini were granted rights to the building in 1948, after squatters were finally evicted. In addition to Risorgimento material, there are also displays illustrating the long history of the Garibaldini, especially the heroism of Garibaldini partisans in World War II. At the top of the gate are the library and archives of the Association. Up to this time, the Museum has rarely been open to the public, but in 1991 Signor Paolo Latini opened the collection to an Academy group, and in 1993 Academy Trustees and Fellows were graciously received there by Prof. Annita Garibaldi Jallet, a descendant of "the General" and his wife Anita.

THE WALL OF POPE URBAN VIII

The new Porta San Pancrazio of 1854 restored control over the Via Aurelia at a spot that had been fortified since the third century. The previous Porta San Pancrazio, designed by Marco Antonio de Rossi in 1642-44, had formed part of Pope Urban VIII's imposing line of walls built to protect the entire Janiculum [fig. 9.2]. Urban's Gate had lasted a little over two hundred years until drastically bombed by the French in 1849. On its external side, it was handsomely faced with ashlar blocks and had four engaged pilasters, two on either side of the single arch. Covering the cornerstone of the arch, Urban's coat of arms interrupted a narrow frieze bearing the inscription ANNO DOM MDCXX (?) XLIV PONTIF MAX A (?). This reading is problematical, recording what is visible on Luigi Rossini's *veduta*, dated 1829 [fig. 9. 3]. Vincenzo Forcella provides the following reading derived from an engraving by Giuseppe Vasi: ANNO.DOMINI. MDCXLIV.PONTIF.XXI (In the year of our Lord 1644, in the 21st year of his pontificate). In the middle of the attic above ran an elaborate inscription announcing to all who entered Rome Urban's achievements in building the new wall:

VRBANVS VIII PONT MAX
ABSOLVTIS CIVITATIS LEONINAE MVNIME[NTIS]
ET MOENIBVS AC PROPVGNACVLIS AD TIBERIM VSQ[VE]
EXCITATIS
IMMINENTEM VRBI IANICVLVM ET
TRANSTIBERINAM REGIONEM CIRCVNDVCENS
PVBLICA EX SECVRITATI PROSPEXIT
(Urban VIII, Pontifex Maximus, after completing the fortifications of
the Leonine City and building up the walls and bulwarks all the way to the
Tiber, [then] by surrounding the Janiculum, which looms over the city [of
Rome] and the Trasteverine region [with fortifications], planned ahead in
regard to the safety of the people.)

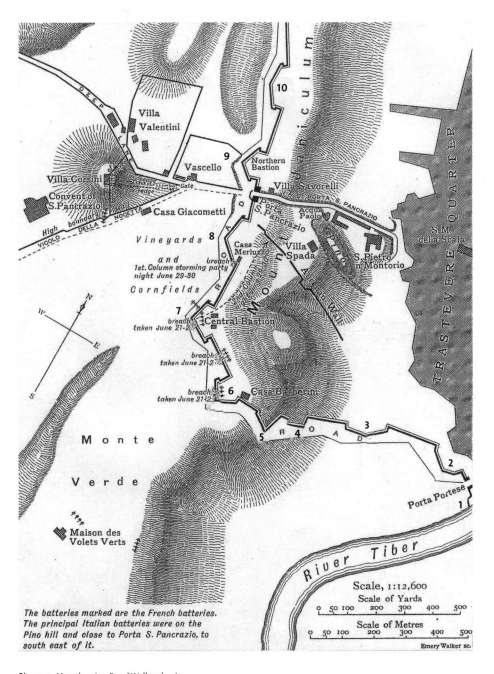

Fig. 9. 2. Map showing Papal Wall and gate in 1849, from Trevelyan, *Garibaldi's Defence of the Roman Republic*, opposite p. 210.

BELOW

Fig. 9. 3. Porta San Pancrazio by
Luigi Rossini, 1829. Note the van-
tage court and inner gate, seen
here through the outer portal.
Reproduction courtesy of the
Fototeca Unione, Photographic
Archive of the AAR (F.U. 6405).

BOTTOM

Fig. 9. 4. Surviving portions of
the Aurelian Wall as it approached
the ancient Porta Aurelia, viewed
from the Porta. Above them is the
Villino Aurelia and below, the wall
surrounding the Villa Aurelia.
Photograph, K. A. Geffcken.

Here again, Rossini's reading of the inscription may need some correction, especially on the right side, where he ran out of space, showing some of the letters in shadow. On either side, engaged, fluted pilasters framed this impressive statement. To left and right of the attic and across the attic roof, a balustrade gave a finished border to the top of the gate. A print by Giuseppe Vasi (1747) shows that in the eighteenth century a little hexagonal tower with a flagpole stood atop the attic.[2]

ALIGNMENT OF URBAN'S GATE AND THE ROMAN PORTA AURELIA

This seventeenth century gate, oriented northwest to southeast, opened into a vantage court with an inner gate set at a contrasting north-to-south direction. The wrench in the different orientations of the portals can be seen in Rossini's print, and today can be glimpsed by looking at the present gate (built 1854) and then at the remains of the Aurelian Wall (A.D. 271-275 / 279) as it approached the ancient Porta Aurelia. These remains consist of two brick projections emerging from the wall beneath Villino Aurelia [fig. 9. 4]. When Pope Paul III strengthened the Porta Aurelia in the sixteenth century, apparently he simply repaired the old outer and inner gates and placed on the inner gate his crest, where it was later described by Nicholas Audebert of Orleans in 1575. Urban's architect kept the old inner gate, but demolished the outer gate, and built a new outer Porta a bit to the west and at a different angle. This shift in alignment was necessary to meet the new Papal Wall approaching from Bastion Eight to the south (in the Academy's back garden) and from Bastion Nine to the north.

The ancient Porta Aurelia always had possessed a single-arched outer gate, a vantage court, and an inner gate. Its name "Aurelia" conveyed, of course, its function as the city's fortified boundary on the Via Aurelia, on the high ridge of the Janiculum before the road leveled off to the west. But as early as the sixth century, it became known also as the gate of St. Pancratius (San Pancrazio) because of the popular pilgrimage center at the martyr Pancratius's burial spot about a half mile outside this gate. In 401-402, the *porta* had already been restored by Honorius when the round towers were given a square facing and the façade a stone curtain. By 1625, as shown in Maggi's plan of Rome, and also in 1633, as shown in Rainaldi's drawing of the gate, the square towers on either side of the outer portal were in ruinous condition, with vegetation sprouting from their dilapidated tops.[3] But the face of the ancient *porta* still had its early fifth century curtain of dressed stone, many blocks of which bore almost illegible inscriptions – that is, blocks reused from tombs (Richmond, 221-22, quoting Nicholas Audebert). Not only this outer gate but also its two towers were removed in the 1640's, probably when Urban's wall and the elegant Porta San Pancrazio were safely completed.

A strong statement of Papal power, Urban's gate could not eventually withstand the punishing impact of nineteenth century bombardment.

...THE ERRANT FRENCH CANNON BALL

In the dim, early morning hours of June 30, 1849, a French column penetrated the Papal Wall and, sweeping through what is now the Academy garden, captured Porta San Pancrazio from the inner side. Although the exhausted Italian defenses between the gate and the Acqua Paola held out for a few more hours, most knew that Rome was irreparably lost to the French. The gate had been a focus of constant activity for over two months – the protective cover behind which troops waited to go into battle, through which ammunition and food were carried out to garrisons at the Vascello and Casa Giacometti, and the portal through which the dead, dying, and wounded were brought back into Rome.

By June 30, incessant French bombardment had left the gate little more than a shell [fig. 9. 5]. The outer face still stood, scarred, up to the tops of the pilasters, but Urban VIII's *stemma* was gone, and the attic was almost entirely blown away. Only a few ribs of the inner attic vaulting remained, almost suspended in air. The inner court of the gate was heaped with rubble and fallen timbers.

Loss of artillery protection and the steady approach of new French trenches further weakened the Porta San Pancrazio. The barricade and battery that stood in front of the gate on the outside had been overwhelmed, the Italian gunners and sharpshooters there blown to bits. Furthermore, the Italian battery stationed on the Papal Wall just to the south of the gate had been seized by the French, who then shifted the Italian cannon to fire on the Villa Savorelli (Villa Aurelia), on the Via di Porta San Pancrazio (Via Garibaldi) and the Villa Spada. Gullies and craters scoured out by shelling pockmarked the entire surrounding territory. Outside the gate, French trenches had reached to within forty to fifty yards, enabling French riflemen to pick off Italian defenders on the wall. Shells falling on or near the gate had also grievously damaged the houses on the corners facing the outer side of Porta San Pancrazio, Casa de Angeli to the north, and Casa Frontoni (where the Bar Gianicolo is now) to the south.[4] The surviving portions of the gate thus stood in the midst of utter destruction.

Several weeks earlier, on June 13, an incongruous comedy and a tragedy took place close to Porta San Pancrazio. At a strategic barricade right by the gate, one of the soldiers, Candido Augusto Vecchi [fig. 9. 6], was briefly buried alive by falling sacks of earth, but another soldier, Colomba Porzi Antonietti [fig. 9.7], was killed by a French cannon ball ricocheting from one of the sacks and the Wall.

Vecchi, a native of Fermo in the Marche, was a captain in the Piemontese army on leave of absence, when in winter 1848-49, he met Garibaldi at Ascoli. He joined Garibaldi's Italian Legion and fought close to "the General" throughout the Roman campaign. He lived to assist Garibaldi in 1860, and then was elected a deputy in Parliament from 1861 to 1867. Vecchi, a fatalist, expected to die at Rome. In fact, he thought his death already overdue by more than two years because a gypsy fortune teller had predicted that he would die a rich man in Rome at 36 (he was born in

Fig. 9. 5. Porta San Pancrazio, by Carlo Werner, July, 1849, showing destruction from French bombardment. Property of the Villa Aurelia, American Academy in Rome. Photograph, A. Ortolan.

Fig. 9. 6. Candido Augusto Vecchi: bust in the Janiculum Park. Photograph, K. A. Geffcken.

Fig. 9. 7. Colomba Porzi Antonietti, who fought beside her husband and died near Porta San Pancrazio on June 13, 1849. Bust in the Janiculum Park. Photograph, K. A. Geffcken.

1810). So, when Garibaldi invited the hungry Vecchi to share his *risotto*, Vecchi readily accepted, even though, as the chief of staff Luciano Manara warned, all officers sharing Garibaldi's meals for three days had been killed on returning to battle. In any event, eating with Garibaldi at Villa Savorelli (Villa Aurelia) was not a tranquil experience, because of the constant intrusion and din of French fire. Resigned, however, to the gypsy's prediction, Vecchi preferred to meet certain death with a full stomach.

After the good *risotto*, he needed a nap because he had been on duty for two nights. While he slept deeply in a borrowed bed at the Aurelia, the enemy bombardment increased, and under its cover, the French began fortifying a new (and too close!) trench. Waking Vecchi, Garibaldi tricked him into alertness by assuring him that he had slept for twenty-four hours. He then sent Vecchi off to choose twelve Italian sharpshooters and lead them to a spot from which they could aim accurately at the encroaching French. Vecchi and his men fired from behind a barricade protected by gabions[5] and sacks of earth close to the gate. The French answered with so many shots that one cannon ball pierced and dislodged a sandbag, causing a whole pile of them to bury Vecchi. Informed that Vecchi was dead, Garibaldi was vehemently blaming himself, when, to his astonishment, Vecchi, very much alive, reappeared announcing, "I was only buried." (Garibaldi 262-63).

But the French ball that tore open a bag of sand was not yet spent. It ricocheted off the Papal Wall and penetrated the lower back of a young officer, who fell first into a kneeling position, and then backwards with hands crossed on chest, crying out, "*Viva l'Italia!*" Immediately, another officer standing nearby fell on the body with kisses and heart-rending sobs. The dying officer was twenty-two year old Colomba Antonietti, and the grieving officer was her husband Count Luigi Porzi. Her body was carried on a stretcher down to the temporary hospital at Sette Dolori on Via delle Fornaci (now Via Garibaldi), where the nuns put a dress on over her uniform.[6] The next day, when her funeral cortege passed over the Tiber to San Carlo ai Catinari, a large crowd accompanied her bier, showering it with white roses. At San Carlo she was buried in the chapel of Santa Cecilia, the chapel nearest the high altar, in the right nave. In 1940, when her skeleton was exhumed for reburial in the new Janiculum mausoleum for the Risorgimento dead, jewelry and religious objects were found with her: a necklace, a rosary, three religious medals, and a button from an officer's uniform bearing the initials CP (i.e. Colomba Porzi).[7]

Colomba Antonietti was born October 19, 1826, at Bastia, a town to the east of Perugia, and she grew up at Foligno. Her husband Luigi Porzi was born at Ancona, though his family were members of the old aristocracy of Imola. When the couple met, he was a cadet in the Papal army. Both families opposed their marriage, but Luigi and Colomba prevailed, and their wedding took place on December 13, 1846. He, however, was sentenced to three months in Castel Sant'Angelo because he had married without permission of the Papal government. But an indulgent commandant at Sant'Angelo allowed Colomba to visit her husband daily. Within a year, Luigi and Colomba had determined to fight for Italian liberty. Colomba cut off her long hair and put on an officer's uniform. She accompanied her husband to Venice in 1848, where they participated as a team in the campaign for Venetian liberation from the Austrians. By the late winter of 1849, Luigi was commissioned a lieutenant in the Second Infantry Regiment, marching toward Rome to defend the new Republic.

Colomba proved herself a dedicated soldier. On May 19 at Velletri, she won praise for her valor, and on June 13, when the French ball struck her back, she was handing her husband ammunition. Urged earlier that day to leave such a dangerously exposed position, she said that her life was *"consecrata all'Italia da gran tempo e che prezzo non aveva per lei se non in quanto poteva giovare alla sua patria sventurata."*[8] (*Ai Caduti* 152). Later, Garibaldi commended her heroic valor in battle (see also "Anita Garibaldi" . . . p. 68). Colomba's bust in the Janiculum Park, sculpted by G. Nicolini, was authorized in 1910 and dedicated April 30, 1911. Her portrait stands in a significant place of honor among major heroes of 1849 like Manara, Masina, and Medici. Vecchi's bust, on the other hand, is not far from Anita Garibaldi's monument and tomb. Its inclusion in the *passeggiata* recognizes Vecchi's long friendship with and unswerving support of Garibaldi.

Candido Augusto Vecchi and Colomba Antonietti are, of course, only two of hundreds who fought at Porta San Pancrazio in 1849 (see, for example, pp. 230-32, on the *tamburino*, who died at the gate). In fact, a large quantity of human bones were unearthed just outside the gate when pipes to the modern Janiculum reservoir were laid (see Chapter 29 on the Michelangelo Façade). After these bones were identified as remains of combatants in 1849, they were added to those placed in the mausoleum of the Risorgimento Caduti on the Janiculum. Today, the periphery of the Porta remains a dangerous area, now from speeding vehicles, as demonstrated in the horrendous death of two pedestrians, a mother and father, and severe injuries to their son, inflicted by a heedless driver in 2004. And there are also, in the vicinity, ancient burials, occasionally brought to light by a gardener's hoe or the laying of a new foundation. Like all Roman roads outside the walls, Via Aurelia was lined with columbaria and tombs, both substantial and modest, and in the later Roman period, by networks of catacombs under and around the church of San Pancrazio.

There was a time, though, in the years just after World War II, when the Piazzale at the gate was more like a village square. Eric Baade describes it as a country scene in Chapter 32 of the present book. Eleanor Clark also described the scene in her *Rome and a Villa* (46): "Go up the hill from Trastevere and sit at the Bar Gianicolo, across from the papal walls and the Porta San Pancrazio. That is the newest and dumpiest of the city gates, a petit-bourgeois triumphal arch in stucco, still it marks an exit, and you are really in the country there; the bar is a village bar; the vegetation is thick and casual: trees, wisteria, an arbor to sit under in the summer, azaleas on the roof, capers and other shrubbery in the city wall."

93

⊞ REFERENCES

Ai Caduti per Roma MDCCCXLIX-MDCCCLXX (Rome 1941), especially Pietro Ascensi, "Antonietti, Colomba in Porzi," 152-53.

Cassanelli, L., G. Delfini, and D. Fonti. *Le Mura di Roma* (Rome, 1974).

Clark, Eleanor. *Rome and a Villa* (Garden City, N.Y., 1952).

Cozza, Lucos. "Mura Aureliane, l. Trastevere, il Braccio Settentrionale: dal Tevere a Porta Aurelia-S. Pancrazio," in *Bull. Com.* 91 (1986), 103-30.

Cozza, Lucos. "Mura Aureliane, 2. Trastevere, Il Braccio Meridionale: dal Tevere a Porta Aurelia-San Pancrazio," *Bull. Com.* 92 (1987-88), 137-174.

Fondare la Nazione: I Repubblicani del 1849 e la Difesa del Gianicolo, ed. Lauro Rossi (Rome, 2001). See especially 120: photograph (July 1849) by Stefano Lecchi, which shows not only the gravely damaged Porta San Pancrazio, but also some of the damaged structure of the Villino Aurelia.

Forcella, Vincenzo. *Iscrizioni delle Chiese e d'altri Edificii di Roma dal Secolo XI fino ai Giorni Nostri* (Rome, 1897), XIII, 39 (no. 48).

The Letters of Margaret Fuller, ed. Robert N. Hudspeth (Ithaca and London, 1988), 241: letter to Elizabeth Hoar, 17th June (1849), in which Fuller copies the entry on the death of Colomba Antonietti published in the *Monitore Romano,* 14 June, 1849.

Garibaldi, Giuseppe. *The Memoirs,* ed. Alexandre Dumas, trans. R. S. Garnett (London, 1931).

Gigli, Laura. *Guide Rionali di Roma. Rione XIII: Trastevere, Parte I,* 2nd ed. (Rome, 1980).

Malizia, Giuiliano. "Un' Eroina per la Difesa di Roma," *Roma Ieri, Oggi, Domani 9,* no. 90 (1996), 42-45.

Marino, Antonio. *Il Gianicolo Illustrato* (Rome, 1922).

Mura e Porte di Roma Antica, ed. B. Brizzi (Rome, 1995).

Nash, Ernest, *Pictorial Dictionary of Ancient Rome* (New York, 1962), II. 206-07.

Richmond, Ian A. *The City Wall of Imperial Rome* (Oxford, 1930).

Trevelyan, G. M. *Garibaldi's Defence of the Roman Republic,* 3rd ed. (London, 1912).

Trevelyan, G. M. *Garibaldi and the Thousand* (London, 1919).

◩ NOTES

1 See Laura Gigli, *Guide Rionali di Rome. Rione XIII Trastevere. Parte I,* 184 and 186 for the complete inscription on the Porta San Pancrazio.

2 Giuseppe Vasi's view of the Porta San Pancrazio (No. 13 in *Delle Magnificenze di Roma Antica e Moderna,* Book I) is reproduced in Gigli 185. See also the *veduta* of Gaspar Van Wittel (Vanvitelli), who worked in Rome from 1674 to his death in 1736 (Marco Chiarini, *Vedute Romane: Disegni dal XVI al XVIII Secolo* [Rome, 1971]. Fig. 59).

3 For Maggi's plan of Rome, see Nash fig. 945, and for Rainaldi's drawing of the gate, see Nash fig. 944.

4 These names appear on the French military map in General J. B. Ph. Vaillant, *Le Siège de Rome en 1849* (Paris, 1851), reproduced in Cozza 153.

5 Gabions were cylinders of wicker filled with earth and stones. Tightly lined up and reinforced with additional mounds of earth or sandbags, they were placed in front of batteries, trenches, and defensive positions. Several gabions appear in the *veduta* by C. Werner reproduced opposite p. 228 in Trevelyan.

6 Artists' depictions of Colomba's death (e.g. *Ai Caduti,* drawing facing 152, and Marino 119) show her wearing a dress in battle, but her biographers state that she wore an officer's uniform. The artists must have felt it immodest for her to wear a soldier's uniform and put a dress on her, just as the nuns at Sette Dolori did for her burial.

7 Photograph of the objects in *Ai Caduti* 42. The button bears not only the initials, but also a death's head with flowing ribbon.

8 Colomba's message was that her life was "consecrated to Italy for a long time and what value did it have for her, if not in how much she [or her life] was able to be useful to her unfortunate country."

ABOVE

Fig. 10. 1. Street marker: Via Fratelli Bonnet, Garibaldini. Photograph, K. A. Geffcken, 2000.

BELOW

Fig. 10. 2. Via Fratelli Bonnet. Photograph, N. Goldman, 2004.

CHAPTER 10

WHO WERE THE FRATELLI BONNET?

Katherine A. Geffcken

Fig. 10. 3. Nino Bonnet (from
the Romagna). Emilio Curatulo,
Anita Garibaldi (Milan & Rome,
1932), opposite 116.

N ext to Via Angelo Masina and Via Carini, no street is probably more familiar to the Academy community than Via
Fratelli Bonnet, where we wait for buses, head toward the
street market, and walk to the Intercollegiate Center [figs.
10. 1 & 10. 2]. Who were the brothers Bonnet, and why do
these Garibaldini have a French name?

There were at least four Bonnet brothers, from Comacchio
in the province of Ferrara. The eldest, Gioacchino (sometimes spelled Giovacchino),
usually called Nino, was born July 26, 1819 [fig. 10. 3]. After surviving many campaigns fighting for the Republican cause, Nino lived to see Italy unified. The twins
Gaetano Romolo and Raimondo Bonnet were born January 4, 1826. In 1848 the
twins joined Angelo Masina's cavalry unit, the Lancieri della Morte, Raimondo as
captain and Gaetano as lieutenant and aide-de-camp to Masina. At Rome on June 3,
1849, Gaetano was killed in one of the heroic but hopeless charges to recapture the
Villa Corsini dei Quattro Venti from the French (see pp. 16, 20). In the same battle,
Raimondo was wounded, but recovered sufficiently to
accompany Garibaldi on the arduous retreat across Italy
in July, 1849. Like his older brother Nino, Raimondo survived to live in a united Italy. The fourth Bonnet, Celeste,
is a shadowy figure; various accounts report that he assisted his brother Nino in patriotic enterprises.

The four Bonnets were sons of an Italian mother,
Barbara Guggi, and a French father, Auguste Étienne
Bonnet, who came in 1811 from France to Comacchio, to
install a salt factory. Augusto Stefano Bonnet, as he
became known in Comacchio, must have prospered
because by 1848 his son Nino not only owned several fine
farms in the district but was a leading citizen of the town.
All the family seems to have shared a passionate, steady
devotion to Republican causes. For instance, Gioacchino's
very name (the Italian version of Joachim) shows family

loyalty to the dashing Napoleonic king of Naples, Joachim Murat (Trevelyan 289). Furthermore, the Romagna was a hotbed of Republican sentiment, constantly pressured by Austrian-controlled Lombardy and Veneto to the north. Indeed, Comacchio stood on the front lines, located in lagoons on the southern edge of the Po delta, just within the Papal States and close to Austrian territory on the other side of the Po.

A small fishing town by the 1840's, boasting especially magnificent eels, Comacchio had been, in the past, a strategic port and valuable source of salt. Founded as Ravenna declined, and situated not far from the site of ancient Spina, Comacchio stood on thirteen little islands linked by bridges over canals, with lands around rich in salt beds and full of game and fish. Ella Noyes describes the view of the area from the campanile of the nearby abbey at Pomposa:

> To the east lies the blue line of the retreated Adriatic, and between you and it
> spreads out a welter of dark earth and shining water, in the midst of which
> rise out the domes and spires of Commacchio [sic], that salt city over which
> the Estensi ruled. All around it are the shallow waters where the lords of
> Ferrara diverted themselves with fishing. The neighborhood of Commacchio
> was their favorite haunt for all kinds of sport . . . . There was wild game of
> every sort (Noyes 407).

By the 1840's the Bonnets not only owned considerable tracts of this territory, but their knowledge of its waterways and hidden paths would play a critical role in saving Garibaldi's life.

Nino Bonnet began his political apprenticeship early, joining Giuseppe Mazzini's secret organization Giovine Italia. By spring 1848, he was a member of the local militia of Ravenna, which crossed over into the Veneto to help defend Vicenza against the Austrians. In order to concentrate troops at the more strategic city of Verona, the Austrians had withdrawn from Vicenza on March 25, 1848. But the Austrians soon tried to take Vicenza back from the Italians in April, and then again in May. On May 23 they began a siege of the city with 19,000 men, while 3,000 Italians inside defended it. After a horrific struggle, Vicenza capitulated to the Austrians on June 10, 1848. The fall of Vicenza was a turning point in the North Italian war for independence. George Meredith, in his novel *Vittoria*, likens the effects of Vicenza's fall to a violent storm that broke over Lombardy and the Veneto: between Venice and Milan there swept suddenly "this unutterable devastation" (377). At Vicenza, Nino commanded the fifth company of the Ravenna *guardia civile*. The Austrians, admiring Italian bravery at Vicenza, released the defeated defenders on condition that they not fight against Austria for three months.

Nino Bonnet returned home to the Romagna, but revolutionary activity in Bologna (from which the Austrians had been expelled in August 1848) soon drew his attention. Angelo Masina, the rich young Bolognese, was recruiting his own company of lancers, and Garibaldi with his Italian Legion drew near Bologna in November. The General, as Garibaldi was always known, came to the Romagna to recruit, knowing that patriots there would readily answer his call. As the November days passed, Garibaldi and Masina moved with their troops east to the Adriatic, intent on sailing to Venice to support the new Republic there or on responding to other calls for help against the Austrians or Neapolitans. Masina and his lancers waited at Comacchio, Garibaldi at Ravenna. When Papal troops arrived at Comacchio, Nino Bonnet organized his town to protect the lancers with barricades and cannon fire against the Papal attack. Then at Ravenna, Bonnet conferred with Garibaldi, whose "air of nobility and heroism" inspired in Nino a lifelong devotion (Trevelyan 289, quoting Bonnet 5-6).

When Gaetano and Raimondo left Comacchio in Masina's company, Nino remained in the Romagna, working for Republican causes and helped by his other brother Celeste. Once again, Nino fought in defense of a major city against the Austrians. He was wounded at Bologna, which fell after an eight-day siege on May 16, 1849. Less than three months later, he had recovered enough to rescue Garibaldi on the beach at Magnavacca near Comacchio.

Meanwhile, the Bonnet twins were acquitting themselves well in battles in and around Rome. On June 2, Gaetano wrote Nino to report that in the battle at Velletri (May 19, 1849) he fought alongside the infantry, advancing even under the town walls: ". . . e posso dire, senza millanterie, che io feci il mio dovere . . . ." (quoted in Ai Caduti 156) ("…and I can say, without boasting, that I did my duty…") Earlier in the day, on the road to Velletri, Masina and his forty odd lancers had successfully charged not only two squadrons of Neapolitan cavalry, but after that success, three to four thousand enemy infantry (Garibaldi 242-43).

On the day after his proud letter to Nino, Gaetano was killed in one of the six charges to recapture the Casino of the Quattro Venti. In which of the charges he fell and in which his brother Raimondo was wounded, I have been so far unable to discover. According to Garibaldi's own account (Garibaldi 249-53), Masina and his lancers figured prominently in the second and fifth charges. In the desperate fifth charge, Masina galloped forward with about twenty lancers, and was struck down on the great landing outside the villa's principal salone (see p. 20). Certainly, if they survived the earlier assaults, the Bonnet twins went down during this fifth attempt. By then the building, held by ever-reinforced French troops, "was growling and darting out flames like a volcano," and in front of it was a scene of unparalleled carnage (Garibaldi 250, 252).

In sending forward Masina's lancers at the Quattro Venti, Garibaldi is sometimes accused of having squandered the flower of the Romagna in a "wild goose chase" (Trevelyan 189). But the surviving Bonnets continued devoted as ever to "the General." After the fall of the short-lived Roman Republic, Raimondo rode out of Porta San Giovanni among the four thousand whom Garibaldi led in retreat on July 2, 1849. Although more than two thousand five hundred drifted away or deserted as the discouraged army eluded pursuers across Italy, Raimondo went all the way to the troops' final refuge high up in the little Republic of San Marino. There on July 31, Garibaldi released his soldiers to return to their homes. Everywhere, the towns, roads, and woods were full of Austrian soldiers, searching for Garibaldi and his men.

Fig. 10. 4. Painting by Matania, 1884, showing the cart transporting Anita to the Guiccioli farmhouse where she died. Emilio Curatulo, *Anita Garibaldi* (Milan & Rome, 1932), opposite 124.

Raimondo was one of the lucky ones who slipped through the countryside safely.

The oldest brother Nino, now back at home in Comacchio, had connections with a well-developed network of communication among patriots throughout the Romagna and the Veneto. He learned that Garibaldi, his wife Anita, his staff, and about two hundred thirty soldiers had successfully made their way to a little port on the Adriatic, Cesenatico. He further learned that there they had embarked on about thirteen fishing boats and were now headed toward Venice, where Manin's republic held out. But Bonnet also knew that the Austrian navy would intercept this little fishing fleet. On the evening of August 2, he joined a crowd on a jetty near Comacchio, all drawn to the shore to watch the colored sails in the distance. Later, that night, from his bed, he could hear the Austrian cannon firing. Again, at sunrise, he joined a crowd of citizens and Austrian soldiers on the pier, where they saw that about ten boats had been captured, but three (or five) were racing toward the shore a little to the north, pursued by Austrian craft. Bonnet breathlessly drove his little horse gig north as far as he could take it, then on foot hurried through the dunes. There he met Garibaldi wading ashore, carrying mortally ill Anita and followed now by only one colleague, the lame Captain Culiolo. The contrast could not have been more dramatic: the neatly dressed, affluent Bonnet, and emerging from the water, Garibaldi still in his red shirt, now stained with sweat and salt water. Bonnet later described these frantic moments, the boom of Austrian guns, Anita's emaciated face, Garibaldi's attempts to support his failing wife. In a pause to rest as they headed painfully and slowly toward one of Bonnet's farms, [fig. 10. 4], Garibaldi said, *"Ah Bonnet! Voi siete il mio angelo salvatore, l'ancora della mia speranza. Voi solo mi restate: tutti gli altri, come mi riconoscono, m'abbandonano."* ("Ah, Bonnet! You are my angel savior, the anchor of my hope. You alone to me remain: all the others, when they recognize me, abandon me.") Bonnet answered, *"Generale, mio fratello Gaetano è morto combattendo al vostro fianco per la romana libertà: io vi salverò o perirò con voi"* (Bonnet quoted in Renzi 95) ("General, my brother Gaetano died fighting at your side for Roman liberty: I will rescue you or I will perish with you.").

Nino Bonnet not only saved Garibaldi at this critically hazardous moment, but although imprisoned by the Austrians, he returned to work for Italian liberty after his release. He served as a battalion commander under Garibaldi in the invasion of Sicily in 1860, and at the battle of Volturno (October 1, 1860) was made a lieutenant colonel on Garibaldi's central staff. In the third war for independence, in 1866, he was promoted to the rank of full colonel in the regular Italian army. Always in contact with major figures in the Risorgimento, he supported Mazzini's goals and generously financed the republican press. A devoted public servant to the last, he was mayor of Comacchio for several years. In 1887 he published his account of Garibaldi's landing near Comacchio, and in 1888 a work on the local laws of his home area. He died at Magnavacca on December 31,1890. His brother Raimondo died just a short time later, within the next year.

◈ REFERENCES

Ai Caduti per Roma MDCCCXLIX-MDCCCLXX (Rome, 1941).

Di Porto, B. "Giovacchino Bonnet," *Dizionario Biografico degli Italiani* (Rome, 1970) 12.263-64.

Garibaldi, Giuseppe. *The Memoirs*, ed. A. Dumas, trans. R. S. Garnett. (London, 1931).

Mancuso, Franco. "Comacchio," *Città da Scoprire* (Milan, 1983) 1.311-14. For more on Comacchio and the salt beds there, see Ingrid D. Rowland, "A summer outing in 1510: religion and economics in the Papal war with Ferrara," *Viator* 18 (1987) 347-59.

Meredith, George. *Vittoria* (New York, 1897, 1922).

Noyes, Ella. *The story of Ferrara* (London, 1904).

Renzi, Renzo. *Ferrara* (Bologna, 1969) 2.94-95, quoting G. Bonnet's *Lo Sbarco di Garibaldi a Magnavacca* (Bologna, 1887). R. Bonnet wrote an account of the retreat across Italy, *Lettera a Belluzzi*, ms. in Bologna.

Trevelyan, G. M. *Garibaldi's Defence of the Roman Republic* (London, 1912).

Trevelyan, G. M. *Manin and the Venetian Revolution of 1848* (London, 1923).

Casino del Giardino Farnese sul Monte Gianicolo

Fig. 11. 1. Villa Aurelia (*Casino del Giardino Farnese sul Monte Gianicolo*). By Giuseppe Vasi, from his *Le Magnificenze* (1760). To the left is the Casino Farnese of Pope Paul III. Photographed by A. Ortolan from the volume in the Rare Book Room, Library of the AAR.

CHAPTER 11

THE HISTORY OF VILLA AURELIA

Lawrence Richardson, jr

W hen Cardinal Girolamo Farnese set out to build what was to become Villa Aurelia about the year 1650, the preliminaries called for both tact and perseverance. Fortunately he was amply endowed with both. The site on which the Cardinal had set his heart was the highest point in the Eternal City, the stretch of the old Aurelian Wall where it approached the Porta San Pancrazio, and this was adjacent to the Vigna Farnese, a property that had belonged to the Farnese family since the days of the Farnese pope, Paul III, a century before. It was only a decade or so earlier that the wall here had ceased to be an important part of the city's defenses, thanks to the new fortifications of the Janiculum begun under Urban VIII Barberini, and the existence of Vigna Farnese very probably tipped the scales in the Cardinal's favor. In due course a papal letter was forthcoming that granted him permission to build, but to build only in a very limited way.

Probably Cardinal Farnese was in large part his own architect, and what he built appeared to Rome not a villa but rather a grand loggia precariously balanced on the picturesque ruin of the Aurelian Wall. On the side toward Vigna Farnese it developed as a house, but to those on the Via Aurelia what was most impressive was the long gallery that crowned the building and was finished at either end with asymmetrical towers, a pair of belvederes from which at one end one looked over the heart of the ancient city and at the other toward Michelangelo's *cupolone* and the green countryside. The view became immediately the most celebrated panorama in Rome. The Cardinal's house was an immense success, and he spent the rest of his life furnishing and embellishing it. He engaged the most expensive painters, Lauri and Schorr, known as "il Tedesco," to decorate its ceilings and never tired of adding to its treasures. He went so far as to bring to Rome expressly to work on the gallery of the villa, the celebrated Carlo Cignani, a painter whose work he had encountered while on a papal mission to Bologna. The project took Cignani three years to complete.

At Cardinal Girolamo Farnese's death in 1668, the villa and its contents passed to the Farneses of Parma. The Cardinal's will expressed a pious hope that the house might serve as a residence for one of the three cardinals to whom he was in some way connected, Sforza, Borromeo, and Savelli, and that eventually it might be

Fig. 11. 2. Engraving by Giovanni Battista Piranesi, detail showing the Villa Aurelia from the Acqua Paola, turned a bit to be seen. Mid-eighteenth century. Hind #21 detail.

reserved for the use of future Farnese cardinals. But such specific plans came to nothing. Sforza, Borromeo, and Savelli never used the villa, and there were no more Farnese cardinals. Yet the Farneses of Parma did rent the property to a succession of prelates — for instance, to Cardinal Maidalchini, two members of the Acquaviva family, and Monsignor de Canillac. In his diary, Francesco Valesio recorded several elegant dinners at the villa (1702, 1732, 1733). But Girolamo's carefully assembled collection of treasures had been largely dispersed, packed up and sent off to help furnish Farnese houses in Parma.

Fortunately shortly after Cardinal Farnese's death, in the course of settling his estate, the papal bureaucracy made a detailed inspection of the property, and record of that has come down to us. The inspector was Carlo Cartari, an *avvocato concistoriale*, a conscientious bureaucrat, and his description of the house is invaluable in the reconstruction of its plan. From the next century comes Vasi's splendid engraving of the garden front [fig. 11. 1], which shows very much what we see today as the principal block, once one takes away the porte-cochère, a nineteenth-century addition. And thanks to the situation of the villa above the Fontana Paola and next to the Porta San Pancrazio, it turns up in the background of views by artists such as Van Wittel and Piranesi so that one can chart its appearance over the years [fig. 11. 2]. But for the plan we must rely on a single description.

The ground floor, we are told, was made up of three good-sized rooms, an entrance hall and two others of equal size, and three smaller rooms. From one of the

smaller rooms a circular stair led to the upper story, and off this stair opened a mezzanine apartment that was the private suite of the Cardinal. In the upper story there
was a splendid gallery overlooking the Via Aurelia and at the end of this a small room
containing an altar for the Cardinal's devotions that was ingeniously designed so that
when it was not in use it all slid together and could be folded away into a single handsome cupboard. Off the gallery were a dining room and a *salone*, both grand reception rooms with panoramic views, and connecting these was a small room with a
ceiling painted with trellises and vines among which perched various bright-colored
birds, a charming room in which the Cardinal was accustomed to sleep during the
worst heat of the summer.

Surprisingly little has changed in the basic layout over the centuries. Most of
the Cardinal's painted ceiling decorations are gone, but the little room painted with
trellises and birds survives, as delightful now as in the seventeenth century, and the
whole of the *piano nobile* preserves its original volumes and architectural character
with remarkable fidelity. All that is really lacking are the decorations, and especially
Cignani's splendid program of mythological subjects that seems to have so enriched
the gallery. On the ground floor the sequence of spaces has not changed either; the
bearing walls clearly reflect the plan of the *piano nobile*. But the central good-sized
room, between the entrance hall and what is now the principal sitting room, has
been broken up to make a stairwell and to house lavatories and an elevator, so that
one no longer sees it as an architectural unit. Originally the sequence of three good-
sized rooms would have been a series of volumes all the same size, reception rooms
in the tradition of seventeenth century villas, in which the program of painted decoration made the significant differences, and the three smaller rooms, which took
their width from the wall on which they were founded, probably reflected a stretch
of curtain between two towers of the fortification, with the towers then carried up
through the building to make the belvederes on the roof. These are the rooms we see
today as the stair lobby, dining room, and pantry of the villa. Midway along the circular stair leading to the *piano nobile* opened the mezzanine suite of the Cardinal's
private apartment. This has now been walled off and is accessible only from the
opposite end of the building, but it is clear that it ran above the smaller rooms founded on the wall and was architecturally determined by the rooms below it.

It is interesting and significant that in the Cardinal's house there is no provision for kitchens and a service quarter. The whole building was an ingenious showpiece, a loggia in which there was no place for an attic or cellars in which to house
the meaner necessities of life. These must all have found their place in the sixteenth-
century casino of Paul III, which was probably completely done over and made to
work as an annex in conjunction with the new house. Unfortunately we have neither
plan nor complete view of it (but see Casino Farnese, pp. 128-33) that will give us any
idea of what it was like and how it functioned. The best we can say is that it seems
to have kept its sixteenth-century exterior shell unaltered.

The Farneses of Parma showed no inclination to sell the villa, although in
1761, at the death of the tenant Abbé de Canillac, there was discussion about putting

it on the market. Family tradition, however, prevailed. Besides, the villa would bring little money, and it was already promised to Cardinal Orsini. Then finally in 1774 it was rented to Count Ferdinando Giraud, the brother of Cardinal Bernardino Giraud, a member of a family of French bankers who seem to have aspired to replace the Farneses of Latera in all their Roman possessions and glory.

Following the death of Ferdinando Giraud in 1816, his heirs, his four sons, Pietro, Giuseppe, Giovanni, and Francesco, simply stopped paying the rent on the Villa Farnese and allowed the building to fall into disrepair. The property of the Farneses of Parma had by this time passed to the Bourbons of Naples through Elisabetta Farnese, the mother of Charles III, and the remoteness of their royal land-lords may have been a factor in the Girauds' thinking at this juncture. But after a decent interval the real estate agents of the Bourbons protested to the Girauds about their derelictions and the deterioration of the fabric of the house. This was to no avail; the Girauds retorted that the contract had been with their father and structural repairs were now the responsibility of the owners. They would not leave nor pay the rent until these were carried out. So in due course, a civil suit was instituted against them, and then the Girauds proved themselves masters of litigation, the delaying tactic and the counter-measure. The suit dragged on, in and out of court for twenty-five years. Finally in 1839 there was a settlement out of court, and in the end the property was sold to the Girauds for the minuscule sum of 600 *scudi*. There must have been more than a little skullduggery involved here; even the land, one would suppose, would have fetched a higher price, and if the house was run down, it was certainly not a total loss. If the frescoed ceilings were water stained and sadly damaged, still at least some of them could have been restored, as the trellis room shows with its exotic birds. In any case, the Girauds made a very good thing of it; shortly after settlement of the suit, they sold the villa in 1841 for four times the price at which they had bought it and without making any repairs.

The buyer was Count Alessandro Savorelli of Forlì, a newcomer to Rome, heir through his mother to the ancient Roman Palazzo Muti-Papazzurri (now Balestra) on Piazza Santi Apostoli and possessor of a large fortune made larger by the grant of a papal monopoly on the supplying of tallow candles for the illumination of churches in Rome. Not surprisingly the count always preferred to live on Santi Apostoli, which is still today probably the most fashionable address in Rome. In all his restorations, he was aided and abetted by his father-in-law, Virginio Vespignani, the reigning architect of the period, the favorite architect of Pius IX and an indefatigable repristinator of Roman churches. In acquiring the Villa Giraud-Farnese, Savorelli was motivated less by his admiration for the house and the possibilities it offered as a residence, than by his need for space to develop his candle factory. Still he entrusted restoration of the villa to Vespignani, who added the wings extending the main block to east and west along the wall, but with such discretion that they neither detract from the architectural unity of the main block nor seem inappropriate additions. Here he located all the necessary outbuildings, a suite of rooms for the family, and a chapel. This must have been the time when the central room on the ground floor was sacrificed to make a stairwell and approach to the new family quarters. And now the old Roman wall disappeared behind a dramatic promenade along the front, under which Vespignani hid several of the workshops.

There seems to be some doubt that the Savorelli family ever really lived in the villa. In the summer they were usually accustomed to repair to a country place at Sutri. And the pervasive stench of tallow and sulfuric acid, which Savorelli also manufactured, can hardly have been an attraction. But perhaps Vespignani did not think of that when he began work. In any case he lavished loving attention on the house, and it must have cost Savorelli a fortune. The *piano nobile* alone was a triumphant wedding of the old and new. Not a single proportion seems to have been sacrificed, but the whole *piano nobile* was completely repaved, replastered, and repainted.

Vespignani had barely finished the work when disaster struck in 1848-49 in the shape of Mazzini and the Roman Republic. Pius IX fled to Naples; Napoleon III sent an army to restore the Pope to his throne; Garibaldi was summoned to help defend the Republic; and Rome prepared to stand siege. The French troops under General Oudinot rolled down the Via Aurelia, the direct road from their landing at Civitavecchia. Garibaldi and his forces faced them first at the Vatican and then at Porta San Pancrazio from April 30 to June 30. He made Villa Savorelli his headquarters from June 4-21, since it commanded so comprehensive a view of the field and the disposition of the defenders. The French set about bombarding the position with cannon, and there are wonderful descriptions of the heroism and the intoxicating exhilaration of the days that followed, accounts of the relentless pounding of the artillery and constant hiss of rifles, of reckless sorties into the Villa Corsini dei Quattro Venti against overwhelming odds, of Garibaldi's calling for fresh bottles and glasses when a cannonball had cleared the table in front of him. When the defense finally collapsed and Garibaldi fled north on July 2, the top of the Janiculum was a spectacle of desolation and carnage. The majestic Villa Corsini was reduced to a chunk of its lofty basement; the church of San Pietro in Montorio was without its apse, from which Raphael's Transfiguration had fortunately been removed; the Villa Savorelli had lost its roof and its south front facing Via Aurelia almost from end to end, exposing the shattered gallery and the rooms of the mezzanine [fig. 11. 3]; and the casino of Paul III was a total loss, a thing of the past.

With the return of the Pope, Count Savorelli, an ardent papist, applied for compensation for the damages his property had sustained, and we can presume he received it, since Vespignani was a member of the papal commission of four on reparations. Savorelli was back in the business of manufacturing candles in the villa by 1850. In 1854 he is recorded in family records as having rebuilt the south front and the great circular stair. Evidently he was not a very popular figure in Rome in those days, however, for he complained of vandalism and asked for police protection of his factory, in addition to a French army patrol. Quantities of sulfuric acid had been poured out on the ground, and the equipment for the candle business had all been stolen during the days of the Republic, destruction that sounds like more than casual war damage, and Savorelli's fortunes were now in relentless decline. He died in

Fig. 11. 3. Villa Aurelia (southern façade), July 1849. By Carlo Werner. Property of the Villa Aurelia, AAR. Photograph, A. Ortolan.

1864, a broken and ruined man, leaving his affairs in a dreadful muddle.

His widow and children seem to have been unequal to salvaging anything from the wreck of their fortunes. At first the villa was put up to let; eventually it was mortgaged to the Monte di Pietà, and in 1879 it was sold for debt to the Cassa dei Depositi e Prestiti. It was put up at auction and bought by Clara Jessup Heyland in 1881. She was the daughter of a rich Philadelphian, married to Major Alexander Heyland, who had been invalided out of the British Royal Artillery in India. He was then so crippled that he was confined to a wheelchair most of the time, and they had retired to Rome hoping to find a climate and an atmosphere that would prove beneficial for him. Mrs. Heyland loved the villa, renamed it Villa Aurelia, and with gusto attacked the project of making it elegant and comfortable — in the unrelenting terms of nineteenth-century Anglo-American comfort. She installed plumbing and invented a diminutive Romanesque campanile, a sort of ruin of the medieval church of SS. Giovanni e Paolo al Gianicolo, to house the standpipe to maintain pressure in her numerous bathrooms, which were higher than any others in Rome; she added the porte-cochère [fig. 11. 4] and the heraldic stained glass in the entrance hall; she put in an elevator and fireplaces in every room; and along the façade facing Via Garibaldi she added, at equal intervals, three great bay windows running the full height of the main block [fig. 11. 5]. The final result, the labor of many years, was a triumph of ingenuity and determination. At the same time she devoted herself to redesigning

ABOVE

Fig. 11. 4. Villa Aurelia restored by Mrs. Heyland showing the porte-cochère addition on the front. Photograph,
Photographic Archive of the AAR.

BELOW

Fig. 11. 5. Villa Aurelia restorations by Mrs. Heyland
showing the bay windows and the trimmed ilex trees in
terraces above the Via Aurelia (today the Via Garibaldi).
Photograph, Photographic Archive of the AAR.

Fig. 11. 6. The Aurelia garden with walks and fountains restored. Photograph, N. W. Goldman, 2002.

Fig. 11. 7. The bay-covered walkway surprise. Photograph, N. W. Goldman, 2002.

the garden. Savorelli's candle-making installations were swept away. A series of long, narrow terraces in front, connected by stairs, now descended toward the Via Aurelia and was planted with beds of flowers under banks of ilex clipped into topiary blocks. The drives and walks of the old *vigna* were redesigned with fountains and pools to punctuate them [fig. 11. 6]. And bay-covered walks were grown to break the vistas and spring little surprises on the visitor [fig. 11. 7]. The whole was a garden that combined, in a very intricate way, the formality of Italian open parterres with the shade and mystery of parkland. Clipped ilex rose to a uniform height under towering umbrella pines; walks and the angles of their turns were laid out with meticulous care [fig. 11. 8]. In all of Rome there is no garden that combines the natural and the disciplined in quite the same way.

As Mrs. Heyland loved her house in Rome, so she loved her native country, and at her death in 1909 she willed the Villa Aurelia to the American Academy in Rome to be its permanent home [fig. 11. 9]. And so it has become, although it took the trustees time to see the advantages of the location and J.P. Morgan's enthusiastic appraisal of the site and his financial backing to make the possibility a reality.

Fig. 11. 8. The turning path of the entrance rising to introduce the visitor to the gardens. Photograph, N. W. Goldman, 2002.

Fig. 11. 9. The formal entrance to the Villa Aurelia. Photograph, Photographic Archive of the AAR.

Fig. 11. 10. The Villa Aurelia Music
Room restored. Photograph supplied
by L. Richardson, jr

In 1945-47, shortly after the Second World War, the Academy undertook a badly needed refurbishing of the villa and restoration of the exterior to the lines of the original loggia of the Cardinal. Mrs. Heyland's bay windows were removed, but the belvedere towers could not be reconstructed on the evidence available. Instead, Mrs. Heyland's highly ornamental chimney pots now provide graceful distinction to its roofline. Vespignani's east wing was kept and Mrs. Heyland's porte-cochère and faintly manorial Gothic entrance hall. The stables and service wing were converted into guest-house flats.[1] The whole outer shell of Cardinal Farnese's loggia could be reconstructed, thanks to the old Roman custom of making terracotta matrices for the stuccowork that are then stored for use whenever the house needs repairs and repainting. The interior volumes are for the most part original, too. But the splendid decoration of the music room is Vespignani's [fig. 11. 10], and the gardens and pleasances that contribute so much to the special character of the house today are Clara Heyland's.

▨ REFERENCES

Aldrich, Amey. *Villa Aurelia* (Rome, 1938).

American Academy in Rome, Finance Office: Property deeds, documents.

Banfi, Florio (Holik Barabas). "Villa Farnese al Gianicolo," *L'Urbe* 26 (1963), 17-25.

Benocci, Carla. "Villa Aurelia si espande: Pio Piacentini come figura di mediazione del 'nuovo' Giardino Americano sul Gianicolo." *Strenna dei Romanisti* (2004), 45-62.

Bignami Odier, Jeanne. "Le Casin Farnèse du Mont Janicule (Porte San Pancrazio), Maintenant Villa Aurelia," *Mélanges de l'École Française de Rome* 91,1 (1979), 507-538.

Connors, Joseph. "Villa Farnese Bourbon Giraud Savorelli Heyland Aurelia," unpublished manuscript.

Roncaglia, Linda. *Villa Aurelia al Gianicolo*. Tesi di Laurea in Storia dell' Architettura Moderna, Università di Roma, 2000.

▨ NOTES

1 In the 2000-2002 renovation of the Villa Aurelia, the *foresteria* wing has been turned into a lecture hall (see Chapter 13).

TOP

Fig. 12. 1. Mrs. Heyland's favorite donkey, not being mistreated, in the garden of the Villa Aurelia. Photograph, Photographic Archive of the AAR.

ABOVE LEFT

Fig. 12. 2. The inscription on the retaining wall below San Pietro in Montorio, commemorating the construction of the road built in 1867. Photograph, E. R. Knauer.

ABOVE RIGHT

Fig. 12. 3. The Via Crucis providing a pedestrian ascent to San Pietro in Montorio from lower down the Via Garibaldi. Photograph, E. R. Knauer.

CHAPTER 12

RUMINATIONS ON MRS. HEYLAND'S WILL

Elfriede Regina (Kezia) Knauer

In 1909, Mrs. Clara Jessup Heyland willed her estate, the Villa Aurelia and its gardens, to the American Academy in Rome; the bequest was accepted on January 3, 1910. Eleven days before her death, Mrs. Heyland added to her will the condition that the Academy ". . . take steps to insure against ill-treatment of horses and animals in Rome, it being [her] hope that [she might] arouse in the students of the Academy of America a deep and last-ing interest in this much needed Charity and Act of Mercy." Why did Mrs. Heyland, a woman once described as "languishing on a blue satin sofa with a basket of kittens, each wearing a blue bow," single out this "Act of Mercy" for horses and animals [fig. 12. 1]?

Occupants of the Academy in Rome as pedestrians often explore many short-cuts to ascend to the top of the Gianicolo via the maze of Trastevere *vicoli* from the city below. The stately curves of the Via Garibaldi, built — according to the Latin inscription [fig. 12. 2] just beyond the recessed gates of the Bosco Parrasio — in the short period of only fifty days, at the expense of Pope Pius IX in 1867, made it pos-sible for the first time to ascend comfortably to the Porta di San Pancrazio by car-riage.

A successful design in city planning, the new road profoundly altered the ancient aspect of the hill and the traffic patterns in the area. Thus, for instance, the surviving one of the two stepped ascents [fig. 12. 3] (furnished with stations of the *Via Crucis*) which leads to Piazza di San Pietro in Montorio [fig. 12. 4], was cut off and is barely noticeable today, although it has been rescued from decades of overgrowth and decay. Other ascending streets further down suffered a similar fate. They abrupt-ly end at the high retaining walls that were needed to support the tracts of Via Goffredo Mameli and Via Garibaldi. One of these streets ends in a flight of narrow stairs that gives access to the first hairpin bend at the merging of Via Mameli into Via Garibaldi. It is aptly called the Vicolo della Frusta, the Alley of the Whip [fig. 12. 5]. Together with Vicolo del Cedro, it once was one of the old, and for a long time unpaved, streets leading uphill. Vicolo della Frusta still hugs a huge medieval wall, one of the few remaining enclosures in Trastevere that once protected individual blocks with their respective gardens. Today this compound harbors the modern Istituto Professionale di Stato per il Commercio Giulio Romano.

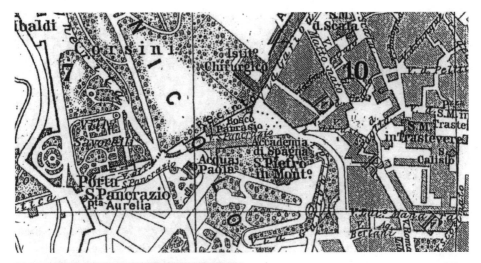

ABOVE

Fig. 12. 4. Detail of the Baedeker map of 1900 showing the layout of the streets during Mrs. Heyland's time at the Villa Aurelia. K. Baedeker, *Italie Centrale*, 12th ed. (Leipzig, 1900). See Fig. 18.2 for Nolli map of the area.

LEFT

Fig. 12. 5. The Vicolo della Frusta, the Alley of the Whip. Photograph, E. R. Knauer.

Fig. 12. 6. Steep steps and pavement of the Salita di Porta S. Pancrazio. Building of Bosco Parrasio on left. Photograph, K. A. Geffcken, 1998.

Fig. 12. 7. Steep ascent on the via Garibaldi, formerly the top of the Via di Porta S. Pancrazio. It was even steeper before earth was removed in the 1880's. The ascent here, and continuing up to the gate, would have caused drivers to whip their draft animals, and Mrs. Heyland in the Villa Aurelia right above could have heard cries from abused animals. Photograph, B. Goldman, 2004.

Vicolo della Frusta was formerly continued by the Salita di Porta di San Pancrazio (originally the ancient Via Aurelia), still today the steepest part of the ascent, a road that runs just below the Villa Aurelia [fig. 12. 6]. With the remodeling of the Gianicolo, the Salita di Porta San Pancrazio became a reserve for pedestrians. Its vertiginous flight of stairs emerges at the northwest corner of the Piazza di Acqua Paola. Only the lower part of this cul-de-sac allows cars access to the Spanish Liceo "Cervantes" on its south side and the Palazzina dell'Accademia dell'Arcadia (Bosco Parrasio) on its north. In its present state, it is hard to believe that this was for many centuries one of the main traffic-bearing arteries of the hill. Heavy traffic must always have traveled the road since the Via Aurelia was one of the major Roman highways leading to the northwest from the Porta di S. Pancrazio (the Porta Aurelia of antiquity) [fig. 12. 7].

When Mrs. Heyland restored the Villa as her residence, renaming it the Villa Aurelia, the Via Garibaldi had already been laid out. It was certainly not yet macadamed, and it surely was not the automobile racecourse it is today. Traffic and transport depended on draught-and-pack animals, whips being much in evidence when the beasts labored their way uphill. The ordeal of the horses and mules, combined with the pathetic braying of donkeys, must have been a constant acoustic and visual presence for Mrs. Heyland, whose residence sat above the highest tract of the Aurelian Wall just inside the city gate.

The name of the Vicolo della Frusta may thus help us not only to visualize the old days and the old ways, but also to understand Mrs. Heyland's deep concern and her last minute provision in the codicil to her will [fig. 12. 8].

ADDENDUM

The archives of the American Academy in Rome have recently been made available on microfilm. The additional material requires a postscript to this chapter since a more fine-tuned approach to the circumstances of Mrs. Heyland's will is now possible. However, the new information does not alter the suggestions made in this article.

The brother of Mrs. Heyland had contested her will, but an agreement was reached between him and the American Academy through De Forest Brothers, 30 Broad Street , N.Y. in November 1910. The terms of her will that were objectionable were eliminated, among them the "condition to support the work of the Society for the Prevention of Cruelty to Animals."

A contribution by Cristina Puglisi and Christina Huemer entitled "La Villa Aurelia da Clara Jessup Heyland all'Accademia Americana" throws additional light on the circumstances. Their presentation will appear in a forthcoming volume containing the papers of a symposium "Intorno a Villa Sciarra. I salotti internazionali sul Gianicolo tra Ottocento e Novecento," held at the Istituto Italiano di Studi Germanici in Rome in March 2005. I am much obliged to both authors for making the new sources available to me.

REFERENCES

For the text of the will:
Valentine, Lucia and Alan. *The American Academy in Rome, 1894-1969* (Charlottesville, 1973), 51.
For the history of the Gianicolo:
Delli, Sergio. *Le Strade di Roma* (Rome, 1975).
Gigli, Laura. *Guide Rionali di Roma. Rione XIII Trastevere*, Parte I, 2nd ed. (Rome, 1980), 152-56, 161, 167.
For the urban development of the Gianicolo:
Frutaz, Amato Pietro. *Le Piante di Roma*. 3 vols. (Rome, 1962), pls. 476, 495, 521, 527, 536f, 552.
For depictions of the relevant area on the Gianicolo:
Borsi, Stefano. *Roma di Urbano VIII. La Pianta di Giovanni Maggi, 1625* (Rome, 1990), Fol. 38/46, showing the region before fortifications of Urban VIII, and Falda map of 1676 showing it after their erection.
Falda, Giovanni Battista. *Roma al tempo di Clemente X. La Pianta di Roma di Giambattista Falda del 1676, etc.*, con introduzione di Franz Ehrle, S. J. Le Piante Maggiori di Roma dei Sec. XVI e XVII, riprodotte in Fototipia a Cura della Biblioteca Vaticana, No. 5 (Città del Vaticano, 1931).
The Pianta Grande di Roma of Giambattista Nolli, in facsimile, with an introductory essay by Allan Ceen; published by Joseph Aronson (Highmount, N.Y., 1984, 1991).

Mrs. Heyland in the Villa garden.

Fig. 12. 8. Mrs. Clara Jessup Heyland in her garden. Man on her right is unknown. Photograph, Photographic Archive of the AAR.

Fig. 13. 1. The restored Villa Aurelia exterior. Note the lemon garden at the entrance designed by Trustee Mercedes Bass. Photograph, N. W. Goldman, 2002.

CHAPTER 13

THE VILLA AURELIA RESTORATION

Norma Wynick Goldman, based on an interview with Cristina Puglisi, Assistant Director for Academy Properties, architect for the Villa Aurelia restoration

Addendum: Notes on the Restoration by the Architects:
Roberto Einaudi, Cristina Puglisi, Fabiana Zeli

The latest renovation (2000-2002) of the Villa Aurelia, the jewel of the American Academy in Rome at the top of the Janiculum, has involved a major restoration of the existing structures and a dedication of much planning and effort to use the space with maximum efficiency, comfort, and elegance. Alessandra Vinciguerra, Bass Superintendent of Gardens, was in charge of seeing that the gardens were restored and maintained. The lemon garden planted in checkerboard fashion before the entrance is the design of Mercedes Bass, an Academy trustee and chair of the Villa Aurelia restoration. [fig. 13. 1].

In the Villa itself, conservation of all the decorative work in the entire building has been done — the gilded ceilings, the wall reliefs and the paintings have all been restored. Even the stained glass in the atrium has been restored. A nineteenth century decorative work under the modern paint was discovered in the atrium showing the Savorelli (see p. 107) coat of arms; the original painting has been restored.

The basic structure of all of the interior floors has been reinforced. Localized underpinning became necessary when it was discovered that part of the façade had no foundations. The exterior walls were injected with cement to stabilize sections that needed to be reinforced where the fabric was weak.

New systems for the whole building were installed: for heating, electricity, plumbing, and elevators. The new heating system is divided into zones so that different areas can be adjusted for occupation or non-occupation to conserve heating. The windows have been double-glazed with thermal insulation as protection from extremes of heat and cold. A brand-new kitchen of stainless steel components has been installed to allow professional catering for festive occasions.

When the main spiral staircase was restored, a beautiful decorative finish was revealed. To satisfy fire and egress requirements, a new stairway connecting the basement with the top floor was installed where the former mezzanine stairway used to be. The two apartments and the three guest bedrooms in the Villa were renovated and will continue to be available for visitors. A new small bedroom has been added. The Biblioteca above the former director's apartment with its lovely balcony has been redesigned for receptions. Furniture and furnishings throughout have also been renewed.

Fig. 13. 2. The exterior decorations restored. Photograph, N. W. Goldman, 2003.

Fig. 13. 3. The floor of the new Conference Room. Photograph, N. W. Goldman, 2003.

On the exterior, all of the decorative elements of gargoyles, wreaths, and capitals have been restored; old broken cement portions have been replaced with new plaster molded reproductions, using matrices from the preserved portions, the restored portions painted to match the original in white ochre, while the walls were repainted a very light terracotta [fig. 13. 2].

The former Apartments Aurelia A and B no longer exist. The walls between the rooms and between the apartments have been removed so that a new large conference room could be created which accommodates 220, a space much needed for large groups and receptions, conforming to local codes for such gatherings. The tile floor for this conference room is made up of lozenges in three shades of gray, forming a trompe l'oeil pattern that ascends or descends, according to how it is viewed [fig. 13. 3]. The terrace-balconies on the east of this wing have been paved and restored outside the newly-formed conference room to provide open-air space for socializing before lectures, at intermissions, and after events. It can be tented for special events and receptions.

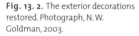

To compensate for the loss of Apartments A and B, four new modern apartments have been created in the former Villino and the Greenhouse. Both units have been completely renovated, each housing two apartments, one on the ground floor and one on the first floor above that, each complete with living room, bedroom, bath and kitchen [fig. 13. 4]. These new facilities have brand-new modern heating, plumbing, kitchen facilities, and electricity. A new Music Studio has been created in the former archaeology workroom.

Fig. 13. 5. Alessandra Vinciguerra, Bass Superintendent of Gardens. Photograph, N. W. Goldman, 2003.

TOP

Fig. 13. 4. The Greenhouse and the Villino
apartments. Photograph, N. W. Goldman, 2003.

ABOVE

Fig. 13. 6. Flowering border along the
stairway to the *villino*.

The long-term garden renovation under the direction of Alessandra
Vinciguerra [13. 5] has resulted in a reinforcement of the original garden design with
continued careful pruning of all the trees and shrubs, the elimination of diseased
portions of the trees, and the establishment of flowering borders along the walkways
and stairways in shades of blue, lavender and yellow [fig. 13. 6].

The renovation of the Aurelia is the latest in a sequence of fine restorations
that the Academy has completed to ensure that its buildings meet present codes and
needs of the Academy community.

⬚ ADDENDUM

NOTES ON THE RESTORATION BY THE ARCHITECTS (2000-2002)

Roberto Einaudi, Cristina Puglisi, Fabiana Zeli

The extensive restoration of Villa Aurelia provided us with the rare opportunity to carry out some detective work and thereby learn more about materials and construction techniques utilized over the history of the building. We looked under existing floorings, paint layers, foundations, and other places usually hidden from view. Most of the time, we specifically searched for clues, but once we literally fell into our discovery.

While we found little that would make us rewrite the history of the Villa, we were able to answer a few questions and confirm some hypotheses. We have organized our notes from below ground up to the roof structure.

Below ground

On the very first day, while we were carefully moving some materials in front of the Greenhouse facing Via Garibaldi, our construction cart suddenly dropped about half a meter. Careful exploration of the newly formed hole in the ground led us to a series of underground vaulted passages about three meters high and of varying widths, with a total length of approximately 20 meters. The general direction of these tunnels is toward the Villino, under the Greenhouse and toward Porta San Pancrazio.

A team of speleologists from Roma Sotterranea, promptly called on the site, carried out a survey of the tunnels (available at the Plant, Planning & Preservation Office of the Academy in Rome). The tunnels were deemed "modern" by Academy Archaeologist Archer Martin, and may have been used for growing mushrooms through the nineteenth century. We also discovered subsequently that the Academy gardeners had already fallen into the same hole some six decades earlier, as documented in the Academy's own Annual Reports. Later we were able to observe that the Academy staff had closed off the original hole with a modern mixture of cement.

While traces of the Aurelian walls that once completely crossed the Villa Aurelia site from the Passeggiata del Gianicolo to Porta San Pancrazio are visible only at the two extremes, the lineal configuration of the Villa, the Greenhouse, and Villino led us to presume that they were founded upon the remains of the ancient walls. The analysis of the uncovered foundations and wall structures indicated, however, that the Aurelian walls in that central area had been completely removed before the construction of the Villa, both to obtain building material for the Papal walls, and to level the site for the Villa gardens. The topmost level of the garden had been lowered so much that the bottom of the foundations of the Roman walls supporting the

Villino were actually well above modern ground level.

During the consolidation work of the nineteenth century wing, previously known as Aurelia A and B, in the northeast corner, we found traces of previous foundations that could have been part of the original Casino by Pope Paul III, on which the modern wall is founded. See Chapter 14 about the "Lost Building," pp. 128-33.

Below floors

After we removed the cement *graniglia*[1] flooring in the ground floor *Salone*, installed by Architect Bruno Zevi in 1945-47, we discovered traces of square terracotta tiles, and four tiles each with a central hole that formed a square in the middle of the room. Clearly, these four tiles marked the place of the four iron columns that supported the wrought iron balcony previously in this room, also removed by Zevi.

Also below the same type of cement *graniglia* floor, in what used to be known as Aurelia A, we found traces of a *Sanpietrini*[2] floor, confirming the prior use of this space as a garage.

When we restored the "mosaic" floor on the ground floor at the bottom of the spiral stairs, we discovered that the green, "stone" tesserae were actually made of glass paste. Similarly, we discovered that the red and yellow "marble" floor in the Atrium was not actually made of stone: it was made of *scagliola*[3] that had badly degenerated and dissolved from the humidity along the walls.

Below paint

During the surface preparation work for the repainting of the Atrium ceiling vault, we discovered below several thick layers of paint, that the central panel was decorated by a coat of arms surrounded by shields with a backdrop of crossed spears. The figure in the middle of the coat of arms was a rampant lion roughly painted when compared to the rest of the decoration, and clearly reworked. The difference in quality was explained by the similarity between the Savorelli and the Heyland family's respective coats of arms. The Savorelli's consists of a rampant and winged griffon with three fleurs de lis above it, while the Heylands' consists of a rampant lion with a sash and the drawing of a tower across it. When the Heylands restored the Villa, the Savorelli rampant griffon was transformed into a rampant lion. The same Heyland coat of arms can be seen in the stained glass windows in the Atrium and above the Villa front door that leads into the Atrium.

On the top floor, during the conservation of the small vaulted ceiling in front of the elevator, which is decorated with birds and trellises, we discovered traces of a painted, geometric design right below the decorative paint layer. Traces of the same geometric pattern were also found below several paint layers on the walls of the Gallery nearby. This confirmed our belief, based on stylistic considerations, that this ceiling was probably painted at the time of the ownership of Clara Jessup Heyland, and certainly dates from after 1849, at which time the Gallery walls collapsed during the Battle for the Repubblica Romana.

On the narrow exterior façade that faces Rome, next to the large arched window that leads from the Music Room to the balcony overlooking Rome, we found significant traces of graffiti incised into the stucco, reproducing the outline of the adjacent window. While the current subdivision of the Music Room window is probably not the original one, the graffito substantiates our hypothesis that the two "windows" visible in the Piranesi print of the Acqua Paola, with the Villa in the background, actually consisted of one real window and one painted one. This is confirmed by the fact that right behind the graffito window and perpendicular to it, is the original structural spine wall for the entire Villa which clearly existed at the time of Piranesi.

On the façades, below exterior paint and stucco[4]

Paint and stucco analyses were commissioned and carried out during the restoration, and the studies are currently kept in the Plant, Planning & Preservation Office in Rome. The difference in the composition of the stucco and the number of exterior lime paint layers clearly indicates the different fate of the north façade facing the garden, from the façades facing the McKim, Mead & White building and Papal walls which were exposed to the cannon balls of the French. These latter façades were rebuilt after the collapse of 1849, and again partially reworked by the Heylands, when they added the bay-windows, which were subsequently removed by Zevi in 1947. While the original stucco of the northern garden façade was still in good shape, that of the west and southern façades, although much newer, as confirmed by a substantially fewer number of exterior lime paint layers, was in worse condition. Metal bars had been used to attach the cast plaster cement column capitals and ornamental figures, causing them to crack and explode, while the initial stucco decoration on the garden façade was still in perfect condition.

Below the terrace roof of the Villa

When we removed the roof terrace above the ceiling in the Dining Room, on the top floor, we discovered finished, painted stucco on the walls above the structural beams that currently hold the decorative ceiling below. This painted stucco still had the holes where the structural wood beams that held the original decorative ceiling used to be. The presence of these holes indicated that the original ceiling of the Dining Room must have hung higher than the current one. This, together with the presence of fragments of finely painted frescos above the vault of the upstairs Gallery looking towards the McKim, Mead & White building (and below the tile roof), confirms that the roof line, and consequently all the ceilings of the top floor, were higher than the current roof and ceilings. It further confirms that all decorative work currently visible on the top floor of the Villa must date from after the destruction of 1849. The fresco fragments above the Gallery vaults, now cleaned and consolidated, may represent the only traces of original decorative work from the time of Cardinal Girolamo Farnese.

⬚ NOTES

1   *Graniglia* is a mixture of cement and small fragments of stone used as inert fillers, smoothly polished.

2   *Sanpietrini* are the typical small basalt stones, with a square surface top, used to pave the streets in Rome.

3   *Scagliola* is a pigmented cement or lime grout mixture made to resemble stone.

4   Stucco, frequently erroneously confused with plaster of Paris, is a mixture of lime and inert materials, usually sand, marble or pozzolana, and contains no gypsum which will expand and crack when exposed to humidity.

Fig. 14. 1. Aerial photograph of the
Villa Aurelia (1970-74), with outlining in bold
black lines to show the approximate location
of the Casino Farnese, now lost. Photograph,
Photographic Archive of the AAR.

CHAPTER 14

THE CASINO FARNESE:
NOTES ON A LOST BUILDING

Katherine A. Geffcken

In his essay on the Villa Aurelia, Professor Lawrence Richardson suggests that the Casino Farnese was probably renovated in the seventeenth century to provide service quarters and kitchen for the new Villa Farnese (that is, the Villa Aurelia), but that the old building seems to have retained ". . . its sixteenth century exterior shell unaltered" (p. 105). Indeed, evidence that Cardinal Girolamo Farnese restored the casino comes from Carlo Cartari's description of the *vigna* and its structures, recorded in 1670. Cartari also remarks that Girolamo decorated the *mediocre habitatione* (modest residence) with *pitture* (paintings).[1] Thus it seems that the Cardinal intended to maintain at least some parts of the casino as pleasant living spaces [fig. 14. 1].

Exactly when Alessandro Farnese (1468-1549) acquired the *vigna*, now the Aurelia property, is not known. Cartari's words (*habitatione fattavi già dal Cardinal Farnese vecchio, che poi fu Paolo 3°*, a residence already completed there by the old Cardinal Farnese, who later became Paul the third) may indicate ownership before 1534 when Alessandro Farnese became Pope Paul III.[2] On the other hand, the Pope's registers for 1537 contain references to payments for the *vigna* (Bignami Odier 508), records that imply a later purchase than Cartari's phrasing indicates. In any case, the *vigna* completed a series of holdings stretching on axis from the Palazzo Farnese across the Tiber to the Vigna Farnese on the river, up to the *vigna* at Porta San Pancrazio.[3] Thus, Paul III could relax not only alongside the Tiber, but also high up on the Janiculum. According to Cartari, the Pope enjoyed the refreshing air of the Janiculum, visiting often his *vigna* there and the house he had built in it (Cartari, quoted in Banfi 17).

Paul III's casino first appears on three maps all made in 1557.[4] They show a small building just to the north of the Aurelian Wall and to the northeast of the Porta San Pancrazio. One half of the structure seems to have an additional upper floor or tower.

Vedute of the seventeenth and eighteenth centuries[5] consistently depict a square casino much smaller than Girolamo Farnese's new seventeenth century villa just to the south of it. To ensure good outlook to the east and southeast, the casino stood at the top edge of the eastern Janiculum slope. From its upper story, the four windows facing east would have offered a splendid panorama. A tempera painting by

Paolo Anesi (1697-1773) in the Galleria Pallavicini conveys its square solidity posi-
tioned amid lush vegetation.[6] From corners of the gabled roof, four chimneys rise,
and also a small tower with crenellations, no doubt the same tower seen on the
maps. This little tower on the roof appears, in addition, in an anonymous view of the
Corsini properties, dated probably about 1700-1740 (see p. 188, fig. 22.3).[7] Against the
southern wall of the casino there was a small one-story building. This small extension stands also against the house wall in Giuseppe Vasi's view of the *"Casino del
Giardino Farnese sul Monte Gianicolo* (the Villa Aurelia) [Richardson, Chapter 11, fig.
1]. Just enough of the sixteenth century house is included in Vasi's view to show elegant framing borders around two of the windows on the ground floor and two in the
upper story. Along at least part of the west façade ran a stone bench. Professor
Richardson has observed that in size and architecture the casino must have resembled the neighboring Villa Lante (ca. 1518-1531).

Various maps, views, and especially information recorded in 1846 by the
stonecutter and mason who restored the casino under the architect Vespignani have
enabled Linda Roncaglia to reconstruct the Cardinal's small house (Roncaglia 14-15,
19). The portion on the south side, only a ground floor, contained the granary or
storeroom and a dining area. Adjoining it, the ground floor of the main house was
divided into a large room with a vaulted ceiling and two small rooms. A stairway led
up to the main floor, where the Cardinal's room had two windows overlooking the
city below. There were three other small rooms, each with two windows. One of
these rooms served as the Cardinal's dressing room. Above was an attic with four
rooms. This main structure measured a bit over thirty-one feet square (Roncaglia
Fig. 6: approximately eleven meters square).

Roncaglia also states (20) that the original approach to the property was by a
twisting road up to the east façade of the casino, as appears in a map by F. Paciotti
(1557). In the first quarter of the seventeenth century, the entrance gate was moved
around to the opposite boundary (Roncaglia 21). This new gate was located on a
road running north from just outside the old Porta Aurelia. In the 1640's this road
was enclosed within Urban VIII's new wall and gate, but the *vigna* entrance remained
accessible, opening onto a carriage-way leading up to the west façade. Nolli's plan
(1748) shows a broad clearing before this west façade and the garden divided into a
grid pattern (see p. 64, fig. 7.2 or p. 150, fig 18.2).

In the century after Cardinal Farnese's death (1668), when the Aurelia property was rented out to various prelates, the casino did not fare well. An inventory
made in 1761 describes its *"finestre, porte, soffiti* [sic], *i quali dipinti in tela quasi tutti
lacerati e sbucati"* ("windows, doors, and ceilings, which, painted on canvas, [are]
almost all torn in shreds and popping out") (quoted in Michel 516-517), and there was
a proposal to pull it down and reuse the materials (Michel 547). But city plans confirm that the house somehow survived until 1849, when throughout the month of
June, French bombardment damaged the house beyond repair, and it was not
rebuilt.[8] At least by the early 1880's the collapsed walls and debris had been cleared
away. We know that much because nothing of the house appears in the famous

Fig. 14. 2. Section from drawing by Q. Cenni, based on Philippet's panorama painting completed 1882-3, depicting the defense of Rome, June 3, 1849. The view faces north from the top of the Villa Aurelia. Note that there is no Casino Farnese. Obviously the Casino had been leveled by 1882. From *Ai Caduti per Roma* (Rome, 1941), following p. 148.

panoramic photograph depicting the conflict of 1849. The enormous original painting, long lost and known to us from this photograph of it, was made in 1882-1883 and exhibited at the 1884 Esposizione Nazionale in Turin.[9] In the photograph, the space where Paul III's casino once stood is filled with soldiers' tents, tables, clotheslines and human figures [fig. 14. 2].

The consistent location of the small casino in all maps and views puts it in the area of the *foresteria* (guest wing), formerly Aurelia A and B, now redone as a lecture and concert hall. Just north of this wing stands Mrs. Heyland's imitation campanile, built to house the standpipe in her water system (see Richardson, p. 108) [fig. 14. 3]. Amey Aldrich mentions a disused well in that area, probably identical with the well appearing in the same spot on Falda's map (1676) [fig. 14. 4] and on Nolli's (1748). From it came the water to maintain the orchard of fruit trees that filled this garden of the Farnese (Roncaglia 20).

Obviously, any surviving traces of the house cannot be observed without exploration and soundings. Surely the casino had a basement, of which vestiges must remain (for recent evidence supporting this observation, see Puglisi et al., p. 125). Once debris from a shattered building is cleared, it is much easier to fill in foundations and cover them over than to dig them out! But hidden walls of Alessandro Farnese's house are only one of many mysteries that lie underground in the Aurelia property. Over the years, various subterranean structures have been found that may-

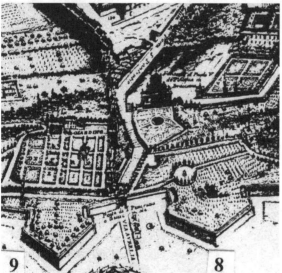

Fig. 14. 3. Mrs. Heyland's imitation campanile, built over the old well that supplied water for Alessandro Farnese's *vigna*. In the background the *foresteria* wing standing on the approximate location of the Casino Farnese. In the far background the Villa Aurelia. Photograph, N. W. Goldman, 2001.

Fig. 14. 4. Section from the Falda map of Rome 1676, showing the Farnese vigna in the left half. The Casino is the light-colored building at the center at top of the square garden plots. To its left is a square plot containing the well.

have been ancient but were possibly reworked in later periods. To my knowledge, no plan or drawing of these underground vaults and corridors exists, probably because exploring them posed too many risks.

REFERENCES

Aldrich, Amey. *Villa Aurelia* (Rome, 1938).
Banfi, Florio (=Holik Barabas). "Villa Farnese al Gianicolo," *L'Urbe* 26 (1963), 17-25.
Bignami Odier, Jeanne. "Le Casin Farnèse du Mont Janicule (Porte San Pancrazio), Maintenant Villa Aurelia," *Mélanges de l'École Française de Rome* 91.1 (1979), 507-38.
Busiri Vici, Andrea. *Trittico Paesistico Romano del '700* (Rome, 1975).
Coffin, David R. *The Villa in the Life of Renaissance Rome* (Princeton, 1973).
Frutaz, A. P. *Le Piante di Roma* II (Rome, 1962).
Gigli, Laura. *Guide Rionali di Roma: Rione XIII Trastevere, Parte I*, 2nd ed. (Rome, 1980).
Hind, A. M. *Giovanni Battista Piranesi: a Critical Study* (London, 1922).
Michel, Geneviève. "Vie Quotidienne au Palais Farnèse," in *Le Palais Farnèse* I,2: *Texte* (Rome, 1981), 509-65. Michel sometimes refers to the Janiculum property as the *giardino della Vignola*.
Roncaglia, Linda. *Villa Aurelia al Gianicolo*. Tesi di Laurea in Storia dell'Architettura Moderna (Università di Roma, 2000).

NOTES

1 Banfi 17-18 gives the text of Carlo Cartari's report, written after Cartari's visit to the Giardino Farnese, 12 March, 1670.

2 Coffin 90 so interprets Cartari's statement. Roncaglia (12) suggests that Alessandro Farnese may have purchased his land on the Janiculum fairly early in the sixteenth century, possibly in the pontificate of Leo X (1513-1521).

3 Alessandro Farnese first purchased (1492) the *vigna* on the north side of the Aurelian Wall between the Lungara and the Tiber, then (1495) the Palazzo Ferriz (later rebuilt and enlarged as Palazzo Farnese). Vasari reports that Michelangelo proposed linking the Farnese properties along the Tiber with a bridge (see Coffin 89-90).

4 Maps by Niccolo Beatrizet, in Frutaz II, No. CXIII; Sebastiano del Rey, in Frutaz II, No. CXIV; and Francesco Paciotti, in Frutaz II, No. CXVI.

5 See, for instance, G. B. Falda's *veduta* (1684), reproduced in Aldrich 26. But in a view of the Acqua Paola (1751), G. B. Piranesi distorts the angle of the Villa Aurelia, omits the Casino Farnese, and cuts away the hillside to show the dome of St. Peter's (in reality, impossible to see from this spot). For Piranesi's Acqua Paola, see Hind 44, no. 21 and pl. XIII.

6 Anesi's painting is reproduced in Busiri Vici 221.

7 On this anonymous *veduta*, see "Casino Riario-Corsini," p. 192, note 5.

8 Evidence for extensive damage to the Casino Farnese comes from the report of the commission that assessed conditions of buildings in July, 1849, published in Paris, 1850. Citing the document, Bignami Odier states, "*Le petit casin de Paul III était écroulé*" (The small casino of Paul III was collapsed). (524).

9 For the panorama painting, see Alessandro Cartocci, "Un Mistero Chiarito: la Pretesa Fotografia di Roma, 3 Giugno, 1849," *Rassegna Storica del Risorgimento* 85.4 (October-December 1998), 505-516. The painter was a Belgian, Léon Philippet (1843-1906), with the assistance of nine or ten other artists. See also Piero Becchetti, *Fotografi e Fotografia in Italia 1839-1880* (Rome, 1978), 22-27; and Valeria Cremona, "Il 'Panorama' di Philippet," in *Fondare la Nazione: i Repubblicani del 1849 e la Difesa del Gianicolo*, ed. Lauro Rossi (Rome, 2001), 128-131.

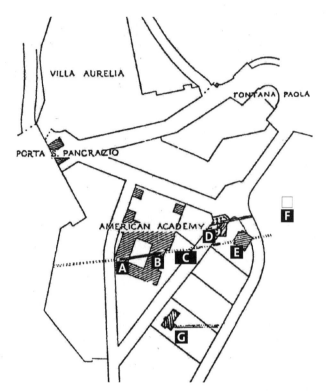

Fig. 15. 1. General plan of the AAR Main Building and its immediate vicinity redrawn from an illustration appearing in the *Memoirs of the American Academy in Rome* (1927), by Van Buren and Stevens, 13, indicating what was known at the time. A-B is the line of the Trajanic Aqueduct under the Academy. C indicates the site of the excavation of the mill by Malcolm Bell and later by Andrew Wilson. D indicates the earlier identification of the mills by Lanciani. E indentifies the Norwegian Institute. F marks the Villa Spada. G. is the Villa Richardson.

Fig. 15. 2. Academy personnel, Fabio Stocchi and Fabrizio Lambiti, opening the trapdoor in the cryptoporticus for the ladder to be lowered into the specus; N. Goldman photographing. Photograph, B. Goldman.

Fig. 15. 3. Adam Rabinowitz and Lynne Lancaster in the Trajanic Aqueduct with a view down the *specus*. Photograph, B. Goldman.

CHAPTER 15

THE AQUEDUCTS OF THE TRANSTIBERIM AND THE AMERICAN ACADEMY IN ROME

Lawrence Richardson, Jr.

Almost everyone who has spent any considerable time at the American Academy in Rome knows that the great Aqua Traiana runs underneath it [fig. 15. 1]. Most of us never saw it, if we even thought that it could be seen. Others knew about the trapdoors in the cellars of the library and in the cryptoporticus on the ground floor [fig. 15. 2], and a hardy few had ventured down the ladder and wandered a little way along the *specus*, the vaulted channel that once housed one of the most abundant of Rome's supplies of water, now only a dank and claustrophobic tunnel [fig. 15. 3]. It did not lead anywhere, and the air was hard to breathe there, so after admiring the reticulate pattern that glows through the hydraulic facing, one soon returned to the upper regions. If one wanted to do more, it was easy to walk down the Via Aurelia to where a section has been exposed at the base of the wall of Villa Doria Pamphilj.

There was, to be sure, the year of the mosquitoes, which focused the interest of everyone living in the Academy for a little while on the aqueduct. The Academy had become all but uninhabitable because clouds of mosquitoes emanated mysteriously from nowhere every night to torment those trying to sleep. Every conceivable breeding spot in the garden was hunted out and drained, to no avail. The commerce in *spirali* (anti-mosquito coils) and bugbombs was brisk, but the mosquitoes rose triumphant over such puny obstacles. Finally it was discovered that they were coming from the aqueduct. Our neighbors on Via XXX Aprile, in the Norwegian Academy, under whose building the aqueduct also passes, had for some reason in construction work blocked the aqueduct, and it was proving the durability of ancient waterproofing by collecting water behind the blockage. Once that was corrected and the dinner table conversation about the episode wore itself out, the aqueduct returned to obscurity.

It came back to attention again, thanks to construction work, first in the excavation for a garage across the street from the Academy that uncovered a part of the old Aurelian Walls. Then again in May of 1990, men working at laying electric cables dug a trench up Via Giacomo Medici and ran it through some ancient construction. Professor Malcolm Bell, alerted by the noise, managed to persuade them to suspend the project for a short time, until he could excavate the site properly and make a

135

record of what was there. It turned out to be the continuation of the conduit under the Academy and parts of the complex that Rodolfo Lanciani had seen in 1886, when the streets on that part of the hill were being laid out. Lanciani had identified this conduit as part of the water mills that were known to be somewhere in the neighborhood, built to take advantage of a good water supply with a considerable head of pressure. They are first mentioned in the fourth century and may have functioned down to the sixth, when Vitiges and his barbarians besieging the city cut the aqueducts (see Chapter 16, following).[1]

Lanciani's drawing of what he was able to see is far from self-explanatory, and he located it on his great map of the ancient city in the widening where Via Giacomo Medici meets Via Angelo Masina in front of Villa Spada, which is a good bit north of where the Academy channel runs. It runs straight from the west corner of the main Academy building to the east corner and reappears in the street about on the property line between the Academy and Villa Bellacci. Moreover the new information we now have about the course of the Aurelian Walls shows that they run only a very short distance south of the new bit of the aqueduct. It seems a good time to pause and reconsider the situation.

There are two aqueducts that enter Rome over the Janiculum, the Aqua Alsietina and the Aqua Traiana. Most of ancient Rome's water came in at Porta Maggiore, where a long tongue of lava spewing out from the Alban Hills makes a natural viaduct on which the channels could be carried without having to resort to the bridges that are so handsome but so costly and laborious to build. Only the Aqua Virgo, which comes in over the Pincian Hill, and the two that come from the west come by other routes. That is partly because there was little good water to be had in the periphery of Rome on the west side of the river, and partly because the Anio Valley through the lower Apennines is so rich in excellent water that there was no point in looking elsewhere. But Augustus wanted to build a *naumachia*, one of those artificial lakes where mock sea battles could be staged, and since it required considerable space to develop such a facility, he very sensibly decided to build it in the Transtiberim next to the villa that Julius Caesar had willed to the Roman people as a permanent park, in the area at the foot of the hill that is now Piazza San Cosimato. It cannot be located precisely, but I have been told by Roman friends that in 1950, when excavations were dug in preparation for the building of the Standa department store on Viale di Trastevere, blocks of travertine were brought to light cut to a curve that might have been the margin of such a lake.

To supply his lake, Augustus had to bring in a new aqueduct, the Aqua Alsietina. Frontinus despised it beyond all others, regarding it as supplying water unfit to drink, to be used only for watering gardens. It was, however, not a very long aqueduct; its sources are near the Via Clodia to the northwest of Rome; and it ran entirely underground. Nor was it very abundant; its volume was only a little more than half that of the Aqua Appia, and not a patch on the Marcia or Claudia. It had to enter Rome at the point later marked by Porta San Pancrazio because of a very narrow ridge that here separates two important watersheds, one marked by the Via delle Fornaci, the other by Viale dei Quattro Venti. The Via Aurelia threads its way between them, and even today the Acqua Paola runs along beside it. In 1926, while digging out the slope above Via XXX Aprile in order to build a retaining wall, workmen uncovered a short stretch of an aqueduct of simple construction, in effect a box drain with walls faced with reticulate and a floor of mortar (possibly lime deposit from the water).² This was evidently originally roofed with slabs of stone, but none was recovered. Only about a meter of the channel could be excavated, but this indicated that it ran almost parallel to the aqueduct under the Academy building, almost due east, but about eighty meters south of that channel, running under the Villa Richardson and the corner of the vacant lot next to this on the northeast. It would have been well located to deliver water to Piazza San Cosimato but outside the line of the Aurelian Walls. Its course outside the new papal wall of Urban VIII cannot be determined, although, since it must have come in along the Via Aurelia on the ridge, we can imagine an arc that would bring it to that point without difficulty. This would, however, pass under, or close to, the Casa Rustica, which is built on an eminence over the ruins of Villa Malvasia, destroyed in the battle of 1849. While it makes almost no difference where its course passed under the Aurelian Wall, since it was underground, how it negotiated the slope of the hill between here and Piazza San Cosimato without building more head than was permissible is a problem. Much of its supply may have been drawn off to water gardens, since this slope was covered with sumptuous *horti* (gardens) as early as the time of Cicero, and very likely there were mill races at mid-slope, for it would seem absurd to waste so much splendid power. But there must have been other slowing devices as well.

A hundred years after Augustus built the Aqua Alsietina, Trajan built the Aqua Traiana, the last of the great aqueducts of ancient Rome. It does not get into Frontinus's account of the waters of Rome, being built in A.D. 109, after his time. It was brought in ostensibly to supply the enormous Baths of Trajan on the Oppius, but the needs of the growing population of the Transtiberim must have been an important consideration, and the demand for more water all over the city may well have been crucial by this time. Its springs were near Trevignano northeast of the Lago di Bracciano, an abundant supply of first-rate water, and a great deal of its course was carried on bridges. It rises high, at about 320 meters above sea level, but soon drops to about 200. Thereafter the gradient is only gentle. The *specus* is relatively high, 1.62 m., with a rounded vault. The construction is of concrete faced with a combination of brick and reticulate, heavily plastered against leakage inside and out [fig. 15. 4].

It was found by chance in the excavation for the Main Building of the American Academy in 1912-1913, at which time the relevant stretch was cleaned, surveyed, and studied. An account of it, the work of Gorham Phillips Stevens and A. W. Van Buren, was published in the first volume of the *Memoirs of the American Academy*. It turned out that Rodolfo Lanciani had already seen another section nearby during the work in laying out streets in 1886, but misplaced it on his map when the street plan was somewhat altered, and he neglected to correct his notes and sketches to

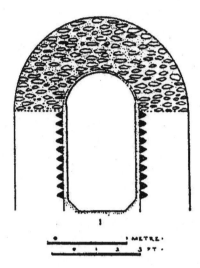

FIG. 15. 4. Drawing of the *specus* by Van Buren and Stevens, *Memoirs of the American Academy in Rome*, 1 (1917), Pl. 15.

take this into account — if he was aware of what had happened. So now we need to move his mill complex some twenty-five meters south to a position just inside the line of the old Aurelian Walls, which may have been built here just to protect it inside the fortification. From here the aqueduct ran in a straight line to the casino of Villa Spada, which is believed to have been built on the ruins of an aqueduct annex, either a reservoir or a monumental fountain, but here more likely the former. And there must have been other mills all down the slope below to exploit the power it would have generated. In fact, however, we know next to nothing about the distribution of the Aqua Traiana in the Transtiberim, and not even on what bridges it crossed the Tiber. The pipes bearing its name all seem to come from the vicinity of the Baths of Trajan.

One may ask why Trajan went to so much trouble to bring water from so far away, when the Baths he was specially concerned with supplying were on the Oppius, and it would seem obviously far easier to bring in a new line from the Anio Valley. But the Transtiberim had always had the poorest water supply in Rome. In theory it got water from most of the aqueducts, but it was always at the end of the lines, and others must have drawn water off in such quantities that what was left was only a trickle, if that. Of course, Transtiberim had its own springs, and some of them were very good. There is one on the slope above Palazzo Corsini that has been the object of considerable contention reaching high places in the days when Queen Christina of Sweden lived there. And there is one on Via Garibaldi under San Pietro in Montorio that has never, so far as I know, gone dry, not even in the great drought of 1949. The Roman altar of Fons had been erected in the area of the Janiculum for a good reason. It seems likely that those in charge of the water system felt that the people of Transtiberim could fend for themselves, if they had to. But Rome was growing very fast, and the planners at the time of Trajan and Hadrian seem to have viewed the Transtiberim as the likeliest area for expansion, or to have had this view forced upon them. And water would be a first necessity. One may wonder whether the numerous *horti* of Cicero's day were not beginning to be broken up to provide less patrician housing and whether Rome was not undergoing a cycle similar to what we see going on there today.

NOTES

1   In 1998 and 1999, Andrew Wilson of the Institute of Archaeology, University of Oxford, carried out further excavations of the aqueduct and mills in the parking lot of the American Academy. His results are reported in *Memoirs of the American Academy in Rome*, Volume 45 (2000), 219-46. He concluded that the mill complex had gone out of use and had been destroyed before A.D. 400, while the aqueduct itself was blocked by a plug of *spolia*, probably during the Gothic siege of Rome in 537. This plug was not removed subsequently, and the aqueduct cannot have functioned thereafter. Since Procopius is explicit in saying that mills on the Janiculum were functioning up to the time of the Gothic siege, Wilson has postulated that the Aqua Traiana must have forked in the neighborhood of Porta Aurelia, one branch being that of the American Academy and Via Giacomo Medici, and the other running somewhere in the vicinity of Via Garibaldi and the Bosco Parrasio. Along this line there must also have been mills that functioned up to the time of the Gothic siege, and this line was then later reopened and repaired and continued to function in the Middle Ages.

2   There is some doubt that the identification of this short stretch as remains of the Aqua Alsietina is correct. Although the masonry was considered to be typically Augustan, what remains is a simple box drain, not the characteristic tunnel of an aqueduct *specus*. It might well be simply another bit of the mill complex connected with the Aqua Traiana.

The Aqua Traiana on the north side of Via Aurelia,
just after its turn into the Aurelia from Via del
Casale di S. Pio V. Note the ancient brick and opus
reticulatum. Photograph. K. A. Geffcken, 2005.

CHAPTER 16

THE MILLS OF THE JANICULUM

Malcolm Bell III

As the utilities trench crept up the slopes of the Janiculum in the spring of 1990, several observers from the Academy kept track of its progress, watching for evidence of antiquities. Not much is known about the slopes below the Academy that drop down towards the Piazza San Cosimato and Trastevere, and any clues are precious. We were especially interested in the area just below the Academy. Would the utilities trench uncover traces of the mills that Rodolfo Lanciani apparently saw near the crest of the Janiculum in 1886? This was, in fact, a topical question, only recently discussed by the distinguished topographer Lucos Cozza, whose meticulous research on the imperial walls of Rome has extended to Trastevere and the Janiculum. Thus when the backhoe crossed the Via Angelo Masina and proceeded up the Via Giacomo Medici and chunks of Roman concrete began to emerge from the trench, the archaeologists were ready, and work was halted. A building clearly lay under the street, but of what sort?

The Soprintendenza Archeologica quickly and cleverly struck a deal with ENEL, the electric utility, and the AAR found itself conducting an emergency excavation. ENEL agreeably offered to remove the asphalt from the enlarged trench, but at a price – the excavation would have to be completed and the trench paved over by the end of May, for the utility was operating under an ironclad agreement with the Italian government requiring the completion of all projects before the beginning of the World Cup in the summer of 1990. We were hostages of international soccer.

There were three weeks in which to complete the project. The Neapolitan utilities workers exuberantly removed the asphalt, and a crew of volunteers from the Academy toiled with admirable devotion and care, amidst the electric cables, gas lines, and water pipes that lay just under the asphalt. The Soprintendenza's support and assistance were instrumental to the success of the project, which soon took on an international aspect. The British School produced both a crew of draftspeople for the drawings and a specialist in Late Roman ceramics for the pottery. The coins were catalogued by a scholar at the Soprintendenza, and environmental remains were examined by a member of the AAR's Palatine excavation. Passersby and neighbors offered constant advice and encouragement, and Academy residents and visiting scholars provided helpful suggestions for the interpretation of the remains. The Neapolitan crew performed stunts with the backhoe, for the entertainment of the ladies.

The concrete walls turned out, after all, to belong to Lanciani's mills, which are now precisely located in the modern city. Prof. Cozza's hypothesis proved to be correct – an error in the *Forma Urbis Romae* had misled previous investigators. The mills are also now much better understood, for prior to the excavation we had only Lanciani's enigmatic pencil sketch of what he saw during the construction of the Via Medici in 1886 [fig. 15. 1].

The structure consists of a massive concrete platform, through which pass three water channels: the central one of the Aqua Traiana, the aqueduct which also passes under the Academy building; and flanking it on either side the wheelraces in which the mill wheels turned, the water that powered them provided by the adjacent aqueduct. These were broad paddle-wheels driven by the current, not "overshot" wheels of the type familiar from examples in the USA that still grind flour in rural areas. The wheels were stacked closely together in the two wheelraces, indicating that this was a major industrial establishment. A set of cogs transferred the movement of the paddle-wheel to a vertical axle, at the top of which was attached the upper of the two millstones. Such mills are described by Vitruvius, and ours is a well-preserved example of the type. Further study of the new evidence will contribute to our understanding of the "Vitruvian mill."

No evidence was found to date the construction of the mills, but they are surely later than A.D. 109, when the Trajanic aqueduct was completed.[1] Two deposits of pottery, lamps, broken mill-stones, rooftiles, and coins were found in the 'gear pits,' the dark spaces beneath the wooden floor of the building where the cog-wheels transferred the motive power of the paddle-wheels to the millstones. These deposits indicate that the mills were abandoned at the end of the fourth century A.D.[2]

The emergency excavation produced new evidence about the topography of the Janiculum, the technology of Roman mills, and the milling of flour in imperial Rome. Another conclusion concerns the strong probability that the rest of the mill lies beneath the side-yard of the AAR.

N.B.: In fall 1991, Italgas, like ENEL in 1990, dug up Via Medici once more, and Professor Bell organized further excavations [figs. 16. 1 and 16. 2]. In the summers of 1998-99, with a group of volunteers from the Academy Summer Session and visiting scholars, Andrew Wilson of the British School conducted excavations of the parking area just inside the gate facing Via Medici [fig. 16. 3], and the results of these further excavations of the mill area have been published in the *Memoirs of the American Academy in Rome*, 45 (2000), 219-46 [figs. 16. 4 & 16. 5]. Wilson presented his findings also at a meeting of the Archaeological Institute of America, and an abstract of his paper is available in AIA *Abstracts* (December, 1999), 64.

TOP LEFT

Fig. 16. 1. Bell's second excavation, fall of 1991, on Via Medici with volunteers Lisa Fentress, Kate Welch, and unidentified third woman. Photograph K. A. Geffcken.

TOP RIGHT

Fig. 16. 2. Unidentified woman excavating the wheelrace during the second season excavation, fall of 1991. Photograph K. A. Geffcken.

BOTTOM

Fig. 16. 3. Wilson's 1998 excavation of the mill in the AAR parking lot: Excavators Sandra Blakely and Andrew Wilson. Photograph K. A. Geffcken.

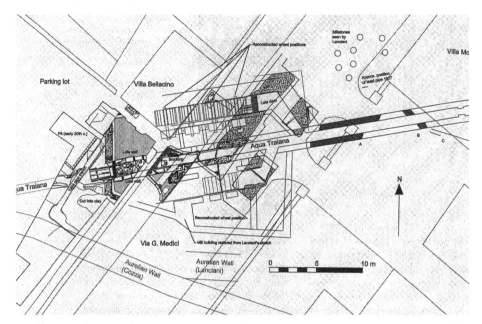

Fig. 16. 4. Composite plan of the Aqua Traiana and the Via
Medici mill complex. To the left, the 1998-1999 excavations; the
three trenches within the street are Malcolm Bell's 1990-1991
excavations. Lanciani's sketch has been redrawn to scale, to fit
the known remains. Drawing from Wilson's article, p. 224, Fig. 4.

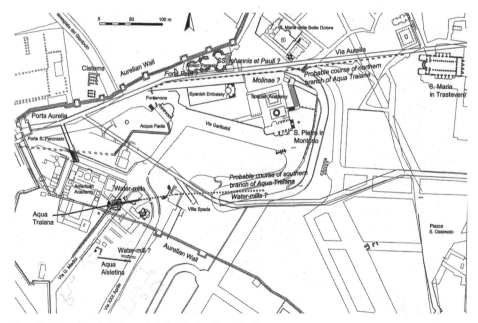

Fig. 16. 5. Plan of the Janiculum salient showing location of the Via
Medici Mills and branch of the Aqua Traiana and suggesting the course
of the northern branch of the Aqua Traiana. From Wilson, p. 240, Fig. 17.

◈ NOTES

1   In an article published in 1993, Professor Bell proposes, on the basis of the evidence, a date in the first half of the third century for the construction of the mill. See Malcolm Bell, "Mulini ad Acqua sul Gianicolo," *Archeologia Laziale* XI (1993), 65-72. (KAG)

2   In the article cited above, note 1, Professor Bell states that the mill complex was abandoned after the third quarter of the fifth century. See his discussion of the numismatic evidence, 70-71. For dating and abandonment of the mill, see also Wilson, *MAAR* 45 (2000), 227 ff. (KAG)

ABOVE

Fig. 17. 1. The print by Giovanni Battista Piranesi showing the Acqua Paola in the mid-eighteenth century, Hind #21. Note the inscription.

LEFT

Fig. 17. 2. The Acqua Paola inscription of Paul V. Photograph B. Goldman, 2003.

CHAPTER 17

THE ACQUA PAOLA FOUNTAIN

Harry B. Evans

his splendid Baroque fountain (often called the *Fontanone*) is best understood by first reading its inscription atop the five arches of its façade [fig. 17. 1]:

PAVLVS QVINTVS PONTIFEX MAXIMVS
AQVAM IN AGRO BRACCIANENSI
SALVBERRIMIS E FONTIBVS COLLECTAM
VETERIBVS AQVAE ALSIETINAE DVCTIBVS RESTITVTIS
NOVISQVE ADDITIS
XXXV AB MILLIARIO DVXIT
ANNO DOMINI MDCXII PONTIFICATVS SVI SEPTIMO [fig. 17. 2]

("Pope Paul V introduced water tapped from most healthful springs in the territory of Bracciano at the thirty-fifth milestone, having restored the ancient conduits of the Aqua Alsietina and having added new ones, in the year 1612 A.D., the seventh of his pontificate").

But Paul V is wrong in his claims: in actuality his engineers restored the conduits of the ancient Aqua Traiana of A.D. 109, not the Aqua Alsietina that the Emperor Augustus had brought to Rome more than a century earlier to supply his *naumachia*, an artificial lake for mock naval battles, in the Transtiber. We might conclude that Paul V may have been attempting to promote himself by associating his work with that of the first *princeps*. However, little was known at the time about the aqueducts of the ancient city, and the course and terminus of the Aqua Traiana were a mystery until the late seventeenth century, when Raffaello Fabretti, a pioneer epigrapher and the most learned antiquarian in Rome at the time, firmly established that it was Trajan's aqueduct that Paul V reworked, not the Augustan Aqua Alsietina, which had also entered Rome over the top of the Janiculum.

Paul V had good reason to construct this monumental display for the aqueduct he introduced [fig. 17. 3]. The Acqua Paola supplied much needed water not only to the neighborhood of Trastevere below it, but also to the Vatican itself, where the present Basilica of S. Pietro was under active construction. Its water was also carried across the Tiber on the Ponte Sisto to supply the neighborhood of the Via Giulia.

Fig. 17. 4. The west façade of the Arco di Tiradiavoli on the Via Aurelia seen from inside the Villa Doria Pamphilj walkway. Photograph B. Goldman, 2004.

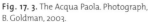

Fig. 17. 3. The Acqua Paola. Photograph, B. Goldman, 2003.

A more modest fountain and inscription of Paul V can be seen today in Trastevere in the immediate vicinity of the bridge, in Piazza Trilussa; the fountain originally stood on the other side of the Tiber, at the southern end of the Via Giulia, but was dismantled and moved to its present position in the late nineteenth century when the modern Tiber embankments were constructed.

Delivery to suburban villas along the route of the aqueduct, like that of the Doria Pamphilj just outside the Aurelian Wall, was no doubt another factor in its planning and construction. We find another inscription of Paul V on the arch carrying the conduit over the Via Aurelia Antica outside the walls, the so-called "Arco di Tiradiavoli" [fig. 17. 4] calling attention to the papal engineering, in much the same spirit as the Claudian inscriptions for the ancient Aqua Claudia and Aqua Anio Novus atop the Porta Maggiore.

The fountain's design is the work of the architect Giovanni Fontana, with the collaboration of Flaminio Ponzio. Fontana seems to have had in mind the triple arches of his own Moses Fountain, the terminus of the late sixteenth century Acqua Felice, when he planned this façade [fig. 17. 5], but the overall design is a significant improvement over the fountain of twenty years earlier. Here the three central arches, like those of the Moses Fountain, are flanked by two smaller ones, creating a much more sweeping façade and space for a much more impressive inscription. Above the inscription in the center is the *stemma* of Paul V, prominently flanked by the eagles and dragons of the Borghese family.[1]

The fountain itself is also a telling example of reuse or recycling of ancient materials so common in Baroque Rome. The four large columns of red granite flanking its three central arches are material from the quadriporticus of the old St. Peter's, at that time being replaced by the basilica we know today; the two smaller grey gran-

Fig. 17. 5. The three arches designed by Giovanni Fontana. Photograph B. Goldman, 2003.

Fig. 17. 6. The structure behind the façade of the Acqua Paola, originally designed to house the watermen, viewed from the roof of the Villa Sforza Cesarini. Photograph B. Goldman, 2003.

ite columns at the ends came from the old basilica itself. The marble slabs of the fountain's façade are material from the Temple of Minerva in the Forum of Nerva.

This fountain was obviously built as a watershow to glorify the pope who built it, but the structure also served other purposes: its attic provided quarters for the watermen [fig. 17. 6], and below its monumental basin (added by Carlo Fontana for Pope Alexander VIII in 1690) are chambers, pipes, and valves for distribution of its water to different districts and areas. One interesting detail can be seen in the fountain's loggia, reached by the gate (sometimes locked, but often open) on the north side (towards the Via Garibaldi and Villa Aurelia). Inside the loggia, a group of post-classical inscriptions documents the distribution system of the Aqua Virgo, an Augustan aqueduct introduced into the Campus Martius by Marcus Agrippa that continued to function through the Middle Ages; its water continues to supply fountains in that area of Rome.

▨ REFERENCES

Aicher, P. J. *Guide to the Aqueducts of Ancient Rome* (Wauconda, Ill., 1995).

Aicher, P. J. "Terminal Display Fountains (*Mostre*) and the Aqueducts of Ancient Rome," *Phoenix* 47 (1993), 339-52.

Bruun, C. "Frontinus, Pope Paul V, and the Aqua Alsietina/Traiana Confusion," *Papers of the British School at Rome* 69 (2001), 299-315.

Cancellieri, C. "L'acquedotto Paolo (Sec. XVII-XX)," in *Il trionfo dell'acqua: acque e acquedotti a Roma, IV Sec a.C. –XX. Sec.*, ed. A. Liberati Silverio and G. Pisani Sartorio (Rome, 1986), 225-31.

Tolomeo, M. G. "La mostra dell'Acqua Paola," in *Il trionfo dell'acqua*, 250-54. *(see full reference above)*

▨ NOTES

1   It was this pope's nephew, Cardinal Scipio Borghese, who in the early seventeenth century assembled the famous collection of art in the Villa bearing the Borghese name.

ABOVE

Fig. 18. 1. The garden today beside and behind the Chiaraviglio. Photograph, N. W. Goldman, 2003.

BELOW

Fig. 18. 2. Nolli map (1748) showing the Botanical Garden: No. 1192 is the Orto Botanico.

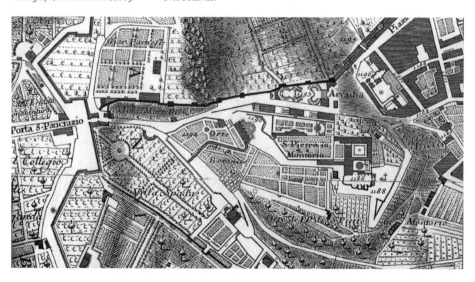

CHAPTER 18

THE BOTANICAL GARDEN OF ROME ON THE JANICULUM

Antonella Bucci

My years as a librarian at the American Academy long stimulated my interest in the Janiculum, especially the Academy's section of the hill. Fortunately, the Academy Library's rare book collection includes several handsome guides dating from 1600 to 1800. When I was leafing through one of these, *Roma Antica, e Moderna o sia nuova Descrizione di tutti gli Edifici Antichi . . .*(1765), I noticed a sentence which, after alluding to the Fontana dell'Acqua Paola on the Janiculum, continues ". . . *dietro al suddetto fonte fece Alessandro VII un bellissimo giardino con ogni sorte di semplici, anche pellegrini, a benefizio degli studiosi della Botanica. Vi aggiunse Clemente XI un Casino, e la Scuola, dove da un Lettore a ciò deputato, si fa di tali Semplici l'ostensione. . . .*" ("behind the abovementioned fountain Alexander VII created a very beautiful garden with every sort of medicinal herbs, even those coming from foreign lands, for the benefit of students of Botany. Clement XI added here a Casino and a School where, by a reader appointed for this task, there is made the demonstration of such herbs. . . "). This statement suggests that the Botanical Garden of Rome of ca.1700 was located where today are the gardens of the Villa Chiaraviglio and of the Sforza Cesarini [fig. 18. 1]. I began to search for other evidence that might confirm this hypothesis. The first confirmation came from the map by Nolli of 1748 [fig. 18. 2], one of the most accurate maps executed in this period, in which appear the words "*Orto Botanico*" on the land situated behind the Fontanone dell'Acqua Paola. I found a second piece of confirming evidence at the Biblioteca Angelica, where I consulted the splendid eight volume work by Giorgio Bonelli, *Hortus Romanus* (1772). In the first volume, a map engraved in green ink by Andrea De Rossi illustrates in great detail the position of the botanical garden, which then extended from the modern Via Garibaldi to Via Medici [fig. 18. 3]. The northern section now lies in the garden of the Villa Sforza Cesarini, divided by the aqueduct of Paul V from the southern section within the garden of the Villa Chiaraviglio. The main entrance to the garden was to the right as one faces the Fontana dell'Acqua Paola. There was a section for seedlings, another for aquatic plants (probably toward where Via Giacomo Medici is now). Some 3,000 different species were represented in the garden, which was well watered by fountains drawing from the Fontanone dell'Acqua Paola. There was also

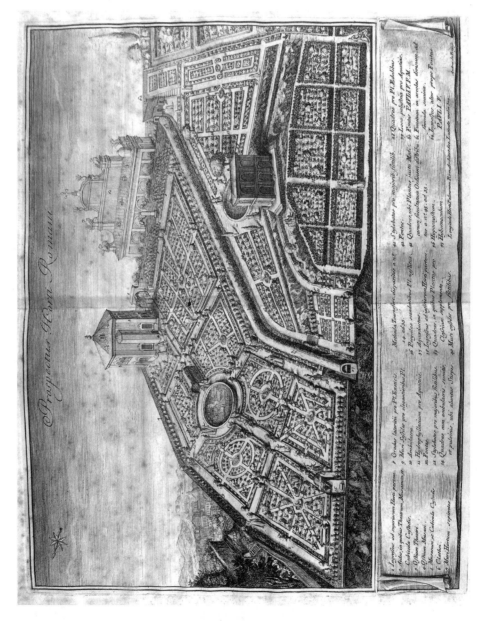

Fig. 18.3. Engraving by Andrea De Rossi from Giorgio Bonelli, *Hortus Romanus.* Vol. 1 (1772), showing the entire Botanical Garden, divided by the aqueduct line leading to the Acqua Paola. Photograph supplied by and with permission from the Biblioteca Angelica, Rome, 2005. To the right is the present garden of the Chiaraviglio [Fig. 18.1]; to the left is the present garden of the Villa Sforza Cesarini.

a building with pentagonal plan, "il Casino di Clemente XI," which the Pope had constructed in 1703 as a lecture hall for botanical instruction, the so-called *ostensioni* (demonstrations). This building was damaged by cannon fire from the French artillery during the defense of Rome in 1849, but traces of its original construction can still be seen at Via Garibaldi, 31a.

Enrico Carano wrote in 1933 that two greenhouses, one heated and one cool, served to protect the plants, adding that the area of the garden measured a hectare and a half. The period of greatest activity for the Botanical Garden was from 1678 to 1708 when its direction was entrusted to Giovan Battista Trionfetti, an expert and enthusiastic botanist, who dedicated his whole life to enriching the garden *"in modo da portarlo ad uno splendore tale da renderlo se non il primo d'Europa certo uno dei più celebrati."* (so as to bring it to a splendor such as to make it, if not the first garden of Europe, certainly one of the most celebrated) (Pirotta and Chiovenda, 6).

Trionfetti maintained that practical experience was very important for students, but since the plants had their own different growing seasons, it was difficult for him to show entire plants to the pupils in the *"publicae ostensiones plantarum"* (public lectures or demonstrations of plants). For this reason he initiated the compilation of an herbarium called *Hortus Hyemalis,* a huge work in 13 volumes that he did not succeed in finishing. It was, however, completed some years after his death.

To find suitable plants, Trionfetti undertook difficult and arduous trips, true adventures, as he describes them. The result was a beautiful herbarium, the oldest known pertaining to Roman plants, preserved today in the Biblioteca Casanatense. Furthermore, there are many documents on the Botanical Garden in the Archivio di Stato and in various historical libraries in Rome.

Despite a position not well suited to a garden because of exposure to the winds, particularly to the *tramontana* (north wind), it remained active for many years, from about 1660 to 1823, when Leo XII inaugurated a new site in the Via della Lungara in the garden of Palazzo Salviati, not far from its modern location in the grounds of Palazzo Corsini.

REFERENCES

Antonella Bucci, librarian at the American Academy from 1974 to 2000, first published a version of this chapter in the *Newsletter of the Classical Society of the AAR* in 1994. It later appeared in an Italian version in a volume on the Janiculum issued by the Finnish Institute: E. M. Steinby, ed., *Ianiculum – Gianicolo, Storia. Topografia, Monumenti, Leggende dall'Antichità al Rinascimento. Acta Instituti Romani Finlandiae* 16 (Rome, 1996).
Bonelli, Giorgio. *Hortus romanus*, Vol. 1 (Rome, 1772).
Carano, Enrico. "Storia della botanica in Roma e nel Lazio," *Le scienze fisiche e biologiche in Roma e nel Lazio* (Roma, 1933), 203.
Pirotta, R. and E. Chiovenda. *Illustrazione di alcuni erbari antichi romani* (Genoa, 1900), 6.
Poggioli, Giuseppe. *Lavori in opera di scienze naturali del già prof. Michelangelo Poggioli ora pubblicati dall'avv. Giuseppe suo figlio* (Rome, 1880).

TOP

Fig. 19. 1. Villa Sforza Cesarini viewed from Via Garibaldi. Photograph B. Goldman, 2003. The circular staircase and all surfaces and decoration were added by architect Pio Piacentini in 1913.

BOTTOM

Fig. 19. 2. Villa Sforza Cesarini entrance on Via Garibaldi 31, adjacent to Acqua Paola. Photograph N. W. Goldman, 2003. The offices of OIGA, a business firm of the Torlonia/Sforza Cesarini family, occupy the *primo piano*.

CHAPTER 19

VILLA SFORZA CESARINI AND THE
PENSIONE FERSEN

Lawrence Richardson, jr

Addendum: Katherine A. Geffcken

The Pensione Fersen, originally located in the Villa Sforza Cesarini (Torlonia) behind the Acqua Paola at Via Garibaldi 31 [fig. 19. 1], was for more than half a century an unofficial annex of the American Academy in Rome. It came into existence more or less by accident. After the first World War, in 1922 the American scholar Esther Van Deman was looking for living quarters on the Janiculum. She wanted to be close to the American Academy, located since 1914 near the Porta San Pancrazio, in order to avail herself of its library, and she was attracted by the view over Rome that she sensed must be commanded from the upper floors of the Villa. The house, now painted pale yellow, and present-ly known as Villa Sforza Cesarini [fig. 19. 2], is an elaborate structure developed from its original core of two eighteenth century buildings (see Bucci, pp. 150-3). It had been leased to the Fersens.

With her customary forthrightness, Esther Van Deman simply knocked on the door and asked to look out over the city from the windows which provided the best view. At that time the *piano nobile* of the villa was occupied by Contessa Fersen and her children, and with their instinctive courtesy and doubtless a bit nonplussed by the direct approach of this intrepid foreigner, they escorted her to the proper room. After a brief examination of the apartment and a more attentive one of the view, Miss Van Deman announced, "I'll take it." It was to be her headquarters for the rest of her life.

At that time the Fersens were one of five émigré Russian families living in the Villa Sforza Cesarini. During the Russian revolution they had been staying at their summer home in south Russia on the Black Sea, when word came that they must leave at once to assure their safety. Like many other Russians in similar circum-stances, they then took ship and, by way of Istanbul, made for the Mediterranean and asylum abroad, wherever they could find an enforced exile most agreeable. Some stayed in Istanbul; others went to Athens and Smyrna; and many emigrated to Rome, which they already knew and loved from trips abroad.

But Countess Fersen had to flee her home without her husband. Count Fersen stood high in the Russian aristocracy, a personal friend of the Czar. Because he held a command in the White Army, he could not leave with his family. The

Fersens had produced four children: Paul, Alexander, Elizabeth (known as Lili), and Olga, the youngest. The health of their young daughter Olga was poor, and there was concern about obtaining treatment for her, as well as finding an accommodating climate. But the Contessa was a resourceful woman, and the family was well connected, and through these connections the Contessa found an apartment in the Villa Sforza Cesarini.

The Fersens, originally of Scottish origin, had split into several branches, one emigrating to Sweden in the eighteenth century, one to Germany, and a third to Russia. When I learned this, it rang a bell in my memory, and I taxed Olga with one of the Fersens having been the Swedish Ambassador, Count Fersen, who was alleged to be Marie Antoinette's lover. "No, No," she said, "that was a different branch of the family." But I believe that she was not being quite truthful, although Nicholas, son of Paul, and his wife Nina Fersen, who now live in the United States, maintain that Olga was right. His name was Axel Fersen (Count Hans Axel Fersen 1755-1810), and he was from the Swedish branch of the family. In any case, the branch of the family that had emigrated to Russia had been Russian for so many generations that all trace of Scotland had long since been erased.

I presume that Miss Van Deman had assumed that, with so many different Russian families in residence in the Villa, it was rented out piecemeal, room by room. Her establishment there with the Fersens almost immediately drew other members of the Academy family to seek accommodations there, and in the period between the two World Wars the guest book came to include a roster of illustrious American scholars. But there was always a substantial contingent of others, chiefly English and Russian, who came from Paris or Vienna or London, friends and relations. Conversation at the dinner table was always lively and scintillating. There have been many stories told of life at the Pensione Fersen in the years between the two world wars, undoubtedly some of them embroidered. The most vivid in my memory is of the annual horse show in the Villa Borghese that took place in May. The whole Russian community of Rome would turn out for this event, dressed to the nines in pre-war finery, armed with parasols and picnic hampers, and they would line the margins of the *galoppatoio*. All those attending, even the women, were great connoisseurs both of horsemanship and the horses themselves. It was a holiday and social occasion not to be missed.

Frank Brown used to tell another story about how the young Count Fersen was extremely fond of watermelon laced with cognac. According to Brown, he conceived the notion that if the melons were raised from birth, as it were, on cognac, they would be especially delicious. To try out his plan one summer he rented a field out beyond the Porta San Pancrazio, planted it with melons, and every morning could be seen armed with a syringe and a bottle of cognac going about in search of the baby melons, which he would then inject. Unfortunately none took to this treatment, and his theory and investment collapsed. Nina and Nicholas Ferson, however, deny that this ever happened.

I first savored the pleasures of the Pensione Fersen just after the second

Fig. 19. 3. Contessa Olga Fersen in the Salone at the American Academy in Rome being presented the centennial medal by Lawrence Richardson, jr. Her good friend Eric Baade is among the group of admirers, the bearded man with glasses. Photograph, AAR Archives in New York.

World War. By that time Miss Van Deman had died (she is buried about fifteen feet from the large tombstone of her Russian friends in the Protestant cemetery in Rome), and the young Count Fersen had emigrated to America and had dropped his title. The Villa had been repossessed by its owners and temporarily surrendered to the state to serve as a hospice for war orphans. The dispossessed Fersens had then found new lodgings in a comfortable villa of vaguely Tuscan character on Viale Aurelio Saffi, just outside the walls where they plunge down the hill to the Tiber. I was young and new to Rome and was put under the tutelage of Madame Sonia de Daehn, the last living granddaughter of Czar Nicholas I. Madame de Daehn was a majestic figure, dressed always entirely in black, who spoke an Edwardian English that was almost unaccented but full of such outdated elegances that one listened mesmerized. I believe that she was then the only other one left, besides Olga Fersen and the de Daehns, Peter and Ketounia, of the Russian colony that had once lived in the Villa Sforza Cesarini. The other lodgers in 1947 were a shadowy lot for me, now far removed in time. Only the Contessa Olga Fersen herself comes vividly to mind. But one of the things I remember best is that the note of one's bill[1] was delivered with such enormous discretion that one had to hunt for it on the breakfast tray on the proper morning; even the servants were not allowed to discuss such sorry matters.

Later still, in the 1960's, the Pensione Fersen had to move again, this time to a large airy flat in one of the new *palazzi* rising off Piazza Cucchi, between the Viale dei Quattro Venti and Villa Doria Pamphilj. My wife and I stayed there one summer, by which time the only permanent paying member of the *ménage* was the Contessa Leonora Lichnowsky, a deep-voiced German aristocrat who had somehow wound up a colorful career of global range employed at FAO.[2] She tended to dominate the conversation at dinner, but with such a range of interests and of experiences to draw on that one was never bored. Eventually she even outlived Olga Fersen, who, despite a brittle frame and frail health, lived well into her nineties (1904-1998) [fig. 19. 3]. Olga lived long enough to receive in 1994 the American Academy's centennial medal, an honor she greatly prized.[3]

NOTES

1   One of the bills made out to Esther Van Deman survived because she had made archaeological notes on the back. The slip of paper is filed in the boxes of Van Deman's notes stored in the Photographic Archive of the AAR. The bill is for February, 1924 @ 34 lire per day: 29 X 34 lire = 986 lire; one extra heat on Feb. 5 = 100 lire; 2 dinners on Feb 21 (probably guests) = 14 lire. A total of 1100 lire, paid, and signed by P. de Daehn. Note found and reproduced by K. A. Geffcken.

2   Food and Agriculture Organization.

3   The awarding of this medal was sponsored by Eric and Isobel Baade, long-time residents of the Pensione Fersen. After the Contessa's death, the family presented the medal to Eric Baade, and now that Eric also has died, Isobel still owns and cherishes the award.

Nicholas Fersen, nephew of the Contessa Olga, died December 13, 2005 at age 85. In the year before his death he gave permission to include this description of the Villa, an excerpt from his autobiography:

"My paternal grandmother . . . looked around, took a deep breath, pooled whatever few valuables had been saved from the general wreck, and opened a boarding house on the Janiculum Hill, within calling distance from the American Academy in Rome. Thus the Pensione Villa Sforza was born in the year 1921. Villa Sforza, the edifice rented for the purpose, defies all description. The original two structures from the Botanical Garden were built onto piecemeal by successive owners who desperately tried to outdo one another in elegance and imagination. Their efforts resulted in the whitest of elephants, a monster loaded with travertine and stucco over-structures, terraces, terraced roofs, balconies, arches, mosaic floors, outrageously false Baroque decorations. A circular marble stairway with wrought-iron banisters ran all the way up to the third and last floor. In any sensible modern structure an equal space would have accommodated four or even five floors! There was an elevator, but I never saw it in working order. Twenty-five odd rooms, some of them cubbyholes, others rivaling a Waldorf ballroom in size and loftiness, were strewn haphazardly all over the map. They were connected by an intricate network of halls, and minor staircases which ran in all directions.... Throw in servants' quarters, kitchens and utilities, plus a garage and laundry building at the far end of the garden, and you see where we stood. The garden may have been 'formal Italian' in Torlonia time, but what I remember was a glorious tangle of laurels, oleanders, cypresses, orange trees and even bamboos – the jungles and battlefields and sailing ships of all my childhood adventures."

 ADDENDUM

VILLA SFORZA CESARINI

Katherine A. Geffcken

The present building at Via Garibaldi 31, in the Sforza Cesarini property behind the Acqua Paola, has as its kernel two eighteenth century structures: the pentagonal tower for the demonstration of plant specimens (*semplici*) dated 1703, and more directly behind the Fontanone a building completed later in the eighteenth century (see Bucci, pp. 150-3 and fig. 18.3), After the Orto Botanico was moved elsewhere in 1823, the State assumed control of the property until 1835, when the buildings and grounds were auctioned off to Antonio Gianni acting in behalf of the archaeologist Antonio Nibby. After Nibby's death in 1839, the property eventually passed to the Torlonia family. By the early years of the twentieth century, the owner was Maria Torlonia, born in 1876 and married in 1897 to Duke

Fig. 19. 4. View of Rome by G. Thomas, engraved by W. Mason, *London Illustrated News*, May 4, 1850, reproduced in *Ai Caduti*. Note the Tower of the Semplici and adjoining building behind the Acqua Paola.

Lorenzo Sforza Cesarini. Her grandfather Prince Alessandro Torlonia (1800-1876) had acquired immense properties, which later were inherited by his four grandchildren, the offspring of his only child Anna Maria and her husband Giulio Borghese Torlonia. But, writing on March 2, 1907, Clara Jessup Heyland (owner of the Villa Aurelia), commented that the Torlonia property behind the Acqua Paola had been uninhabited for "quite 40 years" and strangely "always unletable [*sic*]." The Duke and Duchess Sforza Cesarini, she reported, were asking 350,000 *lire* (about $87,500) for the buildings and gardens.[1]

In 1912 the Academy regarded the Orti Torlonia/Sforza Cesarini, the Villa, and the Villino Bellacci as much desired additions to the Aurelia property and the lot

159

Fig. 19. 5. Section of the drawing by Q. Cenni, based on the panorama painting of Rome from the Janiculum by L. Philippet (1882-3), reproduced from *Ai Caduti*. Note changes in the Semplici and adjoining structure since 1850.

where the Academy Main Building now stands. It was clear that the Academy would need land for future development and for assuring unobstructed views of the city. For months the Academy maneuvered to convince the Sforza Cesarini and, more important, the Duchess's older brother Prince Giovanni Torlonia to accept J. Pierpont Morgan's generous offers. But Torlonia set the prices ever higher; he was genuinely reluctant to sell.

Then, in September 1912, the Academy suddenly learned that extensive alterations and additions had begun at Villa Sforza Cesarini, with the aim of converting it into an apartment house.[2] Conferences were held, Morgan was informed, and the Academy's efforts to buy intensified. But as foundations were laid for the Academy's sculpture studios and the Main Building, Prince Giovanni Torlonia threatened the Academy with legal action because the new buildings, especially one of the sculpture studios, were improperly close to the Villino Bellacci, the home of his mistress Cesarina Bellacci. Realizing that the Prince would win any legal suit and that work on the Main Building would be terminated, the Academy abandoned hopes for the Orti Torlonia. But Morgan agreed, before his death in March 1913, to pay the huge sum of 192,500 *lire* (almost $40,000) to Bellacci for her *villino*, thus averting legal pressure from the Prince. Much attached to her lovely residence, Bellacci (quite legally) took with her all the precious chandeliers and light fixtures, when she moved out.3 About the same time, Maria Torlonia Sforza Cesarini received permission from the city to restructure and enlarge her villa buildings.

The developing shape of the Villa Sforza Cesarini can be traced in various views. George Housman Thomas's drawing, engraved by Walter Mason and published in *The London Illustrated News*, May 4, 1850 [fig. 19. 4], shows the two eighteenth century buildings essentially as they must have been in the days of the Orto Botanico, but marred with damage from shelling in 1849. By 1882, Léon Philippet's great panorama includes a larger building of the Semplici [fig. 19. 5]. A third floor had been added to the tower, and its dimensions much expanded. The style, however, remains fairly simple and the outer walls of the Semplici are still evident.

The house we see today is architect Pio Piacentini's redesigning for the Duchess Sforza Cesarini, a residence highly decorated with elaborate window framing and cornices. Repeated many times in the moldings is the Sforza lion rampant with front and back legs on the trunk of a quince tree. These decorative elements even encircle the elegant round tower that Piacentini added on the north side to enclose the long winding staircase described above by Nicholas Fersen (p. 158). Piacentini also linked the two eighteenth century buildings with new construction that presented a dramatic concave façade to the garden and with stairs to accommodate uneven floor levels in the two buildings. An inscription celebrating the Duchess's embellishment of her villa adorns the concave garden façade:

MARIA TORLONIA
LAURENTII SFORTIA CESARINUS DUCIS UXOR
HAEDES FAMILIAE SUAE
AMPLIAVIT ET ORNAVIT A.D. MDCCCCXIII

(Maria Torlonia, wife of Lorenzo, Duke Sforza Cesarini, enlarged and adorned [this] house of her family A.D. 1913)4 [fig. 19. 6].

In January 1924, discussion about the Villa Sforza Cesarini arose again in Academy circles when Professor Cleveland Chase of Hamilton College proposed that the Academy guarantee the lease granted by the Sforza family to the Daehns/Fersens. Chase saw such a guarantee as a solution to several problems. First, the Daehn/Fersen household would provide an excellent home for Academy female Fellows and for students, both male and female, who were not allowed to live at the Academy. Having stayed at the Villa Sforza Cesarini in 1921-22, Professor Chase recommended it as a beautiful house and garden, with already a distinguished list of guests ("no pension could match the dignity"). Furthermore, the modest rates, he said, were based on the Daehns and Fersens' own cooperative arrangement. Apparently, the Russian tenants had experienced "great difficulty in getting their lease renewed from year to year." An Academy guarantee of the lease for a term of years would ease the situation and "do better by [Col. Peter] de Daehn, a man of

Fig. 19. 6. Concave façade (1913) linking the Tower of the Semplici (left, outside the photograph) and the second eighteenth century building beginning with windows at right. Designed by Pio Piacentini, this façade faces into the garden. The inscription over the arch commemorates embellishment carried out by Maria Torlonia, Duchess Sforza Cesarini. Greenery in the foreground covers the aqueduct of Paul V. Photograph taken from garden of Villa Chiaraviglio. K. A. Geffcken, 2005.

quality and ability." Already the Academy had been employing Daehn, paid by special donations. According to Professor Chase, the Villa Sforza might even be purchased and the Academy should "investigate this opportunity while it is still open."[5]

But Professor Tenney Frank of the Johns Hopkins University, then Professor in Charge at the Academy, argued against Chase's proposal for two reasons. He predicted that the Russians would return to their native country "when security is established there," and that "a boarding house is not equivalent to what the men [who live at the Academy] receive." And then Professor Frank suggested appropriate solutions for housing women within the Academy Main Building.[6]

In the end, however, as we well know, the Russians were not destined to return to their native estates, and housing Academy women would remain a burning issue for years to come. In the meantime, the Daehns and Fersens provided a fine home to Academy scholars, students, and visitors.

◈ NOTES

1   Clara Jessup Heyland to Charles W. Leavitt, 2 March, 1907 (Archives of American Art, AAR Archives/ reel 5755).

2   William Mitchell Kendall to William Rutherford Mead, September 1912 (Archives of American Art, AAR Archives/reel 5756). The news of building activity at the Villa Sforza Cesarini was so alarming to the Academy that Jesse Benedict Carter, Director of the old Classical School and future Director of the Academy, was summoned from vacation back to Rome. On his return, Carter wrote to William Rutherford Mead, 21 September, 1912, that he had discovered why the Academy will never obtain the Torlonia property but that he could not write it. Instead, Mr. Kendall would explain directly to Mead later in New York (an indirect reference to Cesarina Bellacci and her relation to the Prince?) (AAR Archives/reel 5756). For earlier negotiations for the Torlonia and Bellacci properties, see the diary of Gorham Phillips Stevens, 23 May, 1912 (unpublished notebooks, AAR Library).

3   Report from Jesse Benedict Carter, 9 March, 1915 (Archives of American Art, AAR Archives/reel 5765). The lawsuit against the Academy threatened by Giovanni Torlonia is described in this report (it "would have ended fatally for the Academy") as well as in several previous letters from Carter (e.g., Carter to Mead, 29 January, 1913, preserved in AAR Archives/reel 5754).

4   A Latinist might not only prefer to see "Sfortia Cesarinus" in the genitive case, but also question the spelling of *haedes* (for *aedes*). Piacentini's handsome drawings for the villa are filed in the Archivio Capitolino, *protocollo* (register number) 5404, dated 14 October, 1912, and approved 6 May, 1913.

5   Cleveland K. Chase to James Egbert (Professor at Columbia University and Academy Trustee), 28 January, 1924 (Archives of American Art, AAR Archives/reel 5756). While we have usually referred to the Daehns as "de Daehns," Nina Fersen, wife of Nicholas Fersen, has reminded me that the "de" is used properly only between a title (and/or first name) and the surname.

6   Tenney Frank to Egbert, 3 January, 1924 (Archives of American Art, AAR Archives/reel 5756).

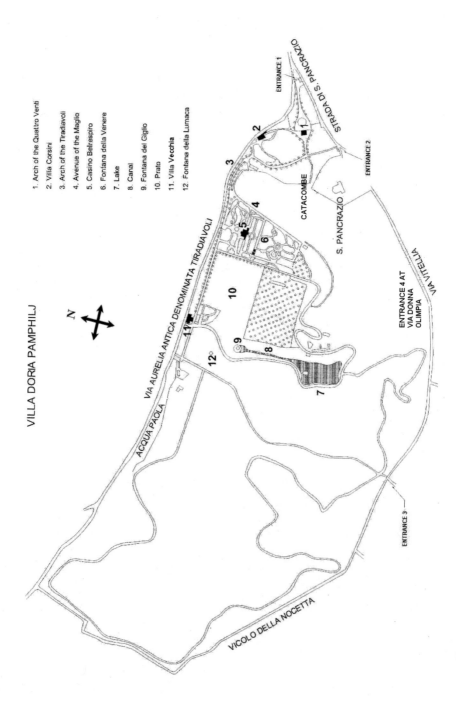

Fig. 20. 1. Map drawing by Elisa Silva, FAAR 2006, showing layout of the Villa Doria Pamphilj, redrawn from map in A. Schiavo, *Villa Doria Pamphilj*.

VILLA DORIA PAMPHILJ

1. Arch of the Quattro Venti
2. Villa Corsini
3. Arch of the Tiradiavoli
4. Avenue of the Maglio
5. Casino Belrespiro
6. Fontana della Venere
7. Lake
8. Canal
9. Fontana del Giglio
10. Prato
11. Villa Vecchia
12. Fontana della Lumaca

CHAPTER 20

THE VILLA DORIA PAMPHILJ

Mirka Beneš

Less than 800 meters distant from the gate of the American Academy in Rome lies the Villa Pamphilj (Pamphili), one of the greatest creations of Baroque Italian landscape architecture. Ever since the Comune di Roma acquired it in 1971, it has become one of Rome's most beloved public parks, and the largest.[1] Here, the visitor finds over two hundred acres of beautiful landscapes, once completely walled in, including a core of formal gardens, in which to wander, stroll, sit and read, picnic, or exercise [fig. 20.1].[2] Built from 1645 to 1670 alongside the Via Aurelia on the Janiculum Hill, the 200-acre villa was one of the key products of the social rise of the Pamphilj family in Rome (the Pamphilj had come from Gubbio in 1465), an effort of generations that culminated in the pontificate of Innocent X Pamphilj (1644-55). It was built for Cardinal Camillo Pamphilj, the 22-year old nephew of the pope, but as it was a key political and social statement for the newly papal family, we can be sure that behind the scenes Innocent X had the final say about the design of the architecture, gardens and their decorations.[3]

In visiting the Villa Pamphilj, you will see a landscape that has undergone numerous transformations over the centuries. It was initially an area of tombs, both Roman and early Christian, along the Via Aurelia, a roadway of commercial and pilgrim traffic linking the sea northwest at Civitavecchia to Rome. From the medieval period to the seventeenth century and beyond, it consisted of a landscape of *vigne*, small agrarian properties from five to fifty acres close to the city, usually with vineyards and trees. Further out were the *casali*, livestock and grain farms from hundreds to thousands of acres in size. From 1645 to 1670 some thirty small *vigna*-owners were displaced from the land that became the great Pamphilj villa estate surrounded by other vineyards. For the next two centuries, till the late nineteenth, the landscape was basically unchanged both inside and outside the villa walls until a Victorian English garden style was transposed onto the seventeenth-century formal core of the Villa Pamphilj. This new garden style followed the destruction of parts of the villa in the war of the Roman Republic, when the pope was allied with the French against Garibaldi in 1849. That Victorian garden has in turn been simplified but also depleted by much public overuse after the Villa Pamphilj opened as a public Roman park in 1971.

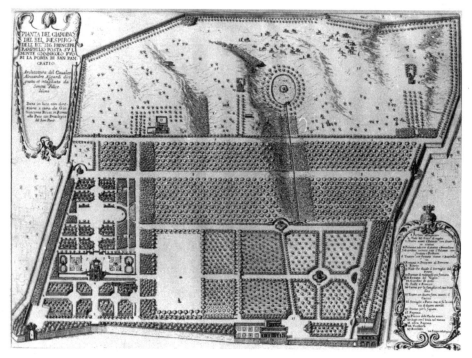

Fig. 20. 2. Plan of the Villa Doria
Pamphilj, by Simone Felice Delfino,
part of Falda's garden series.

You may find it helpful on a visit to bring a photocopy of the Janiculum por-
tion of Giambattista Nolli's 1748 plan of Rome, since no city maps of Rome prior to
Nolli's had represented the areas outside the city walls, nor did Giovanni Battista
Falda's bird's-eye view-map of Rome (1676), which provides wonderful detail for the
Janiculum and the Academy's site. Another photocopy of the villa's plan in the late
seventeenth century would be useful as well [fig. 20. 2].[4] If you go straight out the
Porta San Pancrazio, carefully minding the heavy traffic as you go through the city
wall (fortified in time of war by Pope Urban VIII in 1642-44) you will find after about
a city block straight ahead of you the entrance to the Villa Pamphilj. The present
Villa entrance was set up on former Corsini land following the purchase of this
neighboring Villa Corsini in 1857 by Prince Filippo Andrea Doria Pamphilj. You are
about 80 meters above sea-level here, since both the crests of the Janiculum Hill and
of the Villa are the highest areas of Rome.

To become oriented in a landscape that has undergone many changes since
antiquity, you should know that the original seventeenth-century design of the Villa
Pamphilj — of both the main palace (the Casino) and of the formal gardens — was
oriented to the cardinal points. At the entrance, you are facing due west.

As the ground rises past the entrance gate, you encounter the huge monumental arch the Doria Pamphilj family built in 1859 to commemorate the defeat of
Garibaldi and to honor the fallen French soldiers; it is decorated with ancient reliefs

Fig. 20. 3. Prince Doria Pamphilj's Arch (1859), built on the site of the Casino dei Quattro Venti, east façade. Photograph, K.A. Geffcken, 2002.

Fig. 20. 4. Aqueduct line visible from the pathway inside the Villa garden wall along the Via Aurelia. Photograph B. Goldman, 2004.

from the surrounding tomb areas [fig. 20. 3]. As you come over the rise, you are on the site of the former Corsini casino, called the Quattro Venti, destroyed in the Garibaldi defense.5 You then descend along the nineteenth-century carriageway with umbrella pines nearby, a path that curves through the sloping land in a hairpin turn, a version of English Picturesque style.6 *Leccio* trees, or evergreen holm oaks, native to the Roman Campagna and planted everywhere in Roman villas, begin to surround you, and at the bottom of the turn, on your left you see a deep ravine, which marks the boundary line between the old Villa Corsini and the Pamphilj. On your right you are next to aqueduct arches of Paul V Borghese [fig. 20. 4] running above ground, which flank the Via Aurelia and form the Villa wall at that point.7 On your right, you see above the wall the handsome arch, known popularly as the Tiradiavoli [fig. 17. 4], built over the road by Pope Paul V during his reconstruction of Trajan's aqueduct in 1610-12. It carries the aqueduct across that road. On the Via Aurelia, just beyond this Arch, the seventeenth-century entrance to the Villa once stood, a tall portal in travertine crowned by the papal Pamphilj arms. Today, instead, you face a green metal fence that separates the Villa's palace, the Casino Nobile, and its immediate gardens from the rest of the public park. The Palace and gardens are owned by the Italian Government, the Consiglio dei Ministri, and this fenced portion and the Casino are closed to the public.

If you were a visitor around 1670, approaching through this entrance directly from the Via Aurelia, and not through the Villa Corsini, which was another property, you could enter on foot, or by horseback or by carriage. A beautiful avenue of trees extending three hundred meters, alternating cypress and elms on both sides (some poplars, too, so say the original planting documents), greeted the visitor here, displaying leafy foliage above and trimmed interplanted hedges below. The avenue led to a splendid vista of sparkling water against stone in the Fountain of the Dolphins at the far end. This avenue was called the *"Viale dove si gioca al maglio"* (Avenue of the croquet game), on Falda's bird's-eye plan of the Villa described below. Indeed, seventeenth-century Pamphilj household accounts record that wooden mallets and balls for *maglio* were shipped up to villa from the city palace. Today this avenue is flanked only by holm oak trees, but in the seventeenth century nearly all the avenues of the Villa were lined by elms, poplars, cypress, or pines (*pinus pinea*).[8]

As you look down this long carriageway, you should consult a plan of the entire Villa estate. The two most useful ones are from about 1670, both by the prodigious print and map-maker Falda. One is a bird's-eye view [fig. 20.2], showing buildings and plantings of the Villa Pamphilj in three dimensions; it was published in Falda's famous platebook *Li Giardini di Roma*, which showcased the nine top gardens of Rome circa 1670, from the Vatican and the Quirinal to the Villas Borghese and Pamphilj. The other is a large plan that was published folded inside the platebook *Villa Pamphilia eiusque Palatium* (Rome, ca. 1670), for which the printmaker Dominique Barrière made five stunning etched views of the Villa for Camillo Pamphilj, starting in 1648 with the main palace and ending in 1660 with the park and its antique statues. Both show that the 210 acres of the seventeenth-century Villa Pamphilj were enclosed by a continuous circuit of wall, completed in 1670 and measuring five miles in perimeter. The size and perimeter of the Villa estate were considered marvels at the time, the largest in Rome (the Villa Borghese had a four-mile perimeter). After the size of the Villa Pamphilj was nearly doubled during nineteenth-century land acquisitions, the shape of the Villa estate became that of a half moon, bounded on the north by the Via Aurelia and on the south by the Via Vitellia and the Via della Nocetta, which rejoined the Aurelia.

The plans of the villa, from Falda to a present day plan, reveal that the visitor now stands in the northeastern corner, at the edge of an estate or park, not on axis with the main palace as at the Villa Medici in Rome or the Villa d'Este at Tivoli. This approach to designing the Roman villa as an estate with parkland originated in the late-sixteenth century with the Villa Montalto of Pope Sixtus V (1585-90), which was destroyed to make way for Rome's Termini station, and was soon repeated at the Villa Borghese (1606-33), as can still be seen today. It involved the conceptualization of the villa as a series of great tree gardens or groves, and it kept the main palace hidden as a marvelous surprise, screened by trees and attainable only after wandering through part of the park. And so it is here, where the palace, called the Casino Belrespiro—"lovely breeze," stands amidst trees on high ground in the fresh dry air of the Janiculum overlooking three grand terraced garden levels along a north-south axis below [fig. 20. 5]. You soon reach this central axis, the main north-south spine of the design, after walking the 300 meter entrance avenue, which lies on a diagonal, because of the ravine on the left. Originally, there was a choice of climbing directly up to the Casino Belrespiro or taking this long avenue, which leads into a triangular area of once-formal gardens. On the right there open up successive oblique views of the Casino Belrespiro on its grand podium-terrace [fig. 20. 6].

Turning to face north on the central axis, you stand at the most famous viewing point of the Villa Pamphilj's grand formal gardens [fig. 20. 7]. Both the gardens and the Casino were built as a unit from 1645 to 1648 for Cardinal Camillo Pamphilj,

Fig. 20. 5. Casino Belrespiro from
the northwest, showing the parterres
in front of the Casino. Photograph,
G. Dwyer, 2005.

Fig. 20. 6. Casino Belrespiro photographed
by Georgina Masson. Photograph,
Photographic Archive of the AAR.

and their area was called the Giardino Nuovo to distinguish it from the adjoining Vigna Vecchia, the vineyard along the Via Aurelia farther to the west, which the Pamphilj had bought in 1630 when Camillo's uncle (Innocent X) had first become a cardinal himself. The Casino and its three terraced gardens (the Giardino Nuovo) were designed in the spring of 1645 and built rapidly from 1645 to 1648 [fig. 20. 7]. The design was a collaboration between the Bolognese sculptor Alessandro Algardi (1598-1654) and the Roman architect Girolamo Rainaldi (1570-1655), helped by his son, the famous Carlo Rainaldi (1611-91). Rainaldi senior, who had just been named architect to the Pamphilj family by Innocent X, designed the architectural façades, layout, massing, and imagery of the Giardino Nuovo and its Casino, which form a pendant to the grand city palace he rebuilt for the papal Pamphilj family in the Piazza Navona at exactly the same time, 1645-48. Algardi was in charge of the sculptural decoration, both interior and exterior, and the artistic direction of the overall project, which comprised an enormous amount of sculptural and antiquarian work.9 In many instances Rainaldi and Algardi, reflecting the desire of their patrons, drew on the formal models of ancient Roman villas and landscape architecture, such as Hadrian's Villa, the Temple of Fortune at Praeneste, and Domitian's villa at Albanum.

The Casino Belrespiro is a cube-like palace set into the change in level between two terraces; it is thus two stories high on the north side—the main

170

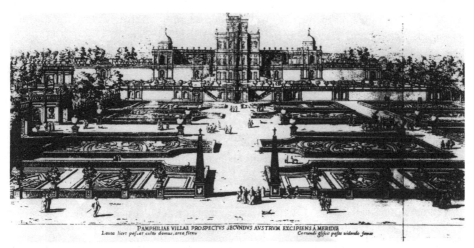

Fig. 20. 7. Drawing of the Villa Pamphilj
*"prospectus secundus austrum excipiens a
meridie,"* 1653-59 from Giovanni Battista
Falda, *Villa Pamphilia* (Rome, 1670).

entrance, and three on the south—the private garden entrance.[10] Oriented to the
cardinal points, it is aligned as closely as possible to the north, in the Vatican valley,
with the dome of Saint Peter's, which can be seen in spectacular views from the roof
level. Surmounted by an attic and belvedere, the Casino's exterior architecture is
magnificent and regal, decorated with membering of clustered pilasters and panels
that form a unity with the bas-reliefs and statues, part ancient, part modern. These
give its façades a rich and refined chiaroscuro effect.[11] Inside, the two main floors
(*piani nobili*) are each organized in a central plan of three bands running north-south,
with a round room at the center surrounded by rectangular rooms. On the *primo
piano nobile* the round *salone* rises in two stories covered by a dome with cryptopor-
ticus-like apertures to let in light. The *pianterreno* is semi-buried to the north because
of the sloping terrain; on this ground level Algardi designed exquisite *stucchi* for the
ceilings of four rooms grouped together, which open onto the private garden.

  With its pearly-white stuccoed façades set against the pines, holm oaks, and
adjacent parkland, the elegant Casino Belrespiro recalls the paintings of Claude
Lorrain, those with enchanted classical palaces amidst pines and the soft grazing
landscapes of the Roman Campagna — and rightly so. This kind of juxtaposition –
light-colored, refined architecture with dark-hued, dense parkland – stems indeed
partly from Claude's pictorial inventions. Both the Villa Pamphilj and Claude's landscapes derive from the same Roman Seicento artistic culture, which employed many
references to the Campagna and to the tension, if not juxtaposition, between urban
buildings and rural landscapes. As if acknowledging the kinship between the Villa
and Claude's work, Camillo Pamphilj commissioned six landscape paintings from
Claude Lorrain. Four can be seen in the Galleria Doria Pamphilj on the Via del
Corso; in Camillo's day two hung, among many other paintings, in the *piano nobile*
room of the Casino Belrespiro overlooking the garden.

The four façades of the Casino were designed by carefully fitting the ancient bas-reliefs, busts, and statues into the architectural framework and membering. Construction and the search for the antiquities to adorn the façades went on simultaneously. The ancient pieces came from a number of find sites, ranging from Nettuno, Viterbo, Porto, and Ostia, to various farms in the Roman Campagna, to the tomb of Cecilia Metella on the Via Appia. In April 1645, from the Metella tomb came the bucrania and garlands placed in the attic of the top storey of the Casino Belrespiro. Hadrian's Villa was also a significant source of marbles, which came in cartloads from the farmland of Giovanni Francesco Bulgarini, whose property stood on the ancient site. The ancient pieces were first reworked by a whole team of sculptor restorers supervised by Algardi, and then they were put together or cut up to fit into the architectural design of each façade. The subjects of the bas-reliefs and busts are occasionally identified in the original purchase or finding documents. A great many reliefs have to do with themes of Bacchus, a topic appropriate for a villa made out of vineyards. They include the hunt, a subject selected for its association with hunting parks in villas, and Imperial Roman portraiture, the abstractions Pax and Concordia, as well as triumphs, all themes fitting the new reign of peace that Innocent X Pamphilj's pontificate hoped to usher in.

Crowned by the Casino Belrespiro at its highest point, the Giardino Nuovo was structured in three terraces or levels. The lowermost level of the gardens, where you enter today, was known as the Giardino del Teatro [fig. 20. 7] because of its former water theater, which is still extant, rebuilt without its water systems after serious damage in the 1849 war. The water theater functions as a retaining wall between this lower level and the park on higher ground to the west, and it derives in concept from those in several villas at Frascati. Two of Barrière's views show the magnificent formal prospects that were originally intended, focusing on the Casino to the north and on the water theater to the west, ornamented with horizontal water displays and flanking rows of fountains and grottoes. The Grotto of Pan to the right of the water

Fig. 20. 8. The fountain with satyrs below the Casino Belrespiro. Photograph, N. W. Goldman, 2004.

Fig. 20. 9. View of the Casino Belrespiro with the Venus fountain in the foreground. Photograph, G. Dwyer, 2005.

theater survives, albeit much restored. The rich architectural-sculptural decoration linked together the Casino, its terraces, and the walls of the water theater, making them seem one continuous L-shaped complex.

Recessed into the main terrace wall of the north-south axis, below the Casino, the central Fountain of Venus in the Giardino del Teatro is an example of Algardi's design and stucco work [fig. 20. 9]. Dog-leg staircases flank this fountain, leading from it to the next garden terrace above — the great podium measuring 45 by 180 meters, which was originally planted with rare and exotic flowers like tulips, narcissi, and anemones. This garden of exotics was called the Giardino Segreto, since *segreto* meant "private" in the seventeenth century. It was also called the Giardino de' fiori (flower garden), a known type by 1640, like the two in the Villa Borghese. From about 1710, it was planted with low-lying parterres of box in the French style, a version still maintained today. Originally two oblong fountain-basins were planned here, but only the west one was built [fig. 20. 5].[12]

The lower Giardino del Teatro level is now covered with grass, its center occupied by a fountain with Satyrs made in 1855 [fig. 20. 8]. However, when first planted in 1645-48, it and the western slopes around the water theater were covered with dense tree gardens organized in regular groves of 600 bitter orange trees (*merangoli*), plus firs, laurels, and ilexes, which were also planted on the topmost terrace next to the Casino.[13] Such groves were called *boschetti*, already well known in sixteenth-century Roman gardens. The lower gardens were thus intended to appear like a sea of trees, above shoulder height when fully grown, amidst which a hippodrome-shaped piazza extended like a clearing out from the water theater; while the Giardino Segreto above remained open like a cleared terrace. Today the *boschetti*, when present on the various garden levels, consist mainly of evergreen holm oaks. All the planting arrangements described here had previously been tried out at the Villa Borghese from about 1606 to 1630.

The Fountain of the Dolphins that once terminated the entrance avenue

Fig. 20. 10. Fountain display,
Fontana del Giglio, from the top
of the canal above the lake.
Photograph, G. Dwyer, 2005.

stood on a podium beneath which the land dropped sharply. It has disappeared, destroyed in the battle of 1849 and replaced by the chapel of the Doria Pamphilj in 1896. This long-gone fountain once looked southward out through a stand of umbrella pines to views over the undulating meadow land called, from the seventeenth century on, the *campagna* of the Villa Pamphilj, in recognition of both its rustic origins and its naturalistic landscaping.

Leaving the Giardino del Teatro southwards past the family-chapel or westward up a ramp of steps, you enter a different realm of the park. Here again, it is good to consult the plans of 1670 or the more recent map of Elisa Silva. You will see that the Villa Pamphilj's overall design juxtaposes a formal garden area with an open park, like the famous Villa Lante at Bagnaia (1568-78) in northern Latium. Here, however, there are more fluid and direct connections between garden and park: long tree-lined avenues once connected the formal gardens to the park and meadows on the south and linked them with the Vigna Vecchia on the west. Some of the ancient holm oaks are still in place, and renewed planting over the centuries has kept many lines of trees in place. Although the Giardino Nuovo was once richly decorated with ancient sculpture and seventeenth century fountains, the park was far less decorated. Only a few fountains, designed by Algardi and others, formed *foci* to the great avenues cutting through the orchards, oak-groves, and pine forest. Most of the fountains are gone now, but a few have been reconstructed in modern times. Wide avenues, like those in the Villa Pamphilj, had been laid out in Roman villas since about 1600 for visitors moving about on horseback or in carriages, which had been introduced to Rome in the later sixteenth century. This mode of circulation made sense in villas that were not gardens but estates, where one could ride for a half-mile before encountering the next fountain or building. One could never have imagined galloping about the Villa d'Este at Tivoli on horseback or in a carriage, even if it were on level ground!

In 1648, the newly completed Villa Pamphilj consisted of the formal Giardino Nuovo on about twenty acres; next to it, along the Via Aurelia, stood the Vigna

Vecchia with its rustic palace (perched on the aqueduct) and a variety of sheds and stables. There was no park yet. From 1650 to 1670, the park was developed by the purchase of over twenty *vigne* of varying sizes and contents, some with rustic buildings, kitchen gardens, and trees, others deserted. The Villa Pamphilj thus grew from twenty to two hundred acres, and the vineyards were all incorporated into a design that divided the Villa into two halves, northern and southern, separated by a fence to keep the animals inside the southern hunting park.

The northern half enclosed the Giardino Nuovo, the Vigna Vecchia, planted mainly with evergreen groves of holm oaks and bitter orange trees, the land between the Giardino Nuovo and the Vigna Vecchia on high ground — known as the Prato (today an open space where soccer is played), and a large stately *pineta*, a forest of umbrella pines that stretched like a transversal band across the estate from east to west. The northern half was traversed by wide avenues for riding or carriage-touring, all organized on a grid, parallel and perpendicular to the Via Aurelia.

By 1670, when Falda made his plan of the Villa, the Fountain of the Sea Snail (Fontana della Lumaca) had been installed in the center of a dense regular grove of bitter orange trees in the Vigna Vecchia. This pedestal fountain with sculpted dolphins and a conch shell had been designed by Gianlorenzo Bernini in 1653 for another Pamphilj garden, and was moved to the Villa by 1670. The present Fountain has been vandalized, but it is a copy of the original (very battered) in the Palazzo Doria Pamphilj downtown.

The southern half enclosed the hunting park, which included open grassland for horseback pursuit of game such as deer, hare, and fowl of all kinds, birding thickets, grazing meadows for livestock, rustic pavilions such as a pheasant house, a dairy farm stabling fifty-some cows, and a lake in one of the valleys fed by a canal that drained natural water sources flowing south from the Via Aurelia [fig. 20. 10]. This area was considered a pastoral evocation of the Roman Campagna with its grasslands. In deliberate contrast to the northern half, the southern hunting park had few avenues. Except for the leveled areas of the Giardino Nuovo and the Prato, no major shifting of earth was done in either half of the park, which was designed, in fact, on the natural terrain sloping gradually westwards but much more steeply to the south.

In terms of its location and concept, the parkland of the Villa Pamphilj, called a *rus suburbanum* in 1670, in some ways emulated the Golden House of Nero in Roman antiquity, a landscaped estate representing *rus in urbe,* or the countryside in the city. The Villa Pamphilj represents, like the Villas Montalto, Ludovisi, and Borghese before it, a major typological change in the landscape architecture of Roman villa design: these seventeenth-century villa gardens, with their vast estates organized around a small core of formal gardens with a casino or small palace as the architectural climax, are truly distinct from their sixteenth-century predecessors in being designed more as parks that evoke the Roman Campagna than as formal gardens.

The original design of the Villa Pamphilj has survived, although all its areas have received the imprint of nineteenth-century planting that favored single trees, often exotics imported from the Americas, instead of dense groves of native trees. In

Fig. 20. 11. Villa Pamphilj garden and Casino Belrespiro. Photograph, K.A. Geffcken.

the later eighteenth century, the Vigna Vecchia area was replanted as a productive agrarian landscape according to agronomic schemes by the landscape gardener Francesco Bettini, although nearly all of his work has disappeared. The original lake, which had — and still does have — an island, was enlarged in the eighteenth and nineteenth centuries, and the canal was widened and restructured. The Lily Fountain was shifted from an eastern position beside the canal head to one directly overlooking it where, in renovated form, it stands today. Despite many changes over time, the Villa Pamphilj and its splendid natural topography remain an extraordinary *rus suburbanum*, an expanse of countryside close to the city, appreciated daily by countless visitors [fig. 20. 11]. Among seventeenth century visitors was Princess Violante Lomellini, a relative of the Pamphilj family, who wrote in 1677 to her mother:

> Prince Pamphilj paid very special compliments to me and to all my retinue with a large banquet in his *Vigna*; the banquet was then accompanied by an abundant and beautiful hunt, where I had great satisfaction without any inconvenience; they killed three boars, two stags, and various hare .... In truth, this *Vigna* is a superb thing, for it pairs the delight of the most beautiful, striking, and tailored garden with the loveliness and amenities of the Roman Campagna. It is enclosed by a five-mile circuit of walls, is very beautiful, and is full of wild goats and hare. It is a marvel that it is just half a mile from Rome.[14]

NOTES

1   By 'villa' is meant what Romans understood in the seventeenth century, i.e. an entire complex or estate that contained a main palace, dependencies, gardens, and tracts of park land. For the history of the Villa Pamphilj, see Armando Schiavo, *Villa Doria Pamphilj* (Milan, 1942); Isa Belli Barsali, *Ville di Roma. Lazio I* (Milan, 1970), 275-297; Carla Benocci, *La villa della famiglia Doria Pamphilj a Roma. Agronomia, paesaggio, architettura nell'Ottocento* (Milan, 1988); Fiorenzo Catalli e Mauro Petrecca, *Villa Pamphilj* (Rome, 1992); Carla Benocci, *Villa Doria Pamphilj* (Rome, 1996); Carla Benocci and Riccardo Vannuccini, eds. *Le virtù e i piaceri in villa* (Rome, 1998).

On the main Casino, see Mirka Beneš, "Alessandro Algardi a Villa Pamphilj," in *Alessandro Algardi. L'altra faccia del barocco*, ed. Jennifer Montagu (Rome, 1999), 49-60; Carla Benocci, *Algardi a Roma: Il Casino del Bel*

Respiro a Villa Doria Pamphilj (Rome, 1999). On the antiquities, see Raissa Calza, ed. *Antichità di Villa Doria Pamphilj* (Rome, 1977); Beatrice Palma Venetucci, ed. *Villa Doria Pamphilj: Storia della Collezione* (Rome, 2001). On the restoration of the villa in 1984, see Luciano Tubello, *Restauri a Roma, Santa Cecilia, Villa Doria Pamphilj, Sant'Eusebio* (Rome, 1988), 77-132. For interpretations of the villa and park, see Mirka Beneš, "Landowning and the Villa in the Social Geography of the Roman Territory. The Location and Landscapes of the Villa Pamphilj (1645-70)," in *Form, Modernism, and History. Essays in Honor of Eduard F. Sekler*, ed. A. von Hoffmann (Cambridge, MA-London, 1996), 187-209; *Idem*, "Pastoralism in the Roman Baroque Villa and in Claude Lorrain. Myths and Realities of the Roman Campagna," in *Villas and Gardens in Early Modern Italy and France*, eds. Mirka Beneš and Dianne Harris (Cambridge-New York, 2001), 88-113.

2   The Villa Pamphilj was expanded westwards during the nineteenth century by many hundreds of acres, but that portion was cut off from the earlier one by the construction of the Via Olimpica for the 1960 Olympics. The two sections are now connected by a bridge over the Olimpica. Walking the circuit of the entire seventeenth-century park can take a good hour and a half, visiting the formal gardens nearest the entrance, about half an hour.

3   The land acquisition documents and construction payments are in the *Archivio Doria Pamphilj, Rome*: Scaffali 97/1-97/23, with payments mainly in Sc. 97/16, 16bis, 17, and 18. Many of the documents are published in Jörg Garms, *Quellen aus dem Archiv Doria-Pamphilj zur Kunsttätigkeit in Rom unter Innocenz X* (Rome-Vienna, 1972).

4   A good plan and view of the Villa Pamphilj are the last plates in G. B. Falda's *Li Giardini di Roma* (Rome, ca. 1675) available in the AAR Rare Book Room; good reprints of Falda's book exist in many libraries. The American Academy's Library also has A. Schiavo, *Villa Doria Pamphilj*, 1942, in which see p. 34 fig. 27 for Falda, and C. Benocci, *Villa Doria Pamphilj*, 1996, in which see e.g. pp. 118-119 for plans of the 1670s and p. 302 for an aerial photo of 1929.

5   See, most recently, Francesco Eleuteri, "Villa Corsini fuori Porta S. Pancrazio a Roma," *Palladio* 18 (July-Dec. 1996), 109-24, and the relevant section in Armando Schiavo's "classic," *Villa Doria Pamphilj* (Milan, 1942), 125-38. Also see pp. 14-21 in this volume in reference to Angelo Masina.

6   Along the way, if it is autumn or winter time and the trees have no foliage, you will get a stunning view westwards of the main palace of the Villa Pamphilj, rising on its terraces across a small ravine.

7   Behind you, on your right, you have just passed the approach to the western, lower level of the Villa Corsini. Formerly stables, this space was converted into a flat, where the late Georgina Masson (pseudonym for Marion Babs Johnson), lived in the 1960s. A friend of the Doria Pamphilj family, Ms. Johnson is still known today for her *Companion Guide to Rome*, which continues to be issued in new revisions, and for her splendid classic *Italian Gardens*. In the latter book, her description of the Villa Pamphilj, her "home" for a while, remains an excellent read. In the last few years a wing has been added to part of the western end of the Villa Corsini, so that the paved court in front of Ms. Johnson's door no longer has its former graceful dimensions. In 1980 Ms. Johnson left her photographic archive to the American Academy in Rome. For further information, see *Georgina Masson 1912-1980* (AAR exhibition catalogue), ed. Alessandra Capodiferro (Milan, 2003). (KG and MB).

8   These lines of trees usually had hedge under- or inter-planting at their base, which meant that from continuous clipped hedges of laurel, box, or other evergreens (to waist or shoulder height of a person) the taller tree trunks rose up like stems with their foliage crowns above. This type of planting, specific to Roman Baroque gardens, was called *spalliere in aria* (hedges in-the-air).

9   Rainaldi also had extensive experience in garden and park design, for example the completion of Vignola's work at Caprarola and the Farnese Gardens on the Palatine, as well as at Parma and Modena in north Italy.

10   The building as executed matches the three views of it etched by Dominique Barrière from 1648 on, except for the wings of one story which terminate in pavilions. Given the vertical rise of the south façade of the Casino, far too narrow and tall as it is, the wings were probably intended from the start, but deemed either too magnificent or too expensive to construct, and they were not built.

11   Variations on this practice of decorating palace and villa casino façades with antique reliefs existed since the early sixteenth century in Rome. Salient examples for comparison include the Casino of Pius IV   177

(Vatican gardens), the Villa Medici, the Palazzo Mattei di Giove, the Casino Borghese dell'Aurora (now Rospigliosi-Pallavicini) on the Quirinal hill, and the Villa Borghese.

12 By late 1646, Algardi had designed a Fountain of the Sea-Tigers with stucco figures for the center of this flower garden terrace, but it was soon after destroyed.

13 One thousand *abeti* (sapling fir trees) were brought in carts from Tuscany in late 1645 and then planted by fourteen men.

14 *Archivio Doria Pamphilj, Rome*, Scaffale 79/80/6, letter of 27 February, 1677.

 ADDENDUM

THE VILLA DORIA PAMPHILJ

Katherine A. Geffcken

In his nineteenth century guidebook *Walks in Rome*, Augustus Hare states that the Villa Doria Pamphilj is "open to pedestrians and to *two-horse* carriages after 12 o'clock on Mondays and Fridays." Though he does not think much of the sculpture adorning the Casino, he greatly admires the gardens of azaleas and camellias and the park. He recommends an excursion along the drives bordering "pine-shaded lawns" and especially urges a visit to the "ilex-fringed terrace" on the north side of the Casino, to see the view of St. Peter's. He also mentions the name "Mary" spelled out in large letters of boxwood, as a memorial to Lady Mary Talbot (died 1858), a daughter of the Earl of Shrewsbury, who married Prince Filippo Andrea Doria Pamphilj.

Thus, the British author Augustus Hare notes the English connection of the Doria Pamphilj, and in fact the head of the house has married a British spouse ever since. The current Prince Jonathan and his sister were English children adopted by the late Princess Orietta and her husband Frank Pogson. In numerous ways the family has nurtured its links to the English-speaking world. Many British and Americans have lived in the Palazzo Doria Pamphilj downtown (which also houses the Anglican Centre, representing the Archbishop of Canterbury and the Anglican Communion in Rome). Other British lived in the Villa Doria Pamphilj as long as it was family property. See above (p. 177, Note 7) for a reference to Marion "Babs" Johnson (pseudonym Georgina Masson), who lived first downtown in the Palazzo and then in the Villa Corsini.

In the 1960's, Academy scholar Berthe Marti became acquainted with Babs Johnson, and through Berthe's connection some of us visited Ms. Johnson's flat, which had been created in the former stables of the Villa Corsini, on its lower, western end. A path through a *pineta* and down a drive led to the stone-paved court before Ms. Johnson's door. Inside, the large space was a bit dark and the furniture heavily upholstered, but Johnson's beloved German shepherd Willy assured lively atmosphere.

In the summer of 1966, Professor Marti "housesat and dogsat" for Ms. Johnson. Berthe's idea for exercising Willy was to drive in her VW through the villa park at wild speed, with Willy running alongside the car. I never learned if Willy was used to galloping in this strenuous way beside Ms. Johnson's Morris Minor. But I well recall the landscape flying past (Berthe liked to have a passenger on these whirlwind tours), the late afternoon light – a deserted country park that could be a painting by Corot come to life. So romantic and idyllic were the pines, ilexes, and the wide-spreading lawns.

Visits to the Villa by Academy folk go back to the first years of our residence on the Janiculum. In his diary entry for February 26, 1917, Gorham Stevens mentions "Base-ball in the Doria Pamphili." (The February date might suggest that Academy Fellows were homesick for reports of Spring Training?). On March 29, 1918, Stevens wrote that he took a walk in the Doria Pamphilj, and on May 20, 1921, he drove William Kendall through the Villa. A partner in McKim, Mead & White and trustee of the Academy, Mr. Kendall always received ceremonial treatment on his regular visits to Rome.

In 1969-70, the Academy had, I recall, twelve passes to the Villa. Most after-noons we would gather at tea in the Academy *salone* and then move on to the Villa. At the entrance our identities were sternly checked by a formidable and large *portiera*. Once into the park, some of us would run (for instance, Ken Worley, Mike Werner, Hugh Lee, Anna Marguerite McCann, and Elaine Gazda), but Patty Waddy and I would walk. I remember the cold dankness rising from the ground, the crunchy pebbles on the carriageways, and the slanted, pale light coming through the pines. We seemed the only persons in a limitless landscape, except for teams of English schoolboys playing their games on the broad level lawn west of the Casino.

This tranquil scene was, however, not undisturbed. Reports reached us that in the night thieves frequently scaled the villa walls and stole works of art, especially heads from sculpture in the park. And indeed we observed the creeping vandalism, the devastating harm to pieces we liked to pass on our walks. Anna Marguerite, in par-ticular, was deeply concerned that a head of Diocletian she admired not be damaged.

Those memorable visits occurred almost in the last days that the Villa was still a private princely domain. The transition to public property has blessed Monteverde with wonderful space to exercise, play, and relax, but destruction of the sculpture in the park has continued at heartbreaking pace.

REFERENCES

Capodiferro, Alessandra., ed. *Georgina Masson 1912-1980,* AAR exhibition catalogue (Milan, 2003).
See especially 14-20 for Milton Gendel's comments on Masson's (i.e., Johnson's) home in the Villa Pamphilj and her dog Willy ("an overweening outsized yellow cur . . . the Abominable Willy," but clearly the center of Ms. Johnson's home life).
Hare, Augustus J. C. *Walks in Rome,* 17th ed (New York, n.d.), 746-47. The first printing of this book appeared in 1871; the seventeenth edition was issued by 1897, when the first owner of my copy inscribed his name in it.
Masson, Georgina (Marion Johnson). *The Companion Guide to Rome* (London, 1965), 88-90.
Stevens, Gorham Phillips. Diary 1911-1932 (unpublished; held by the Library of the American Academy).
Stevens was Director of the Academy 1911-12, head of the school of Fine Arts 1913-17, and Director of the Academy after the death of Director Carter in 1917, until 1932.

Fig. 21. 1. The road from Piazza San Pancrazio
and Via Vitellia up to the Church of San Pancrazio,
with the façade of the church in the background.
Photograph, K. A. Geffcken, 2004.

CHAPTER 21

THE CHURCH OF SAN PANCRAZIO

Katherine Geffcken

On returning to Rome in May 2004, I noticed a banner hanging on the gate of the Church of San Pancrazio, proclaiming the seventeen hundredth anniversary of Pancrazio's martyrdom. I had just missed the saint's big *festa* on May 12, but a small exhibition was still on view in the right aisle. And so, on a lovely Saturday morning, I went to see it. For me, passing through the early seventeenth century gate and walking up the tranquil, shady road to the church always has a calming effect [fig. 21. 1].

On that Saturday inside the church a happy and relaxed wedding was in progress. Several hundred guests were sitting in the central nave, but many others were stretching their legs in the side aisles, and moving outside to talk on their cell phones and smoke. In the left chapel, a young mother was nursing her baby. A small band and three vocalists offered pop music during pauses in the liturgy. One woman I encountered in the left aisle stopped singing along with the vocalists long enough to remark, with some exasperation, that this was a church always in *restauro*. Indeed, both the side aisles have scaffolding and give the appearance of restoration in suspension. Such seems true of San Pancrazio throughout its history, the latest disaster being the collapse of a section of roof in the left aisle in 2001.

An advantage of stopping in during a wedding was that all the lights were on, making it easier to see the *mostra,* which traced the history of the church through old maps, prints, and photographs. Modern images recorded the life of San Pancrazio since it became a parish in 1931. On view, too, were inscriptions from ancient burials in the area and architectural fragments from earlier periods of the building.

Also featured, of course, were depictions and accounts of the martyr Pancratius, who mostly appears as a young warrior holding a shield and spear or sword and standing on a dragon. At first glance, one would think him St. George. But the texts of his "passion" do not identify him as a soldier or dragon-killer. Traditionally, he is described as a fourteen-year-old Phrygian, who, because he forcefully declared his Christian faith before the Emperor Diocletian, suffered beheading on May 12, 304. His body was discarded, it seems, along the Via Aurelia, but then retrieved by a Roman matron named Octavilla (Piazza and Via Ottavilla are named for her). 181

Apparently, she buried the young martyr on her own property between Via Aurelia and Via Vitellia. In the next centuries, Pancratius's grave became an important goal for pilgrims in Rome [see map, fig. 20. 1]. We must imagine crowds proceeding to the church from the northwest on the Via Aurelia or from the city out Porta San Pancrazio. By the sixth century, the Porta Aurelia had become known as Porta San Pancrazio. Such numbers of pilgrims would have especially thronged the church in the heyday of the cult, the fifth, sixth, and seventh centuries.

Barely anything is really known about this prominent Roman martyr. Accounts of his life and death are romantic creations, originating in the period of his great popularity and drawing from other *passiones* like that of St. Sebastian. But most likely, a young Phrygian who sought out an opportunity to confess his faith before the authorities and died for his belief was buried among the tombs, probably above ground, in the area where the church now stands. His eastern origin would coincide with evidence for other burials discovered close by, which show in names and terminology a link with the East. An inscription, for example, commemorating a man named Botrys, in the catacomb below the church, proclaims Botrys as *Christianos*, and the architecture of the cubicula in his section of the catacomb contains Asiatic characteristics. Furthermore, references in Trasteverine burials to *pneumatikoi* suggest the ecstatic practices of heretical Montanists, who originated in Phrygia.

The date of Pancratius's death is, however, problematical. Diocletian was in Rome only briefly, in the late fall of 303. Even more significant is the statement in the *passio* that Pancratius and his uncle and guardian Dionysius were converted by Pope Cornelius (251-253). While Diocletian had become, in traditional accounts, the classic persecutor of Christians without end, Cornelius seems a more telling reference. Thus, Pancratius may, in fact, have died in the middle of the third century. In any case, other martyrs appear to have been interred in the same area, and over time extensive catacombs were carved out of the tufa below, but no other burial attracted such devotion as that shown to Pancratius. Just why remains mysterious. Perhaps the saint's curious role as punisher of perjurers, to which I will return below, may explain his popularity.

This territory between Via Vitellia and Via Aurelia had long contained tombs. In 1933-34, when old pavement in the church was removed, foundation walls of columbaria dating to the first century were observed not far below the church floor.[1] In addition, an ancient road ran diagonally beneath the nave, possibly the Clivus Rutarius, which linked the Aurelia and Vitellia. Further tombs lie under the open space in front of the church. Two of the numerous catacombs tunneled under the neighborhood have entrances within the nave of the church, but these cannot be visited because of cave-ins.

Pancratius's tomb must soon have been protected with fencing, or maybe within a small martyrium. The first recorded structure to honor the saint was, however, built by Pope Symmachus (498-514), not over the tomb but somewhere near it. That Symmachus also constructed baths at the site reflects the need to serve many dusty, weary pilgrims. In the century following Symmachus's reign, surviving inscriptions

FAR LEFT

Fig. 21. 2. In the summer of 2005, fresh repairs were well advanced on the façade of San Pancrazio. Note the central door, with scaffolding. A banner showing the saint in armor adorns the scaffolding. Photograph, K. A. Geffcken, 2005.

LEFT

Fig. 21. 3. A column from Honorius's basilica, now standing in Paizza San Pancrazio. The column is topped with the tower of the De Torres cardinals and a cross. Photograph, K. A. Geffcken, 2004.

demonstrate that devout Christians wished to be buried near the saint.

Aldo Nestori (1960) argued that Symmachus's church could be known from evidence visible in the current structure. On the other hand, Richard Krautheimer (1967) demonstrates that while the church has been repaired or rebuilt repeatedly, from the eighth century to the present day [fig. 21. 2], we can indeed still grasp the great basilica built by Pope Honorius I (625-38), but not Symmachus's earlier church. Masonry in the transepts, apse, and near the façade dating to Honorius's time prove that the enormous length of the basilica we see today is Honorius's : 55.50 meters long. For its time, this size was extraordinary, recalling, Krautheimer writes (173), the great basilicas of the late fourth and early fifth centuries. The honor so paid to Pancratius places him, in the seventh century, among the most significant Roman martyrs.[2]

Honorius's church was much sunnier than the dark building we now visit. Its clerestory then had eleven windows on each side, as well as windows in the apse and transepts. Its central nave was a meter wider, and ten columns on the left and ten on the right supported the arcaded clerestory walls. Today two columns on each side, still quite possibly *in situ* from Honorius's time, separate the chancel from the transept chapels. The annular crypt beneath the raised chancel imitates that at St. Peter's and definitely survives from Honorius's basilica. In fact, sources indicate that Honorius moved Pancratius's body to the new *confessio* under the high altar.

I enjoyed looking for the columns of Honorius's building, all spoils from earlier structures. Nestori (227) claims to have located 18 out of the original 24. I have seen those in easy view: one in Piazza San Pancrazio [fig. 21. 3], one in the driveway up to the church, two reused on either side of the central door, one split lengthwise into shafts to decorate the sides of the lateral front doors, the four in the chancel, and the handsome, fluted pavonazzetto column set up in the nave to hold the Paschal candle. Nestori saw others, whole or in pieces, in the church property and in a loggia in Villa Pamphilj. These in the Villa seem to me good possibilities, in height and diameter. Most of the columns are gray granite, but cipollino and gray marble were also employed, in addition to the one pavonazetto column. A variety of capitals rest on the columns.

A striking characteristic of the four columns in the chancel is the large square socle placed, as an impost, above each capital. According to Krautheimer, such an arrangement would not have occurred after the seventh century, when impost blocks became outmoded (164). In the nave, the pavonazetto column instead sits properly on its socle.

San Pancrazio was perhaps at its most splendid peak in 1249 when Abate Ugone embellished it with cosmatesque inlays. In particular, he erected a magnificent ambo, for reading the epistle, on the right in the nave, and another, larger ambo on the left for delivery of the gospel. These had borders of gold and colored stones, combined with large panels and disks of porphyry and intricate details sculpted in the white marble. In the war of 1798, French troops ripped these apart. Some pathetic fragments are now mounted in the left aisle on a pillar. The French also broke into the relics of S. Pancrazio, tossed them out, and stole precious decoration from the reliquary.[3] Indeed, they left the church in almost total ruin (templum . . . direptum expilatum. . . see Krautheimer, 157). The building suffered again from human desecration and also cannon balls in 1849.

The basilica we visit today is dominated by Cardinal De Torres's early seventeenth century renovations. Lodovico De Torres, a Roman descendant of a great Spanish family, was archbishop of Monreale, made cardinal in 1606, then appointed head of the Vatican Library. After his death in 1609, his projects at San Pancrazio were completed by his nephew Cardinal Cosimo De Torres.[4] Evidence of the De Torres family is everywhere: the carved tower, their emblem, atop the column in Piazza San Pancrazio, and in relief on the keystones of gates, and in the magnificent coffered wooden ceilings. In the nave, Lodovico replaced Honorius's columns with five gigantic pillars on either side, and he reopened the side aisles, which had been walled off in the fifteenth century. The clerestory surfaces, their windows eliminated, were decorated later in the seventeenth century with putti and garlands in stucco. Antonio Tempesta frescoed the upper chancel walls, and on the exterior façade, doors and windows were redone.

Among newer additions is the marble baptismal font now in the left transept chapel. Elegantly simple, it was brought to San Pancrazio from SS. Celso and Giuliano, near Ponte Sant' Angelo, after the latter church ceased to be a parish. It derives importance from being the font at which Eugenio Pacelli (Pius XII) was baptized on 4 March, 1876.

I mentioned above that St. Pancratius acquired a role as avenger of false oaths.

The Saint's power was apparently quick and dramatic, as several accounts attest. Before even reaching the chancel, the perjurer would become a raving maniac or fall down dead on the spot (see, for instance, Jacopo de Voragine [thirteenth century], *The Golden Legend,* as "Englished" by William Caxton [1470] [London, 1900], 182-84.) As I watched the wedding that fresh summer morning, I wondered if the couple were aware of the saint's interest in vows and oaths. Clearly their pledges were all made in good faith, as both continued to the end of the ceremony in glowing health.[5]

REFERENCES

Cecchelli, Carlo. *Monumenti Cristiani-Eretici di Roma* (Rome, 1944).

Cecchelli, Margherita. *S. Pancrazio: Le Chiese di Roma Illustrate* 124 (Rome, 1972).

Crook, John. *The Architectural Setting of the Cult of Saints in the Early Christian West* (Oxford, 2000).

D'Achille, Anna Maria. "La Basilica di San Pancrazio: Via Aurelia Miliario Secundo," in *Le Virtù e I Piaceri in Villa,* ed. Carla Benocci (Milan, 1998), 21-35.

Franchi de' Cavalieri, Pio. "Della Leggenda di S. Pancrazio Romano," *Studi e Testi* 19 (1908), 77-105.

Guérin, P. *Les Petits Bollandistes* 15 (Paris, 1883), 487-89.

Krautheimer, Richard, Spencer Corbett, and Wolfgang Frankl. *Corpus Basilicarum Christianarum Romae: The Early Christian Basilicas of Rome* III. (Rome, New York, 1967), 153-74.

Nestori, Aldo. "La Basilica di San Pancrazio in Roma," *Rivista di Archeologia Cristiana* 36 (1960), 213-48, and plates I-IV.

NOTES

1 In 1933-34, professional excavation unfortunately did not take place. The floor was quickly repaved, and an opportunity for careful exploration lost.

2 The phenomenal popularity of Pancratius is astounding. So many of his relics were distributed that surely a miraculous "reproduction" took place (*Petits Bollandistes* 488). As early as the sixth century his relics were requested from abroad. His name appeared in Europe in many forms: Pancrazio, Pancrace, Brancas, Brancaccio, Blancat, Planchas, Planchais, Planchers, Plancart, Crampas, Cranpace, Brachs, Branchais, Blanchars, Blanse, and most important for English speakers, Pancras. His popularity in Britain originates with St. Augustine's foundation of a church dedicated to St. Pancras at Canterbury, ca. 600. Augustine's interest in Pancras may derive from his time as prior in Gregory the Great's monastery on the Caelian. Pancratius seems connected with the Caelian. He and his uncle Dionysius are said to have lived there. M. Cecchelli (40, n. 8) suggests that by the sixth century, there may have been an oratory of the martyr on the Caelian.

3 The head of Pancratius has been returned to San Pancrazio from the Lateran, where in 1308 it is said to have dripped with blood.

4 The De Torres cardinals, as well as the earlier Abate Ugone, are remembered in modern street names in Monteverde.

5 I learned at San Pancrazio that the State now owns the basilica and is responsible for upkeep of the structure. The parish is served by discalced Carmelites, who first arrived there in 1662. Previously, the religious of Sant' Ambrogio had been in residence, and before them, Cistercians (1257-1430). For over 600 years, Benedictines were in charge, installed there by Gregory the Great (590-604). Gregory is reported as founder of the monastery attached to the right side of the church, originally named St. Victor (San Vittore). This monastery is now owned by the Daughters of St. Mary of Providence, and operated as a home for elderly convalescent women, the Casa di S. Pio X. The receptionist nun proudly described to me her institution and their restoration of the monastery, between moments of intently watching the Olympics on her television set.

Fig. 22. 1. The equestrian statue of Garibaldi atop the Monument on Piazzale Garibaldi above the site of the former Casino. Photograph, B. Goldman, 2003.

Fig. 22. 2. Part of the northeastern façade of the Casino Riario-Corsini *pianterreno*. The cannon emerges at noon from the central door onto its firing platform. Note the tourists on the Piazzale Garibaldi above admiring the view. Photograph, K. A. Geffcken, 1997.

CHAPTER 22

THE CASINO RIARIO-CORSINI, QUEEN CHRISTINA, AND THE FATE OF THE GIARDINI CORSINI

Katherine A. Geffcken

T he cannon shot off at noon from the Janiculum is a familiar sound in Roman daily life, but probably few people know more than that it comes from somewhere close to Piazzale Garibaldi, [fig. 22. 1], from the mass of trees that here and there block the spectacular view.[1] In fact, the cannon is housed in the surviving *pianterreno* of the Casino Riario-Corsini, on which the east corner of Piazzale Garibaldi rests [fig. 22. 2]. The casino as a free-standing structure was doomed when the equestrian statue of Garibaldi [fig. 22. 1] was set in place behind it in 1895.[2] Just six years before, the casino had been reconstructed in pretentious pseudo-Gothic style as a *Vedetta Apennina* (a lookout toward the Apennines). In its brief existence, the *Vedetta* lured many to its upper floor for the magnificent panorama. But since it detracted from the design of the Garibaldi monument, the City in 1899 authorized destruction of its tower and upper floor and the leveling of the *piazzale* forward to the east, with the ground floor to support the front of the belvedere. The casino had been built in a slight dip in the Janiculum ridge and just a bit down the eastern slope from the highest ground [fig. 22. 3]. With the new terracing, the midpoint of the *passeggiata* became a large level space buttressed by retaining walls on the east and the Papal Wall on the west.

The Casino Riario-Corsini (not to be confused with the Casino Corsini dei Quattro Venti outside the walls[3]), though altered from time to time, dated back more than three hundred years. It was the topmost element in properties on the right bank of the Tiber that members of the Riario family assembled in the Renaissance. These holdings stretched from the Via della Lungara to the Janiculum summit. In 1511, along the Via della Lungara, Cardinal Raffaele Riario constructed a *palazzo* on a *vigna* he had acquired in 1492 (Borsellino 24). One hundred years later, in 1593 (1592 in one document), *abate* Galeazzo Riario purchased from the Odescalchi the casino and *vigna* located above on the Janiculum, this property extending from the *vigna* of the Casino Farnese (in the Villa Aurelia garden) to the boundary of the Villa Lante (Borsellino 22). Thus, by 1593, the Riario possessed the magnificent expanse from the *palazzo* on the Via della Lungara through the gardens and vineyards up to the casino on the top of the hill.

Among many notable persons who leased these properties, the most intrigu-

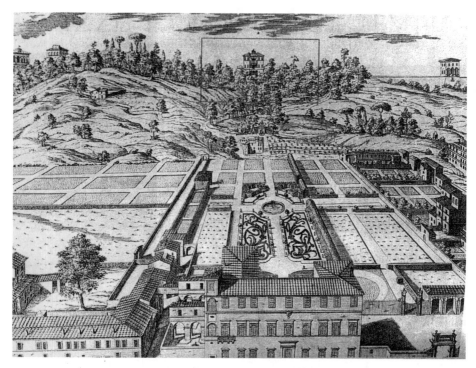

Fig. 22. 3. Perspective view showing the Riario-Corsini property from the Via Lungara (foreground) up to the Casino Riario, probably about 1741. The square drawn on the *veduta* draws attention to the Casino Riario. The view shows the Palazzo Riario before redesigning and enlarge- ment by Ferdinando Fuga. On the ridge of the Janiculum appear, from left to right, Villa Aurelia, Casino Farnese (now lost, see Chapter 14), Casino Riario (in the center), and Villa Lante at the far right. From Barcham, 488, Fig. 35.

ing was Christina, Queen of Sweden [fig. 22. 4], who lived in the casino from July 1659 to 1663 (with time away from Rome in 1660-1662), while the *palazzo* underwent renovations to ensure its suitability to her rank and tastes. Then, from 1663 until her death in 1689, Christina and her court occupied the *palazzo*. By this period in her Roman career she needed some distance from the downtown city. Christina was not always an easy guest. After her conversion to Catholicism and abdication of the Swedish throne, she had been welcomed at Rome with triumphal ceremony in 1655.

But with her strong personality, independent ways, political schemes, and lavish living, she soon became an embarrassment to the Pope. When she arrived for her second stay in 1658, Pope Alexander VII even suggested she not live in Rome (Masson 299). But Cardinal Decio Azzolino, with whom Christina was by now deeply infatuated, patched up her relations with the Pope and arranged for her leasing the Riario property, thus removing her almost into *villeggiatura*. There Christina's court became a center for the arts, for music and conversation, and for appreciation of her splendid collection of paintings and sculpture.[4]

A perspective view [fig. 22. 3], dated variously from the last quarter of the sev-

Fig. 22. 4. Portrait of Queen Christina by Sébastien Bourdon 1652 or 1653 when Bourdon spent a year at the court in Sweden. Later images of Christina portray her in male garb. Photograph, Swedish National Museum.

Fig. 22. 5. This section of the Falda map 1676 shows the Casino Riario on the left with four garden plots behind it.

enteenth century to approximately 1741,[5] shows the layout of the *palazzo*, garden, and casino. Dense natural growth and trees on the hillside cut by a driveway winding back and forth to the top contrast with the axial formality of the gardens below. The casino had two upper stories with many windows from which to enjoy the view. It had its own surrounding terracing and, as Falda's plan of Rome (1676) shows, there was a formal garden behind with a gate opening onto the road running just inside the Papal Wall [fig. 22. 5].

Georgina Masson lists some of the plantings specified in Queen Christina's lease of the Riario properties: spring bulbs, "pergolas of jasmin [*sic*] and secret gardens filled with orange and lemon trees . . ." (Masson 303).

In addition to her passion for politics, philosophy, and the arts, Christina liked gardens. Masson evokes "the languorous heat of a Roman summer" when in July 1659 the Queen moved into the casino. It had "only nine rooms [on the upper floors?] but it also had its own enclosed gardens filled with the music of fountains and the scent of orange and lemon blossom . . . this romantic little house, hidden away among the ilex groves . . ." (303-04). With the long views of Rome below and cool Janiculum breezes, Christina and her court lived a cultivated life in their *villeggiatura*.

In 1736, Cardinal Neri Corsini and his brother, Prince Bartolomeo III, acquired this entire stretch of Riario property from the Lungara to the Janiculum. Though adaptations had been made in the *palazzo* over the years, the Corsini architect Ferdinando Fuga extensively renovated and enlarged the building, thus producing the façade we see today on the Lungara. But as the Corsini primarily lived at Florence, the *palazzo* was often leased. Finally, in 1872, as the real estate boom hit the new national capital Rome, *Principe* Tommaso Corsini prepared to sell this Trastevere property, commissioning his Roman agent Paolo Pollastri to draw up plans. Pollastri's plan and elevation of the casino show that by this time the house was L-shaped with a ground floor of service rooms and a single upper story of four vaulted rooms, one with a loggia on the northeast façade (Borsellino 234). In the early nineteenth century, the house had undergone some drastic changes. The architect Giacomo Palazzi had removed the west section of the casino and the upper floor in 1810-1811 (Borsellino 22), so that viewed from the east the house had become broader and squatter. In the 1849 bombardments, it had suffered only minor damage because the Italian defenders had not placed a trench or artillery between the house and the Papal wall. The French concentrated their fire instead on Porta San Pancrazio, Villas Aurelia and Spada, and Casino Malvasia.[6]

Pollastri's plans as well as nineteenth century photographs demonstrate that the casino was not axially aligned with the gardens and *palazzo* below. From its beginning it had obviously been oriented to give a wide panorama of views, to Mt. Soracte and the Sabine Hills on the northeast side and to the Alban Hills on the southeast. Numerous nineteenth century *vedute* of Rome and especially of the Corsini property below were drawn from its loggia or from the terrace in front of the casino (Borsellino figs.100-103, 108). In many of these, the irregularly shaped terrace and parapet just in front of the casino appear in the foreground. This terracing survives today in front of the *pianterreno* wall. To the south side of the terrace one print (Borsellino fig. 100) includes the *pozzo* seen in Pollastri's plan.

After these Corsini properties were sold in 1883, the boundary line between the part below, bought by the State, and the remainder above, purchased by the City, was set at an unfortunate level. Had the dividing fence [fig. 22. 6] been placed just fifteen feet higher on the hill, the elegant niche at the top of the Corsini gardens would not have been cut off from the rest of the gardens below and thus left to vandalism. Situated about thirty feet

Fig. 22. 6. The niche of the Giardini Corsini showing the fence that separates the property of the City and that of the State. Photograph, K. A. Geffcken, 1997.

below the casino terrace, this tall niche included a large togate statue placed on a funeral cippus (CIL VI. 3513, once in Queen Christina's collection). The cippus is still in place, but the statue fell from its pedestal about 1970 and has since disappeared (Borsellino 66). Today, garbage litters the walk on the *Comune* side just in front of the niche.

On taking over the Corsini gardens, both the State and the City (but most of all the City) set about destroying the magnificent ilexes and pines. Already in the twelfth edition of his *Walks in Rome*, Augustus Hare commented on "the fury of the Government against trees" (II. 478-479), and in his seventeenth edition (1905) he wrote, "Instead of preserving the magnificent avenues of immemorial ilexes (the finest in the world except those of Albano), to give dignity to their drive along the Janiculan, the authorities, with the hatred of trees till quite lately usual here, at once ordered their destruction. The injury to Rome was so great that the Queen of Italy was induced to go in person to intercede in their behalf, but was told that it was useless, as the trees were already sold for firewood! It was under these trees that Queen Christina delighted to preside over . . . [recitations of poetry]."[7]

Just below the top of the slope, some of the original great ilexes do survive, and below, the properties owned by the State are, for the most part, beautifully maintained as the Orto Botanico of La Sapienza. But as the late Carlo Pietrangeli pointed out, the designs of a garden such as the Riario-Corsini and of a botanical garden are antithetical (in de Vico Fallani, 10). The splendid

Fig. 22. 7. Le Undici Fontane, Villa Corsini, in 2001. This water display was called "the eleven fountains" because, when it was in full operation, five jets rose on either side and a high jet rose in the center at the top. The system has now only a modest jet at the top, which trickles down the levels, but all is much cleaner than when I first photographed it in 1997. Photograph, K. A. Geffcken.

parterres have been replaced by exotic plantings, many interesting in themselves. High up and hidden away are an incongruous Japanese teahouse, pool, and garden. Though paths and lawns are well maintained, major elements of the Corsini design, such as La Scalinata delle Undici Fontane [fig. 22. 7], have been left to disintegrate, overgrown and full of slime (see Borsellino figs. 87-89).[8]

As for the casino at the top, several projects were proposed in the late nineteenth century for its restoration and enlargement.[9] But the City's selection of P. E. DeSanctis's design to rework it as a Gothic castle was bizarre. The surviving *pianterreno* does not suggest an attractive building, even though the view from its upper story was as dazzling as what we see today from Piazzale Garibaldi — if we can ignore the ever-growing row of tawdry souvenir stalls doing business near the belvedere. Better to imagine Queen Christina's *serate* in this garden high above Rome and to admire the dense old ilexes below the parapet that survive from the Corsini *gran macchia*.

◈ REFERENCES

Ai Caduti per Roma MDCCCXLIX-MDCCCLXX (Rome, 1941).

Berggren, Lars, and Lennart Sjöstedt. *L'Ombra dei Grandi: Monumenti e Politica Monumentale a Roma (1870-1895)* (Rome, 1996).

Borsellino, Enzo. *Palazzo Corsini alla Lungara: Storia di un Cantiere* (Rome / Fasano, 1988).

Catalano, Mario, and Ezio Pellegrini. *L'Orto Botanico di Roma* (Rome, 1975).

Christina, Queen of Sweden, Exhibition Catalogue (Stockholm, 1966).

Coffin, David R. *Gardens and Gardening in Papal Rome* (Princeton, 1991).

de Vico Fallani, Massimo, *Storia dei Giardini Pubblici di Roma nell'Ottocento* (Rome, 1992).

Frutaz, A. P. *Le Piante di Roma III* (Rome, 1962).

Gigli, Laura. *Guide Rionali di Roma: Rione XIII Trastevere, Parte I*. 2nd ed. (Rome, 1980).

Hare, Augustus. *Walks in Rome*, 12th ed. (London, n.d.).

Hare, Augustus. *Walks in Rome*, 17th ed. (London, 1905).

Masson, Georgina, *Queen Christina* (New York, 1968/69).

◈ NOTES

1 Instituted by the Papal government in the nineteenth century, the cannon was first fired from Castel Sant'Angelo, then from Monte Mario, and beginning in 1904 from the Casino Riario-Corsini.

2 On the politics connected with the Garibaldi monument and the decision to place it in the Janiculum park, see Berggren and Sjöstedt 83-94, 218-19, 239-41, 262-67, esp. 218-19.

3 On the Casino Corsini dei Quattro Venti, see pp. 16-21. Corsini ownership of the Quattro Venti property preceded acquisition of the land extending from Via della Lungara.

4 Another notable tenant of the casino was Federico Cornaro (1579-1653), who in 1645 paid a lifetime rent to Ferdinando Riario (see William L. Barcham, *Grand in Design: the Life and Career of Federico Cornaro, Prince of the Church, Patriarch of Venice, and Patron of the Arts* [Venice, 2001], 310, 398, 402, and figs. 34, 35).

5 The exhibition catalogue *Christina, Queen of Sweden*, 319-20, attributes this view to G. B. Falda, within Christina's lifetime, but D. R. Coffin dates it later, early in the period of Corsini ownership (ca. 1741) because of the French influence in the garden design (Coffin 123). The view shows the *palazzo* before Fuga's reworking and extending the structure.

6 The panoramic drawing by G. Thomas, engraved by W. Mason, and published May 4, 1850 in the *London Illustrated News*, shows the casino standing with no major damage (reproduced in *Ai Caduti* opposite p. 320).

7 For the hundreds and hundreds of oaks, ilexes, elms, etc. removed from the Corsini heights in 1883 to clear the new Passeggiata, see de Vico Fallani 245.

8 On a return visit to the garden in August 2001, I saw that the Undici Fontane have been cleaned up. There is still a great deal of moss, but the design of the stepped fountains is clearer. Only gentle trickles of water move down. To bring them back to their original exuberant sprays would doubtless require replacing *calcare*-jammed pipes. And of course the ornamental sculpture and urns are long gone.

9 For many nineteenth and twentieth century projects for the Janiculum (fortunately never realized!), see J. Rasmus Brandt, "Roma Capitale e il Gianicolo. Progetti urbanistici nel cassetto," *Acta Instituti Romani Finlandiae* 16 (1996).

Cemetery of Santo Spirito

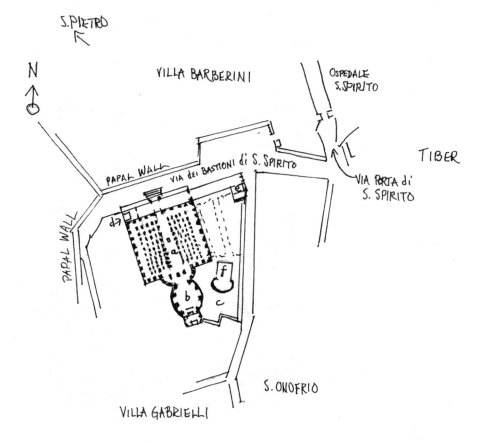

Fig. 23. 1. Plan of the Cimitero di Santo Spirito and environs. Drawing by K. A. Geffcken.

a: Cimitero di Santo Spirito

b: Capella di SS. Crocifisso

c. Terra Santa

d. Capella di S. Maria del Rosario (?)

e. Storerooms, etc., for Pia Unione

f. Theater

BURIALS ON THE JANICULUM:
THE CEMETERY OF SANTO SPIRITO

Katherine A. Geffcken

After the defeat of Garibaldi and the Italian forces at Rome in 1849, many dead lay on the field and in churches and hospitals. Some of these bodies were sent home to their families, but more than 3,000 were buried in the Cimitero di Santo Spirito, on the northern end of the Janiculum in a peaceful corner shaded by magnificent cypresses. This burial ground was not a military cemetery; it normally received the bodies of those who died at the Hospital of Santo Spirito below, near the Tiber. Over the last century, this cemetery has been so obliterated that, at first, traces are hard to find. Only the cypresses still flourish, seen above the wall protecting the Pontificia Universitas Urbaniana de Propaganda Fide. One description of the cemetery compared its evocative atmosphere to that of the Protestant Cemetery near the Pyramid of Cestius (Canezza 57), but at the latter, no such startling and macabre spectacles were staged as those that drew viewers to Santo Spirito during the November Octave of the Dead.

The original cemetery serving the Hospital of Santo Spirito was down on the Tiber bank, but frequent floods made the location far from hygienic. In the reign of Pope Benedict XIV, during the 1740's, the architect Ferdinando Fuga was commissioned to design an extension of the hospital and a new cemetery uphill in a *vigna* belonging to the hospital. This *vigna* stretched southwards from the high Papal Wall at the section known as the Bastion of Santo Spirito [fig. 23. 1]. For the cemetery, Fuga's plan dated 1745 shows an elegant open square enclosed by a high wall containing, on all sides, arched niches separated by pilasters. The square was oriented roughly northwest to southeast and was approached by a long *salita* that began where the Papal Wall makes a sharp turn west just outside the Porta Santo Spirito. This straight *salita* arrived at the main entrance of the cemetery, which was centered on the northwest side of the square, a travertine portal topped by the *stemma* of Benedict XIV. Recalling scenes of his childhood in the nineteenth century, Alessandro Canezza describes the *salita* as lined with mulberry trees and holm oaks, but earlier in the century Antoine Jean-Baptiste Thomas's lithograph shows it instead as a street full of wretched beggars accosting the approaching mourners and promising prayers for the dead in return for alms [fig. 23. 2].

Fig. 23. 2. The *Salita* to the Cemetery of Santo Spirito: Beggars and Mourners. To the left, the Bastion Santo Spirito, and at the bottom of the *Salita*, the Santo Spirito Hospital. From Antoine Jean-Baptiste Thomas, *Un An à Rome et dans ses Environs* (1823), Photograph, A. Ortolan from the facsimile edition (1971) in the Rare Book Room, American Academy in Rome.

On entering the cemetery, the visitor saw, opposite in the southeast wall, an exedra and entrance to a small, domed church. There is confusion in accounts about the name of this church. Two chapels were associated with the cemetery, the Capella del Crocifisso and the Capella di Santa Maria del Rosario. The best evidence names this original chapel at the head of the complex the Capella del Crocifisso, designed by Fuga. Above this southeastern wall rose Sant'Onofrio, higher on the Janiculum. Inside, the chapel nave held three altars on each side, set into recesses in the curved walls. Contrasting with the outward curving nave walls, the sanctuary extended in rectangular shape to the southeast.

In the open cemetery square there were, lined up in rows, 103 slabs with round metal rings for lifting, each covering a deep vaulted chamber below for the dead. In 1775, the Pia Unione della Beata Vergine del Rosario was granted responsibility for burying those who died at Santo Spirito. The Unione decorated the niches of the interior cemetery wall with paintings of the Stations of the Cross and other religious subjects and built a small oratorio, Santa Maria del Rosario, in the corridor on the entrance side of the cemetery. Then, in 1788, a triangle of land to the east of Fuga's cemetery was surrounded by a wall and also set aside for burials. Here, in this Terra

Santa, many families acquired, over time, their own burial areas (Canezza 59). Funeral monuments, trees and ivy made the Terra Santa a park-like spot. In this area were buried most of the 3,000 Italians (and also some of the French casualties) who died in the 1849 conflict.

Fig. 23. 3. Burial in the Cemetery of Santo Spirito: members of the Pia Unione prepare to lower a body into a vault, while in the right background other members say prayers above a shrouded body. From A. Thomas (above). Photograph, A. Ortolan.

The Pia Unione was not a confraternity in the usual sense, and in fact was the only such group to perform its duties in ordinary clothes and not in the usual hooded, long garment. Its members were mostly artisans and shopkeepers from all parts of Rome. Each evening, a half hour after darkness, no matter the weather, a team of the Unione gathered at the mortuary of the hospital. According to the practice at Santo Spirito, the dead had been left in their beds for two hours, then removed to the mortuary for twenty-four hours (Morichini 45).

In its sick wards, Santo Spirito was primarily a fever hospital for men.[1] In 1840, for example, it treated 18,759 patients in its 1,616 beds, and lost 1,490 of them, approximately four a day (Morichini 58). The Unione placed these dead, wrapped in a sheet, on a bed or barrow with long sides extending as handles, and then lifted these barrows onto a horse-drawn wagon. Preceded by a crucifer and priest and carrying torches, the Unione members led the wagon up the hill, chanting prayers and repeating *"Viva la Croce"* as they went. When the slab designated for the day was raised, they lowered the corpse, stripped of its sheet,[2] into the vault by a system of

Fig. 23. 4. Tableau of the Final Judgment at the cemetery of Santo Spirito, 1813. The vaults have been opened and bodies of the recently deceased displayed near the apertures. From A. Thomas (above). Photograph, A. Ortolan.

chains [fig. 23. 3]. This procedure continued daily until 1870, when new legislation forbade burials within the City. Indeed, Morichini, writing in 1842, describes the increasingly foul air at this part of the Janiculum caused by the daily opening of the vaults (Morichini 47). Even so, members of the Pia Unione and their families gathered for vespers at the cemetery on designated Sundays. Canezza, whose father was an officer of the Unione, movingly describes these Sunday trips to services in the chapel and visits at family graves in the Terra Santa.

In 1806, the Unione began to put its artistic talents to work by staging ghoulish pageants or tableaux during the Octave of the Dead in November. Antoine Jean-Baptiste Thomas depicted, in a lithograph, the "Final Judgment" of 1813, a horrible scene in which bodies of the recently dead are shown lifted out of the vaults or hanging in the vault openings, gazing toward heaven.[3] A wax angel suspended above them blows a trumpet and points skyward [fig. 23. 4]. In 1820 a theater was built in the Terra Santa to house these gruesome spectacles. Subjects presented in other years included the martyrdom of Santa Filomena, the martyrdom of Peter, and yet another pageant about Saint Peter illustrating the text *Tu es Petrus,* and involving nine life-size wax figures adorned with real hair and beards and wearing appropriate clothing (Negro 363).[4] These spectacles, as well as the nightly burials, seem to have attracted many curious tourists (Martinelli 77-78).

In 1891, plans were launched to relocate the hospital for the insane, then occupying a long building stretching along Via Lungara, the *Manicomio* (hospital for the insane) of Santa Maria della Pietà. The hospital authorities had already extended the *Manicomio* by installing a community for pensioners and "the tranquilly ill" in the Villa Barberini just on the north side of the Papal Wall and in the former Villa Gabrielli just to the south of the cemetery. But as the encroaching new Tiber embankments doomed the *Manicomio* itself to demolition, the cemetery was expropriated for a new asylum building. The last Sunday vespers at the cemetery took place in Lent of 1891, and the Unione then had the heavy task of transferring the burials by night to the new cemetery, Campo Verano. Canezza reports that from the original 103 vaults were extracted 60,000 intact skulls and that the total volume of bones measured more than 1,865.76 cubic meters. For a time, the Terra Santa was left untouched, and marbles and inscriptions remained in or near the site. But, in the end, the tunneling of the Traforo Principe Amadeo and the realignment of the Via del Gianicolo brought irreversible changes to the terrain. Despite care exerted to remove all burials, some bones were overlooked. As foundations were laid for later buildings, bones emerged from the soil.[5] Canezza reports that some monuments and epitaphs ended up in dumps and some at the Amministrazione Provinciale.

In 1914, the *Manicomio* moved to Monte Mario, and in 1925 the Congregation de Propaganda Fide acquired the property. The Congregation adapted the existing buildings, which had been built on foundations of the cemetery walls, and added further structures in 1929, 1931, and 1973. When I visited this campus of the Pontificia Universitas Urbaniana de Progaganda Fide in July, 1998, I was able to see the periphery of the old cemetery in the long façade and east and west wings of the former *Manicomio*. The old covered portico that extended northeast from the cemetery still exists, though much changed by later modifications. At roughly its midpoint, a small campanile marks the spot where, beneath, there had been a chapel, now converted into a cinema. This room does not seem to me, however, to be located on the site of the chapel of Santa Maria del Rosario, but is rather an adaptation of a middle section of the corridor. Yet, running in front of the buildings within the university grounds, a portion of the old *salita* does survive, now bordered with rows of pines and ilex. And though not *in situ* as described by Canezza, a gray granite column topped by a cross still stands in the grounds. Canezza recalled it placed in front of the theater in the Terra Santa, with a lamp perpetually lit before it (Canezza 59). But the lamp, with its white and turquoise glass windows, is no longer present.

⊠ ADDENDUM

The description above of the Pontificia Universitas Urbaniana remains valid (in 2001) within its own walls, but the northern Janiculum outside its gates has been forever changed by the new underground garage, built for the Papal Jubilee. Masses of earth under Monte S. Spirito and on the Janiculum slope have been moved, in fact revealing some new archaeological sites and destroying others.[6] The

Via del Gianicolo now has separate ascent and descent lanes, on either side of the *traforo* entrance. The new ascent, which skirts the S. Spirito bastion, was formerly a pedestrian walkway on the line of the old *salita* shown in Thomas's lithograph. The winding approaches to and exits from the garage have reduced to a small plot the park of Cardinal Antonio Francesco Orioli, which lay between Via Urbano VIII and Via del Gianicolo. The near loss of this little modern park is not serious (it was often littered with debris from the homeless who took refuge there), but the expropriation of the Orti Torlonia on the east side of the Via del Gianicolo has significantly changed the character of the northern Janiculum. These *orti* were quiet spots, a remnant of the rural Janiculum of earlier days. Behind slightly crumbling walls, an old man tended his fruit trees and goats. From the higher Parco Orioli you could look down on this scene, a half-abandoned landscape with its rustic sheds and vegetation. Now the garden has disappeared in a no-man's land of raw, bulldozed earth. For more information, see Lorenzo Bianchi, *Roma: Il Monte di Santo Spirito tra Gianicolo e Vaticano* (Rome, 1999), 205-12. Future plans announced in 2002 include redesigning a garden in the *orti*, to serve a new hotel located in the former Conservatorio Torlonia on Via Sant'Onofrio.[7]

▦ REFERENCES

Amadei, Emma. "Il Culto dei Morti nella Roma dell'Ottocento," *Capitolium* 32.11 (November, 1957), 27-29.

Armellini, M. *Le Chiese di Roma dal Secolo IV al XIX.* Rev. ed. C. Cecchelli (Rome, 1942), 806-07.

Canezza, Alessandro. "L'Ignoto Sepolcreto dei Caduti per Roma," in *Ai Caduti per Roma* MDCCCXLIX-MDCCCLXX (Roma, 1941), 57-62.

Colonna, Flavia. "L'Opera di Ferdinando Fuga nell' Ospedale di Santo Spirito in Saxia di Roma," in *Ferdinando Fuga: 1699-1999: Roma, Napoli, Palermo,* ed. A. Gambardella (Naples, 2001), 293-303, esp. 296-300 on the cemetery.

Fedeli Bernardini, Franca. *Tratti e [ri]Ritratti di un Manicomio* (Rome, 2003).

Gigli, Laura. *Guide Rionali di Roma: Rione XIII Trastevere, Parte I,* 2nd ed. (Rome,1980), 222-27.

Letarouilly, Paul. *Édifices de Rome Moderne* (1840, reprinted Princeton, 1982).

Martinelli, Vincenzo. *Dal Tevere al Gianicolo: L'Ospedale del Bambin Gesù tra Cronaca e Storia* (Rome, 1980).

Morichini, D. Carlo Luigi. *Degl'Istituti di Pubblica Carità ed Istruzione Primaria e delle Prigioni in Roma Libri Tre.* 2nd ed. (Rome, 1842). I. 35-60.

Negro, Silvio. *Seconda Roma, 1850-1870* (Milan, 1943), 362-64.

Pane, Roberto. *Ferdinando Fuga.* Ed. R. Mormone (Naples, 1956).

Thomas, Antoine Jean-Baptiste. *Un An à Rome et dans ses Environs, recueil de dessins. . .* (Paris, 1823). Thomas (1791-1834) was at the French Academy, Villa Medici, from November 1816 to December 1818.

◈ NOTES

1 The hospital also housed an orphanage for babies deposited in its famous Ruota degli Esposti and dormitories for the *zitelle* (unwed females, many of whom had been abandoned as babies in the Ruota). The Ruota (wheel) was a turntable where abandoned infants (*esposti*) could be safely left to be taken in by the orphanage. A special section of the cemetery was designated for babies who died in the orphanage. There was also a clinic that treated both men and women.

2 Morichini, 47, says that the Pia Unione wrapped the body decently in *una veste nera* (a black garment or cloth covering). Thomas, in his lithograph, shows the body naked, but he may had chosen to do so in order to show a strapping male body limp in death.

3 As Thomas did not arrive in Rome until 1816, he must have reconstructed this spectacle of 1813 from eyewitnesses.

4 Emma Amadei, 29, notes that the Santo Spirito Cemetery often based its pageants on paintings, e.g., *The Resurrection of the Son of the Widow of Nain* (Luke 7.11-17) by G. B. Wicar (1762-1834).

5 I learned about the later finding of bones from personnel at the Propaganda Fide. In particular, I am grateful to the archivist of the university who showed me the inscription dated 1944, recording the cemetery and the removal of bones. Permission to walk in the Propaganda Fide grounds enabled me to understand the topography of the cemetery. For example, running along the modern Via Urbano VIII, the perimeter wall of the campus is a reworking of the old wall of the Terra Santa.

6 For an account of emergency excavations in the area of the Traforo Principe Amedeo and the Rampa Torlonia, see Carla Socrate and Sabina Ventura, "La Domus Imperiale sotto il Gianicolo," *Forma Urbis* 7.7/8 (July and August, 2002), 4-14. Also on future use of the Orti Torlonia and Conservatorio Torlonia and on the excavations, see Lilli Garrone, "Torlonia-Campidoglio, il patto del Gianicolo," *Corriere della Sera: Cronaca di Roma* (July 19, 2002), 43.

7 See Garrone (above, note 6).

Fig. 24. 1. Achille Pinelli, San Pietro in
Montorio, watercolor, 1833; Museo di Roma.
Photograph, Istituto Centrale per il Catalogo
e la Documentazione, E24516.

CHAPTER 24

SAN PIETRO IN MONTORIO, BRAMANTE'S TEMPIETTO, AND THE SPANISH CROWN

Jack Freiberg

Roma patria communis, the ancient dictum celebrating Rome as "common homeland," applies in a special way to Trastevere and the Janiculum hill, inhabited in antiquity by peoples from the farthest reaches of the empire. Today, the Janiculum hosts not only the American Academy, but also the Norwegian and Finnish Institutes, and the Spanish Academy, the last since 1876 accommodated in a portion of the monastery of San Pietro in Montorio. Spain's institutional presence on the Janiculum began in the 1480's when King Ferdinand of Aragon undertook the rebuilding of the preexisting monastery of San Pietro in Montorio on the present site [fig. 24.1]. The coat of arms of Ferdinand and his wife, Queen Isabel of Castile, appears prominently on the façade of the church and throughout the interior, while the names of later Spanish kings who continued that patronage are also present. The interest of the Spanish royals in San Pietro in Montorio was stimulated by the pious tradition identifying the site as the place where Saint Peter had been martyred by crucifixion. During the Middle Ages, this central act in the establishment of the Roman church was said to have occurred near the basilica Constantine the Great had built above the Apostle's grave at the Vatican. But in the mid-fifteenth century an alternative identification of the martyrdom with San Pietro in Montorio was introduced, and this subsequently gathered force, receiving the support of the popes and the faithful, including the kings of Spain.

The monastery occupies a scenic position commanding magnificent views of the city for which the Janiculum was famous in antiquity. Vestiges of ancient Roman construction beneath the monastery and in its immediate vicinity suggest that even in antiquity this was prized real estate. A religious foundation dedicated to Peter first appears in the literary record in the thirteenth century, but as early as the eighth century Peter was associated with that area of the hill. Notwithstanding its spiritual dignity, the monastery was no longer in use when Pope Sixtus IV took steps to revitalize it in 1472. In that year he ceded to his fellow Franciscan and personal confessor, Amadeo Menes de Sylva (d. 1482), the "monastery of San Pietro in Montorio in the Trastevere region of the city where it is said that Saint Peter, Prince of the Apostles, suffered martyrdom on the cross." In a later document the pope described the property as consisting of a church, monastic residence, cloister, unnamed buildings, stalls for animals, a garden, and a vineyard. Sixtus turned the complex over to Amadeo with the stipulation that the friar undertake its restoration.

Amadeo was born in Portugal of a noble family, his mother Portuguese, his father of Castilian descent, and in keeping with this dual heritage identified himself as *Hispano*, referring to the Roman province *Hispania* that encompassed the entire Iberian peninsula. In 1452 he arrived in Italy, joined the Franciscan brotherhood at Assisi, and developed a rigorous interpretation of the Observant reform that attracted numerous followers, especially in Lombardy. To further the expansion of his group, Amadeo solicited financial support from high-ranking sponsors, providing them in turn with spiritual aid. This was precisely the relationship he established with King Ferdinand of Aragon. In 1480 the king wrote to Amadeo announcing his intention "to found a votive church [dedicated] to Saint Peter in that place where the Prince of the Apostles was martyred." The king had previously assumed the vow in connection with Amadeo's assistance in assuring the birth of a son. By the date of the letter, Ferdinand and Isabel's heir, Juan, was two years old, having been born on June 30, 1478, the day following the feast of Saints Peter and Paul when the martyrdom of the Apostle is commemorated.

Construction of the church and monastery came in the following decades, supervised by the king's representatives in Rome. Despite the incomplete state of documentation, the letters Ferdinand wrote to his agents establish him as a fully engaged patron keenly aware of the project's importance for promoting the prestige of the Crown, even if financial resources were not always available to move the project to a speedy conclusion. He encouraged the agents to consider the friars' choice of an architect, reviewed financial accounts, and examined a plan of the church and monastery. In 1498, with works nearing completion, he expressed appreciation for the care with which the project had been pursued, declaring that it had brought him great merit and satisfaction. San Pietro in Montorio was consecrated in 1500 and two years later Bramante's famous Tempietto was founded on the presumed site of the Apostle's martyrdom.

The decoration of Ferdinand's church was far less opulent than what one sees today. During the sixteenth and seventeenth centuries San Pietro in Montorio became one of the most venerated sites in Rome, a status reflected in the splendid works of art commissioned by popes, cardinals, and high-ranking residents from many of the great masters of the age: Raphael's Transfiguration of Christ formerly on the high altar; a lost Stigmatization of Saint Francis painted on Michelangelo's design; Sebastiano del Piombo's robust Flagellation of Christ (also based on Michelangelo's drawings); and works by Vasari, Ammannati, and Bernini, among others. In an ironic twist, the fame of these artists and the prominence of the patrons, have made it difficult to recover the meaning the site originally held for the Spanish Crown, and to appreciate how that meaning was expressed in the architecture of both the church and the Tempietto.

THE CHURCH

As one looks toward the Janiculum from the city, the towering travertine facade of San Pietro in Montorio is conspicuous, silhouetted against the verdant backdrop, the first Renaissance monument to take full advantage of the prominent setting on the hill. Its position would have been even more impressive had Pope Paul V not built the colossal fountain of the Acqua Paola in the immediate vicinity (1612). This scenographic location was enhanced in the early seventeenth century when King Philip III funded the rebuilding of the terrace on which the church rises, added the double ramp stair leading to the single doorway into the church, and raised the fountain based on the royal coat of arms and known as *La Castigliana* (lost in the bombardment of 1849). When, however, the church was built by King Ferdinand in the late fifteenth century, it dominated the hill in austere isolation [fig. 24.2].

The position of San Pietro in Montorio on the crest of the Janiculum recalls the dramatic site occupied by the head church of the Franciscan order at Assisi. Elements of the architecture of San Francesco at Assisi had long been applied to the order's satellite foundations as a sign of spiritual affiliation. This source provided the model for several of the features distinguishing San Pietro in Montorio from other churches built in Rome during the same period, reinforcing the association with the Franciscans originally owed to Amadeo. As at Assisi, the façade of the Janiculum church is defined by a compact aedicula divided by two horizontal moldings that create three distinct levels, the whole crowned by a prominent pediment. Each level is distinguished by a central feature set in vertical alignment. On the interior of the church allusions to Assisi are amplified,

Fig. 24. 2. Giovanni Battista Falda, *Nuovo teatro delle fabriche et edificii, in prospettiva di Roma moderna* (Rome 1665-69), pt. 3, pl. 31. Photograph, Bibliotheca Hertziana, U. Pl. D19933.

CHIESA DEDICATA A S·PIETRO APOSTOLO, DETTA IN MONTEORIO SVL GIANICOLO DE PADRI REFORMATI DI SAN FRANCESCO .
Architettura di Bramante.

Gio·BattaFalda dis et fece   Per Gio Iacomo Rossi in Roma alla pace et Priu del S·Pont .

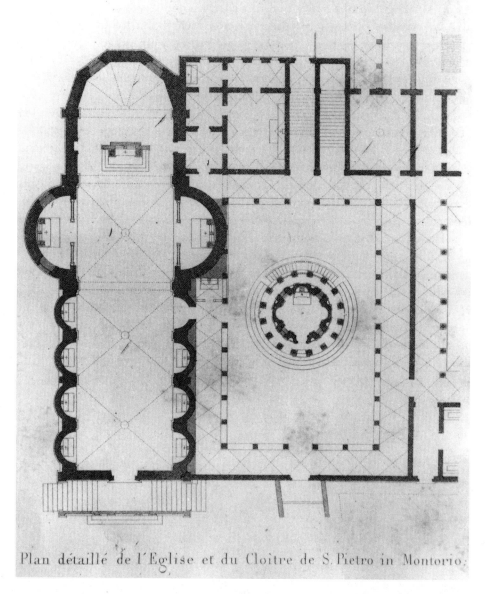

1. Fontaine aujourd'hui détruite.   2. Eglise S.Pietro in Montorio.   3. Entrée du Couvent

Plan détaillé de l'Eglise et du Cloître de S.Pietro in Montorio.

Fig. 24. 3. Plan of monastery of San Pietro in Montorio from Paul Marie Letarouilly, *Édifices de Rome moderne...* 6 vols. (Liege, 1849-66), plate vol. 3, pl. 44. Photograph, Bibliotheca Hertziana, U. Pl. D10749.

most directly at the liturgical core, where a polygonal apse consisting of five facets and crowned by a fan vault repeats the arrangement seen in the church dedicated to the order's founder [fig. 24.3].

Other architectural features address the dedication to the Apostle, which would have been meaningful to the Spanish royals no less than to the Franciscans. One recalls that support of the papal office was a central feature of the Franciscan mission, expressed for example in the famous episode when Pope Innocent III had a vision of the humble Francis supporting the Lateran basilica, the pope's episcopal church and Rome's cathedral. On the Janiculum, the extended choir, preceding the polygonal apse, recalls Pope Nicholas V's ambitious scheme of the 1450's, partially carried out, to rebuild the Constantinian apse of old Saint Peter's as a monumental aula for the majestic papal ceremonial. This Petrine reference is augmented by the eight apsidal chapels lining the nave of the church, four to a side, whose original semicircular contours were fully visible on the left flank before subsequent interventions produced the hodgepodge seen today. The motif of repeating extradossal apses along the flank of a church was introduced to Renaissance architecture by Brunelleschi, but its origins are found in the papal audience hall Pope Leo III constructed around 800 at the Lateran palace, which survived until dismantled in the late sixteenth century. The location at Rome's cathedral lent the Leonine hall particular authority, as did its function in the most august papal ceremonies.

The physical and conceptual nexus between the Franciscan and Apostolic themes expressed in the architecture of San Pietro in Montorio is provided by one of the most striking aspects of the structure, the dilated lateral apses that propel the discrete swelling rhythms of the nave chapels toward a dramatic culmination in the choir. The configuration is a variant of the so-called triconch that had a prestigious lineage beginning in antiquity, but is especially relevant here for its Christian use in churches and chapels serving as mausoleums. The martyrial aspect of the foundation where Peter was said to have been crucified is thus addressed, reinforcing the idea carried by allusions to the churches at Assisi and the Vatican, burial sites, respectively, of Francis and Peter.

The architect responsible for designing San Pietro in Montorio is unknown. Recent attention has focused on the attribution first proposed by Vasari in the sixteenth century to Baccio Pontelli, who is sometimes credited with construction of the bridge built by Sixtus IV to span the Tiber, giving access to Trastevere and the Janiculum from the city. It is probable that the design of the church was negotiated with Ferdinand's agents in Rome, and especially the Spanish-born Bernardino Carvajal, a significant patron in his own right. Judging from the surviving correspondence, the king seems to have participated as well. In an early letter concerning the project he advised that the church should balance the elevated nature of royal patronage with the ideals of humility and poverty followed by the Observant Franciscans. This paradoxical requirement of the commission was addressed by assimilating the majestic forms of official, papal architecture from the Vatican and Lateran to elements drawn from Francis's own church at Assisi.

THE TEMPIETTO

At the time San Pietro in Montorio was consecrated, during the Jubilee year of 1500, the spot identified with Peter's crucifixion, located in the cloister to the right of the church, lacked monumental architectural definition. By the mid-fifteenth century it was distinguished by two columns, the same ones now seen flanking the entrance to the crypt of the Tempietto on the interior. A radical redefinition of this sacred site came in 1502 with the foundation of Bramante's shrine, preceding by some years the architect's own grand design for rebuilding the Apostle's church at the Vatican. The names of Ferdinand and Isabel and the date 1502 are recorded on the ritual foundation stone, which came to light during renovations to

Fig. 24. 4. Bramante, Tempietto. Photograph, Bibliotheca Hertziana, U. Pl. D10880.

the crypt in 1628, and is today mounted on the forward face of the altar in the subterranean chapel.

The "little temple," as the shrine came to be called, is defined by a circular chamber surrounded by sixteen freestanding columns, surmounted by a hemispherical dome elevated on a drum pierced by windows [fig. 24.4]. The Doric entablature, here making its debut in Renaissance architecture, sports Christian liturgical vessels in the metopes. A balustrade joins the two levels and adds a festive touch to the ensemble, reminding one seventeenth century observer of a royal crown. The subtle play of the materials Bramante employed – grey granite Roman spoils for the shafts, white marble for the capitals and bases, and cream-colored travertine for the rest – animates this superb melding of horizontal and vertical elements, solids and voids. Had Bramante's plan to restructure the surrounding cloister with a circular, columned portico been realized, the sacred center where the cross of Peter was believed to have been planted in the earth would have been even more dramatically emphasized.

Bramante based the design in part on the peripteral tholos temple, a legacy of ancient Greece adopted by Roman architects for temples dedicated to, among other deities, Vesta and Hercules. Vitruvius's discussion of the type, and surviving examples such as the temple in the Forum Boarium, fueled the interest of the Renaissance. Nevertheless, construction of an edifice so reminiscent of the pagan world remained a purely theoretical proposition before the Tempietto. In the sixteenth century the Tempietto was praised in the highest terms and its reputation sealed by the claim first made by Sebastiano Serlio in 1537 and reiterated by others that with it Bramante had revived the principles of classical architecture. From the start artists studied every dimension of the shrine to fathom the splendor of antique architecture, now presented in an unfragmented and thus more perfect form. Even today, visitors to the Tempietto encounter aspiring architects earnestly studying the work, just as their Renaissance predecessors did.

The original political meaning of the Tempietto is less completely understood. A balanced assessment of Bramante's design that accounts for both the elevated status of its patrons and the spiritual meaning of the site requires attention to how the structure's marked classical features evoke Spain's own considerable contributions to ancient Rome. In this context, architectural sources sometimes considered in discussions of the Tempietto assume rich nuances of meaning. A case in point are the ruins of Hadrian's villa in Tivoli which Vasari claimed Bramante studied when first in Rome. The spectacular concentric circular plan of the so-called Maritime Theater, well known to Bramante's friend and fellow architect Francesco di Giorgio, may have provided one source for the comprehensive design of the Tempietto and its encircling cloister. Hadrian, like his predecessor and kinsman Trajan, had been born in the Roman colony of Italica located near Seville; both were celebrated in Spanish chronicles of the Middle Ages and Renaissance for territorial conquest and proto-Christian virtue. Association of the Tempietto with Tivoli is confirmed by the learned antiquarian Andrea Fulvio, who would have known Bramante directly. His claim that the Tempietto was created in "similitudinem" of the famed tholos temple dramatically perched on the acropolis of ancient Tibur warrants serious attention. Fulvio's identification of the temple with the local sibyl Albunea draws this monument directly into the theme of Rome's Christian destiny. Like her more famous sister at Cuma, in Christian tradition the Tiburtine Sibyl was said to have prophesied the birth of Christ, in this case revealing a vision of the Virgin and Child to Hadrian's distant predecessor, Augustus.

Other features of the Tempietto, extraneous to the ancient tholos, suggest that Bramante drew on collateral models of centralized architecture that relate more directly to the martyrial function of the site, namely, late antique mausolea. Note especially the tomb of Theodoric the Great (d. 526), the imperial-minded king of the Ostrogoths, located in Ravenna. Only in this type do we find an underground crypt and a drum that supports a dome whose hemispherical contour is fully visible from the exterior, features also seen at the Tempietto. The tomb of Theodoric was widely celebrated during the Renaissance for its awe-inspiring dome carved from a monolithic block of stone. This monument would have carried especially meaningful associations for the Spanish Monarchs since the Royal House of Castile, from which Ferdinand and Isabel both descended, had long traced its lineage to the Visigothic kings of Spain. The Visigoths were credited with unifying the Iberian peninsula, something even the Romans had failed to do, until the Moslem invasions of the eighth century shattered that unity. When the troops of Ferdinand and Isabel conquered the Kingdom of Granada in 1492, concluding eight centuries of struggle to force the Moslems from the peninsula, this political and religious consolidation was restored. The foundation of the Tempietto ten years later, in 1502, marks the anniversary of that momentous event, and suggests the hope for success in expanding the recovery of Christian territory to the Holy Land.

The Tempietto gains added significance as an expression of the temporal and spiritual aspirations of the Spanish Crown through reference to one of the most potent architectural symbols of Jerusalem, the Dome of the Rock (Qubbat as-Sakhrah). Built by the Moslems on the Temple Mount in the late seventh century, this descendant of the same Roman mausoleum type was assimilated to Judeo-Christian history, identified as *Templum Domini*, and included in countless images of the Holy City. The proposal that it provided an ideal model for the Tempietto's centralized plan and dome elevated above a drum is surely correct, further suggesting how Bramante's structure was intended to evoke the idea of Christian triumph by eliding Rome with Jerusalem, Peter with Christ. By undertaking construction of the Tempietto in 1502 King Ferdinand's vow to construct the church on the site of Peter's martyrdom was fulfilled, and the initial concern with dynastic succession that had prompted it was amplified to embrace the more universal Christian goal of reclaiming the Holy Land.

T he reading offered here of San Pietro in Montorio and the Tempietto suggests a coordinated program in which the spiritual dignity of the site and the preeminence of the Spanish Monarchs merged. The link between the Franciscan order and the papacy expressed in the form of the church was complemented in Bramante's shrine by reference to the heritage of imperial Rome in both its pagan and Christian phases. The nuances of meaning which emerge from a consideration of the architectural sources of these structures identify the Spanish Royals as defenders of the Christian nation. This role was directly acknowledged in the title, "Catholic kings," bestowed by Pope Alexander VI upon Ferdinand and Isabel in 1496, in gratitude for their support of the "Apostolic Seat." The pope thus honored the Monarchs' tutelage of the Universal Church and the principle of Petrine primacy upon which it is based. A proclamation of that same custodial role was inscribed on Rome's sacred landscape, high up on the Janiculum hill at San Pietro in Montorio.

REFERENCES

Bruschi, Arnaldo. *Bramante architetto* (Bari: Laterza, 1969), 463-527, 986-1035.
Cantatore, Flavia. "La chiesa di San Pietro in Montorio a Roma: Ricerche ed ipotesi intorno alla fabbrica tra XV e XVI secolo," *Quaderni dell'Istituto di Storia dell'Architettura*, N.S. fasc. 24 (1994) [1997], 3-34.
Cecchelli, Margherita. "Un monastero altomedievale a S. Pietro in Montorio," in *Ianiculum-Gianicolo, storia, topografia, monumenti, leggende dall'antichità al rinascimento, Acta Instituti Romani Finlandiae*, 16, ed. Eva Margareta Steinby (Rome: Institutum Romanum Finlandiae, 1996), 101-07.
Günther, Hubertus. "La ricezione dell'antico nel Tempietto," in *Donato Bramante, ricerche, proposte, riletture*, ed. Francesco Paolo di Teodoro (Urbino: Accademia Raffaello, 2001), 267-302.
Howard, Deborah. "Bramante's Tempietto: Spanish Royal Patronage in Rome," *Apollo* 136 (Oct. 1992), 211-17.
Riegel, Nicole. "San Pietro in Montorio in Rom, Die Votivkirche der katholischen Könige Isabella und Ferdinand von Spanien," *Römisches Jahrbuch der Bibliotheca Hertziana* 32 (1997-98 [2002]), 273-319.

Readers interested in San Pietro in Montorio may consult Professor Freiberg's recent article: "Bramante's Tempietto and the Spanish Crown," *MAAR* 50 (2005), 151-206.

Fig. 25. 1. The coat of arms of Count Abele Graziadei on the façade of the Villa Richardson. Photograph, K. A. Geffcken, 2002.

BELOW

Fig. 25. 2. The Villa Richardson, at that time Villa Graziadei, viewed from the Villa Aurelia, showing the site of the foundation for the AAR Main Building. On the corner to the left: Villino Bellacci; behind it, across Via Medici: Villa Stolberg; to the right, next to the vacant lot: Villa Graziadei (Villa Richardson). This shows the Villa before the Richardson addition of the porte-cochère and the big bedroom above it. Photograph, Photographic Archive of the AAR, 7 August, 1912.

CHAPTER 25

THE VILLA RICHARDSON

Lawrence Richardson, jr

I n the early years of the twentieth century, when the American Academy was under construction at Porta San Pancrazio, the Villa Richardson on Via Giacomo Medici was the residence of Conte Abele Graziadei [fig. 25. 1]. Graziadei seems to have been involved in numerous real estate transactions in that part of the Janiculum and had been of service to J. P. Morgan in the acquisition of the land and buildings for the Academy before the first World War. His nephew, Avvocato Ercole Graziadei, was in time to become the Academy's lawyer in Rome and to serve the Academy for many years. The villa was a comfortable house in the Tuscan style popular toward the end of the nineteenth century set at the top of a precipitous slope, so that it had a commanding view over the southern reaches of Rome when it was built in 1901. A tower atop it with an open loggia added by Graziadei in 1911-12 expanded that panorama toward the east and north [fig. 25. 2].

In 1925 the villa was bought by William Symmes Richardson. Richardson, a partner in the architectural firm of McKim, Mead and White, had been injured in a fall from a horse and was paralyzed below the waist. He had been a friend and close associate of Gorham Phillips Stevens, who at that time was Director of the Academy, and they were both members of the firm of McKim, Mead and White, and loved Rome. Since he could then no longer practice his profession, he decided that he would like to spend the rest of his days in Rome acting as mentor for the Fellows of the Academy in architecture, showing them aspects of Roman and Italian architecture that they would not ordinarily encounter. He was appointed Annual Professor in the Fine Arts for the year 1925-26. His parents were elderly and well-off, and they then simply pulled up stakes and moved their household to Rome [fig. 25. 3].

The house was remodeled to include an elevator that would accommodate Richardson's wheelchair, and an apartment was added for him over the new porte-cochère [fig. 25. 4]. A motor car was acquired and modified so that he could be rolled into it with his wheelchair. Thus with minimal fuss he was installed as adjunct faculty next door to the Academy. He made further changes in the house in due course, notably the installation of door frames and fireplaces rescued from dilapidated palazzi. The great renaissance fireplace in the *salone* that one could almost walk into, if he ducked his head, was subsequently dismantled and relegated to the cellar by the

ABOVE

Fig. 25. 3. Rear view of Villa Richardson, as seen from the interior, garden side. Scaffolding indicates that Richardson's reconstruction has begun (1926). Photograph, American Academy in Rome Archives, Archives of American Art, reel 5795, frame 201, reproduced with permission.

BELOW

Fig. 25. 4. The Villa Richardson today, viewed from a second floor window, Academy Main Building. Photograph, B. Goldman, 2002.

United States ambassadors to the Holy See, in favor of a diminutive replacement more in the taste of Westchester County. Richardson also recast the garden front of the house and redesigned the rear garden in an ingenious series of shallow terraces descending to Viale XXX Aprile.

In the course of time Richardson and his parents died, and the house became the residence of his sister Ethel, a charming woman with considerable qualifications as an architectural historian and with an inexhaustible fund of knowledge about Rome and the Roman countryside. She lived in the villa until the second World War made it imperative for any American citizen who could to leave Rome, at which time she stored most of her furniture in the chapel of the Villa Aurelia and retreated to New Jersey. After the war, late in the fall of 1947, she returned to Rome to find that her house had been taken over by squatters, war refugees who could not be removed without legal action. She then took up residence in the Hotel Hassler at the top of the Spanish Steps while she instituted proceedings, but these dragged on, month after month, through the spring of 1948 without positive result or even visible progress.

Finally she despaired of any early resolution of her suit and decided to return to the United States, but almost as soon as she left Rome, there was a break-through, and the squatters decamped. She had donated her furniture to the Academy when it seemed unlikely that she would soon be reinstated in her house; thus on her return she had to see to refurnishing the house, as well as restoring the gardens, but these were projects that she undertook with enterprise and enthusiasm. She had a wide circle of friends in Rome, and in the post-war years the villa was a familiar landmark for old Fellows of the Academy returning to Rome, and she was a warm and generous hostess for many new ones. She lived until 1963 and then the house by the terms of her brother's will passed to the American Academy. Thereafter it served as the residence of Joseph Deiss as Vice-Director of the Academy and then of Frank Brown as Professor in Charge of the Classical School.

When it became advisable to let the Villa Aurelia to serve as residence for the Indian ambassador to the government of Italy, the Villa Richardson became for a

Fig. 25. 5. The Villa Richardson side garden (old Lot #5), viewed from a second floor window of the Academy Main Building, as one looked into the garden during a 4th of July celebration when the American Ambassador to the Holy See was hosting the annual party. Photograph, N. Goldman, 2002.

while the residence of the Director of the Academy, and Henry Millon and John D'Arms lived there. But with the reclaiming of the Villa Aurelia and the return of the Director to residence there, the Villa Richardson had no obvious role to play in Academy life and needs. There was some talk of turning it into flats for Fellows with children, but this idea was abandoned when it became known that the United States government would have an official ambassador to the Holy See and that he or she would need a residence, for which purpose the Villa Richardson seemed almost ideal both in size and location. Since then it has served to house a succession of these ambassadors, and it has been modified (some would say vandalized) to suit their various tastes and requirements [fig. 25. 5]. One would hope some day to reclaim it for the Academy, for it is a gracious house of rich associations for many of us. But that is something that must be left to time to decide.

CHRONOLOGY OF THE VILLA RICHARDSON

Katherine A. Geffcken

Up to the late nineteenth century: the lot on which Villa Richardson stands was part of the Villa Sciarra.

1901: Signor de Moucheron[1] files plans for the villa; *ingegnere* Adolfo Rossi and *intraprendente* Luigi Antonelli, 5 June 1901; approved 8 July 1901; official stamp August 1901. (Archivio Capitolino 61388).

1904: Signor de Moucheron files plans for a gardener's and gatekeeper's house (now called the "Richardino"); *ingegnere* Francesco Saverio Rossi and *intraprendente* Luigi Profili, 9 April and 14 May 1904; approved 22 June 1904. The document states that Moucheron has lived in his villa since 1902. (Archivio Capitolino 52022).

1911-1912: Count Abele Graziadei, now owner of the villa, asks for permission to demolish an unstable little tower atop the tower of the villa and to build, in its place, a belvedere, 6 and 19 December 1911, approved 20 January 1912, inspected 2 March 1912 (Archivio Capitolino 5350).

1918: Graziadei sells his villa to Leone Caetani, Duke of Sermoneta, who already owns property adjacent to the west on Via Giacomo Medici. (Diary of G. P. Stevens,[2] 11 November and 17 December 1918).

1919: Caetani has bought the Graziadei villa for "his mistress and her three children" (Diary of G. P. Stevens, 3 June 1919). [In fact, the mistress Ofelia Fabiani had only one child, her daughter Sveva by Caetani.]

1921: Caetani sells the villa to Livio Tovini, vice president of the Italian House of Deputies. Caetani and mistress depart for British Columbia, Canada. (Diary of G. P. Stevens 24 November 1921). Caetani buys property in Canada and settles there permanently with occasional trips back to Europe.

1925: Through negotiations carried out by Gorham Stevens, Director of the Academy, William Symmes Richardson purchases the villa. (Diary of G. P. Stevens, 28 January 1925). With the collaboration of Stevens, Richardson enlarges and embellishes the villa. (Diary of G. P. Stevens 1925-26 *passim*).

1925-26: W. S. Richardson leads a successful effort to purchase Lot #5 (garden to the side of his villa on Via Giacomo Medici) for the Academy. (Diary of G. P. Stevens 1925-26 *passim*, especially 1 and 2 December 1925, and 14 June 1926).

1931: W. S. Richardson dies 5 April, leaving his villa to the Academy subject to life use by his sister Ethel Bancroft Richardson.

1963: Ethel Richardson dies 18 May, and the villa becomes Academy property.

NOTES

1 A recent article by G. Doti provides the full name of Moucheron: Abate don Pietro de Moucheron. This man may well be identical with the author of three volumes held in the Vatican Library: Pierre Antoine de Moucheron, Comte de Moucheron, priest, born 1858. At Rome in 1900, Moucheron published an account of his family, *Notes sur Ma Famille*. Doti's article, "Un Nuovo Episodio Urbano tra Otto e Novecento. Il Quartiere di Villa Sciarra al Gianicolo" appears in *Roma Moderna e Contemporanea* 10.3 (Sept-Dec 2002), 421-54.

2 The unpublished Diary of G. P. Stevens is held in the Rare Book Room of the Library of the American Academy in Rome.

Fig. 26. 1. Monument to the *Caduti*, seen from its SE side. Photograph, K. A. Geffcken, 2002.

CHAPTER 26

MONUMENT TO THE *CADUTI*: THE FASCIST MAUSOLEUM FOR THE RISORGIMENTO DEAD

Katherine A. Geffcken

If on an early summer evening you walk down Via Medici to the Acqua Paola, you may see busy preparations for entertainment offered after dark around the fountain, and then, across the street, *carabinieri* guarding the Spanish Embassy. Turning right on Via Garibaldi, you glimpse on your left the apse of S. Pietro in Montorio and on your right an expanse of roughly mown grass presided over by magnificent pines, cedars, and a few palms. Here and there on the grass, people play with their dogs, owners and animals full of energy again in the cool of the evening after a slow, hot day. In the midst of this scene stands incongruously the Fascist shrine Ai Caduti per Roma 1849-1870, its rigid travertine structure contrasting with the gracefully sloping park and dark green trees. No monument better demonstrates both Fascist propagandistic use of Risorgimento history and also Fascist reworking of ancient Roman images [fig. 26. 1].

Once owned by S. Pietro in Montorio, this area was called Il Pino because an enormous umbrella pine dominated it, and it was chosen by the Fascist regime as the site for the mausoleum because in 1849 the principal Italian battery stood here. But when Italians fired their guns from this spot against the French, the terrain did not slope so gently. As contemporary views show, it rose to a pronounced hill, high enough for strategic placement of the battery. Incessant French shelling, however, churned up the earth of Il Pino into an impassable chaos of deep craters, destroying artillery, gun crews, and the great pine.[1]

The Zona Sacra Gianicolense, as the round markers at each end term it, was inaugurated by Mussolini on cold, rainy November 3, 1941, but this act was not the first attempt to commemorate the war of 1849 on the Colle del Pino. Soon after the unification of Italy in 1870, an association of Risorgimento veterans, the Società dei Reduci delle Patrie Battaglie, began campaigning for a suitable monument on the Janiculum. On April 24, 1877, the city council of Rome granted about one thousand square meters of the Colle del Pino for such a memorial. There was talk of a large tribute to Garibaldi with the bones of the dead interred beneath. But the monument was not built. Instead, the equestrian statue of Garibaldi, surrounded by busts of many Garibaldini, was erected in the Janiculum park (see pp. 186-87, fig. 22. 1).

Yet the veterans did not give up, and on October 12, 1879 a solemn procession of six wagons brought across the city from Verano about seven and a half cubic meters of bones and ashes. Five of the wagons carried remains of those killed in 1849; the sixth held the bodies of men killed in 1870. These remains were all placed in a small ossuary constructed just for that purpose, at the edge of the piazza in front of S. Pietro in Montorio.

Everyone knew, however, that the dead of 1849 were buried in many more places than Verano — for instance, in private family chapels and plots, in the Cemetery of S. Spirito (see pp. 194-201), in S. Carlo ai Catinari (see p. 92), and in pits or trenches wherever men fell on the battlefield. But efforts to erect a proper mausoleum languished, and the small ossuary on the Janiculum, nearly forgotten, began to fill with water and disintegrate.

But when the Fascists came into power, they saw everything about the Risorgimento as useful for their political message. Building a big monument to the fallen of 1849 coincided exactly with their *"massiccia propaganda nazionalista"* (massive nationalistic propaganda) (Berggren and Sjöstedt 38). The proponents were still the veterans, now called the Società Giuseppe Garibaldi, but this time, in 1937, led by Garibaldi's grandson Ezio, they reached the ears of Mussolini. Things still moved slowly, but with Il Duce's approval, the Society commissioned their member Giovanni Jacobucci, an architect, to design an ossuary mausoleum "of lines austere in a Roman style" (*"di linee romanamente austere"*) (*Ai Caduti* 28).

Meanwhile, in January 1938, the old ossuary was opened and found to be in such deplorable state that whatever bones and remains could be collected were transported temporarily back to Verano. Finally in 1941, mostly because of Mussolini's *"ferrea volontà"* (iron will) (*Ai Caduti* 30), Jacobucci's monument was ready to receive the relics of the dead, carried once more across Rome from Verano and from other burial spots around the city.

The parade accompanying the dead was endless: the red-shirted Legione Garibaldina, many other military units, and representatives with their banners from eighteen cities and towns that had valiantly participated in the Risorgimento. On the Janiculum waiting for the ceremony were direct descendants and other family members of the dead, who had come from all over Italy, especially from the North, which had lost so many in the struggle. In the crowd, too, was the one man still surviving who had been wounded in the insurrection of 1867, the Roman Enrico Biagioli. The mood of the onlookers was suitably enthusiastic, the spectators all well organized for a Fascist display promoting military glory and ultimate victory. But by 1941, Italy was far into the grim years of World War II, and this inauguration differed not only in its pretentious scale, but also in its underlying intention from that of 1879. In that earlier year at the little ossuary, many veterans of the Risorgimento were still alive to celebrate their hard-won victory.

Although at first glance the monument to the *Caduti* seems starkly simple, examination shows that it is highly programmed with significant details. In fact, it is a heroon, with an altar above and the dead buried below, all surrounded by its temenos marked off by a balustrade. Yet any reference to Hellenic tradition, such as columns or capitals, is absent. All details are presented in the Fascist mode of *romanità* ("Roman-ness"): for instance, the laurel in relief on the balustrade, the eagle within a wreath sitting on the central keystone of the front and rear façades, the short Roman sword, sometimes garlanded with laurel, and the Roman wolf. The sculpted fasces that once decorated the corners on the outside of the structure have been removed.

At the entrance to the precinct, two handsome flagpoles seem to guard or announce the monument. Centered within the travertine-paved temenos, is a high, square hypaethral structure, a roofless quadriportico, with three arched openings on each side. This structure stands on a podium with eight gently rising steps. The tall, undecorated arches, each with a prominent keystone, closely resemble those cut into the four sides of the Palazzo della Civiltà e del Lavoro at E.U.R., the so-called "Colosseo Quadrato." Here, running high above the arches is a plain cornice, and above the cornice an attic, a bit less in width than the main structure below.

The floor of the quadriportico is paved with an inlaid marble design of swords and fasces, and in the center of the floor is a large altar of pink granite, which contrasts in color and busy detail with the plain, creamy travertine surrounding it. All sides of the altar are carved in relief with designs suggesting legionary standards. The front and back sides, for example, show the wolf standing atop a tablet bearing SPQR, and underneath, a medallion with a turret-crowned female head – and there are additional details below. At the four top corners are lions' heads linked with a garland.

Inscriptions play an important role in this monument. Carved without any ornamentation and then attached in relief, they convey brute strength. On the four square pillars at each corner of the podium are dates and names of significant places in Risorgimento history. The two pillars on the left side refer to 1849 (the front pillar, for example, bears inscriptions recalling Garibaldi's defense: "1849/VASCELLO/ CASA GIACOMETTI" and "1849/30 APRILE/3-30 GIUGNO"). The dates and names on the two pillars at the right corners refer to events in 1862, 1867, and 1870. On either side of the eagle over the front central keystone are "1849" and "1870." On the attic above, is the inscription: "AI CADUTI PER ROMA"; on each of the other sides in the attic is repeated Garibaldi's famous call "ROMA O MORTE."

Inside the walls above the arches are eight lines by a poet dear to the Fascists, Gabriele d'Annunzio. They come from his *"La Notte di Caprera"* 18.98-107 (underlining indicates those words carved on the monument):

"Giovani, avanti,   chè vinceremo anche oggi!"
Non con lo sprone   ma col suo grande cuore
Ei sollevò   il suo cavallo a volo:
Nel balzo il bianco   mantello palpitò
Come la bianca   ala della Vittoria.
Il giovenile   grido coperse i tuoni
Del monte, dietro   il galoppo senza orma.
Nella fumèa   del vespro, intorno a Roma,

Erano ovunque	la ruina e la morte.
Ma chi morì,	morì vittorioso. (for translation, see p. 228)

D'Annunzio's emphasis on victorious death and the image of Garibaldi riding with his mantle like the wing of Victory create intense drama, as a viewer follows the inscription around the walls.

Atop the pillars at the four corners of the podium are bronze bowls. Wolf heads holding rings decorate the bowls. Filled with fuel and burning at night these containers must have been indeed dramatic (see photograph facing p. 24, *Ai Caduti*).

At the back of the monument, steps lead from left and right down to the burial chamber underneath. The double door to the chamber is rugged bronze and carries in high relief yet more references to military standards, arranged from top to bottom thus: eagle, lion within a wreath, turreted crown (or city wall), a garlanded medallion, and below, another medallion dated XVIII-EF (eighteenth year of the Fascist era). On the walls of this lower back area are various inscriptions, including Mussolini's authorization, a quotation from Ezio Garibaldi, and dedications by Risorgimento associations. Exactly facing the door is a relief showing a Roman trophy (helmet, cuirass, and tunic), with standards behind and shields and weapons piled in front [fig. 26. 2].

Inside the burial chamber, a mixture of marbles creates a richly colored, highly polished, if chilly atmosphere. The inlaid pattern of the floor repeats the design of the pavement above, and in the center a sturdy round pillar supports the altar overhead. The pillar is decorated with alabaster crosses, palms, and the inscription "ET FACERE ET PATI FORTIA ROMANUM EST" ("both to do and to suffer [from] valiant deeds is Roman", from the speech of C. Mucius Scaevola in Livy 2.12.9). The ceiling is entirely covered with brilliant gold mosaic reminiscent of Byzantine and Mediaeval churches. In the mosaic are quotations, including words from Mazzini and Mussolini. Indeed, throughout this monument, architecture, decoration, and inscriptions work together to convey their message, glorious death for the *Patria*.[2]

Recessed into the chamber walls and closed with inscribed mar-

Fig. 26. 2. Monument to the *Caduti*: relief (on lower back door level) facing door of ossuary. Photograph, K. A. Geffcken, 1999.

Fig. 26. 3. Monument to the *Caduti*. Alphabetized list of the dead in the ossuary. Note inscription for Angelo Masina at top right and ceiling of gold mosaic. Photograph, K. A. Geffcken, 1999.

ble plaques are the actual receptacles for the bones. The spaces number ninety-six, into each of which two containers can fit. In 1941, 187 sets of remains were interred, leaving the possibility of adding five containers thereafter. When one considers that on June 3 alone, Garibaldi lost approximately a thousand men,[3] it becomes apparent at once that a pathetically small proportion of the dead lies here. But all the known names are recorded on the marble plaques. In addition to these listings from official records, there were of course many unknown dead and missing.

In alphabetical order, the citations begin with surname, followed by the first name, and finally the native city or town of the deceased [fig. 26. 3]. Below the most significant names is added either a simple biographical notation or a quotation, for instance, from Garibaldi or d'Annunzio. Here is what was carved for Angelo Masina:

MASINA (DE MASINI) ANGELO. BOLOGNA
    COMANDANTE I LANCIERI DELLA MORTE
    "CHI LO VIDE SV DI VN FOCOSO DESTRIERO
    PRECIPITARSI NELLA MISCHIA ED AFFRON_
    TARE IL PERICOLO OVE MAGGIORE SI
    SENTIVA FIERO DI ESSERE ITALIANO"
        GIVSEPPE GARIBALDI   (for translation, see p. 228)

And for Enrico Dandolo:

> DANDOLO ENRICO ANNI 22 VARESE
> CAPITANO BERSAGLIERI LOMBARDI
> "STIRPE DI DOGI SANGVE REPVBBLICANO
> CHE TINSE GIÀ DI SVO COLORE I
> FIANCHI DELLE GALERE" (D' ANNVNZIO)

(for translation, see p. 228.)

D'Annunzio's tribute to Dandolo comes from *"La Notte di Caprera"* 16. 104-106.[4] Enrico Dandolo's bones, however, are not in this mausoleum. He and several others listed here were buried in family tombs (cf. pp. 45, 73).

In the burial chamber, one man who died in 1849 received especially notable recognition, an imposing porphyry sarcophagus set within a green marble frame and under a large marble tablet inscribed, in raised letters, GOFFREDO MAMELI/ 1827-1849. Below this inscription, also in relief, is a lyre backed by a sword, and on the sarcophagus itself, a gold star, referring to the star in the Mameli coat of arms. Spread eagles on left and right frame gilt carved words of Mameli's mother Adelaide, dated Genova, 22 August, 1849: "Her grief for her lost son is profound, but as he is a martyr, she does not weep"[5] [fig. 26. 4].

Why such an honor for this particular man? Mameli was a passionate, gifted

Fig. 26. 4. Monument to the *Caduti*. The ossuary tomb of Mameli. Photograph, K. A. Geffcken, 1999.

youth whose poetry stirred patriotic emotions in the Risorgimento and who, like d'Annunzio, became a favorite of the Fascists. Every Italian today knows Mameli's *"Fratelli d' Italia,"* which was set to music by Silvio Novara and which has been, since 1946, the official Italian anthem. Its text exhorts patriotic endeavor and national unity [fig. 26. 5].

The son of a naval officer Giorgio Mameli and Adelaide dei Marchesi Zoagli, Goffredo was born September 5, 1827, at Genova, and grew up delicate and privileged. While at university in Genova, he was ardently aroused by Mazzini's goals for a unified Italy. He took part in many of the rapidly occurring events in Northern Italy, such as the *Cinque Giornate* at Milano, and when Pope Pius IX departed for Campania and the new Republic was inaugurated, Mameli made his way to Rome. At first a soldier in the Italian Legion and then aide-de-camp to Garibaldi, he was at Garibaldi's side on June 3, during the bloody, day-long struggle for the Casino dei Quattro Venti. But as he watched the desperate action, he felt he should be in the midst of the battle. Thus, when Garibaldi sent out a last group of twenty men in a hopeless attempt to push the French back, Mameli asked to join it. Only six men returned from this suicidal assault. Mameli himself was struck in the left leg.[6]

Mameli's wound was slight, but the treatment he received in the hospital set up at S. Trinità dei Pellegrini was not professional even by 1849 standards, and gangrene set in. On June 18 the leg was amputated, but instead of controlling the infection, the surgery seemed to stimulate it. Mameli suffered indescribable torture, finally dying on July 6. In his last ten days he was often delirious, but his was a quiet delirium in which he softly sang his patriotic pieces and talked about his hopes for Italy. By his bed, for many hours, sat and waited the chief organizer of the medical stations, Cristina di Belgiojoso. Many years later, in 1888, an inscription memorializing Mameli's death was placed on the façade of the hospital.

Fig. 26. 5. A bust of Mameli was decreed in 1885 completed in 1887 by Hemperoni, and placed in the Janiculum park. Photograph, K. A. Geffcken, 2005.

Mameli's body has had four tombs. First he was buried in Santissime Stimmate di S. Francesco at Largo Argentina. Then, after the unification of Italy, on June 10, 1872, he was provisionally interred in a spot along the wall in Verano. Next, on July 21, 1891, his remains were disinterred and examined. The skull was covered with a glass bell; the left

Fig. 26. 6. Tomb of Goffredo
Mameli at Verano, 1891. Body
removed to Janiculum in 1941.
Photograph, K. A. Geffcken, 1998.

femur showed the cut of the amputation. The bones were then sealed in a zinc urn together with a copy of *"Fratelli d'Italia"* and a parchment signed by various authorities including his brother Marchese Giovanni Battista Mameli. The urn was placed in a white marble casket, which in turn was sealed in an elaborate tomb in Verano. This monument, with the carved figure of the dead soldier-poet is still extant, though Mameli's body is no longer there [fig. 26. 6].

Mameli's remains were next disinterred on September 15, 1941, and the zinc urn was stored in the Victor Emanuel monument, to await inauguration of the new ossuary on the Janiculum. Finally, on November 3, 1941, the urn was carried out of the Vittoriano and, in the parade to the Janiculum, given a special place of honor. In the ceremony at the monument for the *Caduti*, Mussolini presided over placing the urn in the porphyry sarcophagus prepared for it.

Sometimes called the Tyrtaeus of the Risorgimento, Mameli lies, one hopes, in his final tomb, and one also hopes that his and others' bones will not again be moved to promote some new political agenda. In the meantime, this monument to nineteenth century warriors vividly illustrates how Fascism misappropriated the Risorgimento, to legitimize itself, to propagandize its concept of "Roman-ness" (*romanità*), and to glorify death in battle.

NOTES

1   See the views in *Ai Caduti* 34 and opposite p. 320 (the latter, important drawing by G. Thomas, engraved by W. Mason, was published in the *London Illustrated News*, May 4, 1850). In a letter to Charles Leavitt (March 2, 1907), Clara Jessup Heyland stated that Maffeo Sciarra (as owner and developer) had taken down the hill opposite the Villa Aurelia about 70-80 feet (Archives of American Art, Archives of the AAR, reel 5755). Mrs. Heyland may have referred to the Colle del Pino or possibly to land where the Academy Main Building now is located.

2   For the texts of the inscriptions, see *Ai Caduti* 32, 34.

3   For estimates of the Italian killed and wounded, see Trevelyan 189-190, and 344-45.

4   The text of the inscription differs from d'Annunzio's poem in two details. First, d'Annunzio gives a Latin flavor to line 104 by using the spelling *republicano*, which the carver has regularized to the Italian *repubblicano*. Second, *fianchi* ends line 105 in d'Annunzio's text.

5   The lyre and sword in the relief above Mameli's sarcophagus refer to words Mazzini wrote in Switzerland in October 1849. They were later used in the preface to the first edition of Mameli's poetry (Genova 1886) and were carved on Mameli's tomb in Verano: *"E lira e spada staranno giusto simbolo della sua vita sulla·pietra che un dì gli erigeremo in Roma nel Camposanto dei Martiri della Nazione."* (for translation, see p. 228) Mazzini was well acquainted with Mameli's family, especially with Mameli's mother Adelaide.

6   Garibaldi's and Emilio Dandolo's accounts of this sixth and last charge differ. Garibaldi says that Dandolo and Mameli came to him and suggested the charge (Garibaldi 253). Dandolo says that Garibaldi asked for twenty men and an officer for a difficult enterprise, that he volunteered but was astonished that only he and twenty men were asked to retake the Quattro Venti, a feat not accomplished by many Italian assaults throughout the day (Dandolo 192-94). Dandolo does not mention Mameli, but that may not be surprising since in writing he focused especially on his own battalion of *bersaglieri*, to which Mameli did not belong. It seems certain, however, that Mameli was wounded in the late afternoon.

TRANSLATIONS

D'Annunzio, *"La Notte di Caprera"* 18.98-107
"Young men, forward, / because we will win also today!"
Not with the spur / but with his great heart
He lifted / his horse into flight:
In the leap the white / cloak fluttered
Like the white / wing of Victory.
The youthful / shouting hid the thunderous sounds
Of the mountain, behind / the gallop that left no [hoof] print.
In the mist / of the evening, around Rome,
There were everywhere / ruin and death.
But [those] who died, / died victorious.

Inscription for Masina:
Masina (De Masini) Angelo, [from] Bologna.
Commander [of] the Lancers of Death.
"Who[ever] saw him astride a fiery warhorse
Hurl himself into the fray and confront
The danger where greater
Felt himself [the observer] proud to be Italian." Giuseppe Garibaldi

Inscription for Enrico Dandolo:
Dandolo, Enrico – 22 years – [from] Varese
Captain [of the] Lombard Bersaglieri –
"Race of the doges – Republican blood –
that stained already with its color the sides –
of the galleys" (d'Annunzio)

For Mameli:
"Both lyre and sword will be a just symbol of his life on the stone that one day we will erect to him in Rome in the cemetery of the martyrs of the nation."

⊞ REFERENCES

Ai Caduti per Roma MDCCCXLIX-MDCCCLXX (Rome 1941), *passim*, especially 4-51, 322-28. This volume describes in detail the work of the Commissione Esecutiva per il Mausoleo Ossario Gianicolense.

Berggren, Lars, and Lennart Sjöstedt. *L'Ombra dei Grandi: Monumenti e Politica Monumentale a Roma 1870-1895* (Rome,1996), 35-38, 218-21.

Cardilli, Luisa. *Il Verano* (Rome, 1995), 13 (on Mameli).

Checchi, Eugenio. *Giardini Storici Romani: Pincio e Gianicolo* (Milan, 1897), 613-16.

Dandolo, Emilio. *I Volontari ed I Bersaglieri Lombardi* (Milan, 1850/repub. Milan, Rome, Naples, 1917).

De Vico Fallani, Massimo. *Storia dei Giardini Pubblici di Roma nell' Ottocento* (Rome, 1992), especially 266 (Jacobucci's plan for the Janiculum *ossario*).

Falasca-Zamponi, Simonetta. *Fascist Spectacle: the Aesthetics of Power in Mussolini's Italy* (Berkeley, Los Angeles, London, 1997), especially 90-99 and 240 (note 49, on the Roman eagle).

Garibaldi, Giuseppe. *The Memoirs of Garibaldi,* ed. Alexandre Dumas, trans. R.S. Garnett (London, 1931).

Huetter, Luigi. *Iscrizioni della Città di Roma dal 1871 al 1920* (Rome 1959), 366-69 (inscriptions about Mameli).

Marino, Antonio. *Il Gianicolo Illustrato* (Rome, 1922), 104-106 (on Mameli).

Stone, Marla. "A flexible Rome: Fascism and the cult of *romanità,*" in *Roman Presences,* ed. Catharine Edwards (Cambridge, 1999), 205-20.

Stone, Marla Susan. *The Patron State: Culture and Politics in Fascist Italy* (Princeton, 1998), 136, 164-66, 194.

Trevelyan, George Macaulay. *Garibaldi's Defence of the Roman Republic,* 3rd ed. (London, 1919).

ABOVE

Fig. 27. 1. La Scalea del Tamburino, ascending from Viale Glorioso. Photograph, K. A. Geffcken, 2002.

BELOW

Fig. 27. 2. La Scalea del Tamburino, descending to Viale Glorioso. Photograph, K. A. Geffcken, 2002.

CHAPTER 27

THE DRUMMER BOYS OF 1849 AND
LA SCALEA DEL TAMBURINO:
THE STAIRWAY OF THE DRUMMER BOY

Katherine A. Geffcken

Nowhere is the steep elevation of the Janiculum more evident than in the precipitous slope covered by the Scalea del Tamburino [fig. 27. 1]. Known sometimes in American Academy circles as "The Glorious Steps," this wide and breathtaking *scalinata* links Viale Glorioso below with the curving end of Via Dandolo above [fig. 27. 2]. It thus provides a challenging shortcut between Trastevere and the Janiculum. The stairway was constructed on land just outside the ancient Aurelian Wall, on a hillside formerly part of Villa Crescenzi [fig. 27. 3], which had been absorbed into Villa Sciarra. Planned in the 1880's along with other new streets in the neighborhood, the *scalea* was dedicated in 1891 to the memory of the drummer boy (*tamburino*) Domenico Subiaco, who died at Porta San Pancrazio on June 30, 1849.

A sixteen-year-old *contadino*, Domenico came from the village of Ripi, south of Frosinone in the Ciociaria. He was the son of Giovanni Subiaco and Angela Maria Paparelli, and he beat the drum for the First Infantry Regiment. Early on June 30, 1849, the last morning that the Italians defended Rome, Domenico set the rhythm for his regiment to advance up to the eighth bastion of the Papal Wall (the eighth bastion is part of the Papal Wall enclosing the back garden of the Academy). The Italians were then engaged in a final desperate effort to push the French back. As fighting near Porta San Pancrazio became more intense, the regiment moved toward the gate, and Domenico climbed onto the roof of the Porta. He stripped off his jacket and begged his comrades below to hand up to him loaded rifles. Totally exposed to enemy fire, he managed to shoot ten or twelve times before being hit in the left side. As the force of the bullet threw him backwards, he fell dying from the gate roof.

This account of Subiaco's daring and death comes from an eyewitness, Camillo Ravioli (quoted in *Ai Caduti* 190). Ceccarius (pseudonym of Giuseppe Ceccarelli), however, tells a variant, that on June 3 as Domenico fired a gun taken from a fallen comrade, he was shot in the forehead by a French bullet, and died near a stairway. Hence, Scalea del Tamburino seemed an appropriate name for the new flight of steps on the side of the Janiculum. Ceccarius's version (*Ai Caduti* 79), one suspects, may derive from a bit of rationalizing aetiology. Or, possibly, stories about more than one *tamburino* have become confused. For instance, at least one drummer named

231

below was killed on June 3.

The list of those who died at Rome in 1849 shows that Domenico Subiaco was one of nine *tamburini* who perished. The others were:

- Ignazio Calzolari, 19, from Ferrara, drummer for the Union Regiment; died June 12.
- Santo Carignano, age not known, from Fivizzano (Apuania), drummer of Legione Reduci; date of death not recorded.
- Vincenzo Fioretti, age not known, probably from Trevi, drummer of the Sixth Infantry Regiment; died June 27.
- Giovanni Gionchini, 16, from Rimini, drummer of the Sixth Infantry Regiment; died June 3.
- Agostino Minghetti, age not given, from Faenza, drummer of Mellara's *Bersaglieri* Battalion; date of death unknown.
- Pasquale Ottavianelli, 21, from Vallerano (Viterbo), drummer of the First Infantry Regiment; date of death unknown.
- Gaetano Paltrinieri, 17, from Crevalcore (Bologna), drummer of the Union Regiment; date of death unknown.
- Attilio Zampini, 14, of Rome, drummer of the Speranza Battalion; died June 30.

Because the *tamburini* beat the drum for infantry assaults, they must have been extremely exposed to enemy fire. The list above shows that three units lost two drummers each and that in four instances the date of death was not even recorded.

By naming the stairway for the *tamburino*, instead of specifically for Subiaco, the dedicators clearly meant to honor not only Domenico's bravery, but also that of all the other young drummers. At Frosinone, Domenico is remembered with a bronze monument and at Ripi by an inscription.

▦ REFERENCES

Ai Caduti per Roma MDCCCXLIX-MDCCCLXX (Rome, 1941), 72-79; 157-94 (list of the dead at Rome). The eyewitness account of Subiaco's death on June 30 (quoted in *Ai Caduti* 190) comes from Camillo Ravioli, *Notizie dei Corpi Militari Regolari che Combatterono a Bologna, Ancona, Roma, 1849* (1884).

Gigli, Laura. *Guide Rionali di Roma: Rione XIII Trastevere. Parte V* (Rome, 1987).

Pocino, Willy. "La 'scalea del Tamburino,'" *Il Tempo* (July 2001). Gigli p. 131 cites an article by Willy Pocino that I have not been able to consult: "Domenico Subiaco di Ripi, Il Tamburino della Scalea Gianicolense," *Lazio Ieri e Oggi* 15.12 (1979), 282-83.

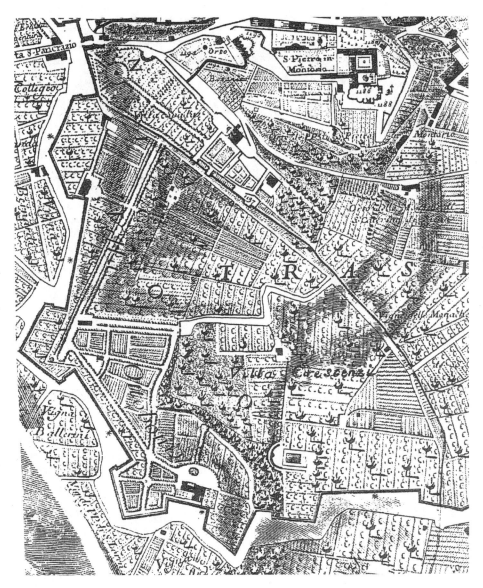

Fig. 27. 3 Section of the Nolli map (1748) showing Villa Crescenzi in the middle, and to left Villa Sciarra, named Ottoboni here (which in the nineteenth century absorbed the Crescenzi), and the Aurelian Wall, their boundary on North and East.

ABOVE

Fig. 28. 1. Entrance to Villa Sciarra opposite Via Pietro Roselli. Photograph, N. W. Goldman, 2005.

BELOW

Fig. 28. 2. Carriage entrance opposite Via Nicola Fabrizi. This entrance was designed by architect Pio Piacentini for Wurts in 1908-1909. Photograph, Katherine A. Geffcken, 2005.

CHAPTER 28

THE VILLA SCIARRA

Katherine A. Geffcken and Norma Wynick Goldman

O n Via Calandrelli, just inside the 1925 double arches cut into the Papal Wall, opens an upper entrance to the garden park of the Villa Sciarra. [fig. 28. 1] This entrance is directly opposite Via Pietro Roselli, as one comes down the hill from the American Academy's back gate. For those wishing to follow the way visitors entered the Villa Sciarra in its days as a private park, farther down Via Calandrelli is the main carriage gate, decorated with sculpture on its side posts. This gate lies opposite the upper end of Via Nicola Fabrizi where the bus makes a sharp turn to complete its ascent up the Janiculum. [fig. 28. 2]

Villa Sciarra as a public park today contains only the kernel of the great villa and *azienda agricola* that once stretched on the Janiculum over the entire terrain between the Papal Wall and the Aurelian Wall. In the nineteenth century at its greatest extent, the Sciarra covered all the Academy's land from the *cortile* in the Main Building back to the Papal Wall and all the territory southeast of the Academy from the Papal Wall to the Viale Glorioso, land today occupied by houses, apartments, and institute buildings. Just within the present boundary line on Via Dandolo is the excavated Syrian Sanctuary dating to the Roman period, cut into the hillside on what is now the lowest part of the Sciarra property. [fig. 29. 1] Above the Sanctuary is a modest caretaker's cottage on the right and atop a flight of steps a larger house on the left. Above both of them, a jungle of wild woodland occupies the lower stretches at the park's southeastern slope.

In 1886, the owner of the Villa, Maffeo Barberini Colonna di Sciarra (usually known as Maffeo Sciarra, 1850-1925) and the Compagnia Fondiaria Italiana proposed a division of this handsome estate into two parts: the main Casino Barberini-Sciarra and its surrounding gardens to remain in Sciarra's hands (this property we know today as the public park), and the rest to be divided into lots for residential development. In this way, land became available for the future Academy site and for all the apartment buildings and convents on Via Nicola Fabrizi, Calandrelli, Dandolo, XXX Aprile, and Casini.

The park today, although much limited in size, is a mecca for neighborhood elders on their outings and for mothers with small children. All flock inside to enjoy

Fig. 28. 3. Birdcage.
Photograph, G. Dwyer, 2005.

its pleasant shade, swings, large bird cage with strutting peacocks, sculptured fountains, and its benches where chatting parents, nannies, and grandparents sit to supervise children at play. Many breeds of dogs find exciting smells as their owners at brisk pace exercise them and themselves. The *uccelliera* houses not only a peacock and peahen, but also pigeons, and ducks that fascinate all visitors. [fig. 28. 3]

There are two other minor entrances to the park: one beside the Syrian Sanctuary below on Via Dandolo, and the other across the street from Salvator Mundi Hospital on Viale delle Mura Gianicolensi. Within the villa, two main carriageways lead through the gardens toward the Casino Barberini-Sciarra, which now houses the Italian Institute for Germanic Studies in Rome. In addition, a myriad of other footpaths wind and circle amidst decorative vegetation, pools and sculptural arrangements.

Like several other passageways in the Sciarra, Viale Adolfo Leducq was named by city authorities for a Garibaldino. A Belgian, Leducq was a captain in the Italian fifth infantry regiment, who died fighting on April 30, 1849. Others remembered in the names of pathways include Paolo Narducci, Gustavo Spada (see p. 58), and the American writer and volunteer nurse, Margaret Ossoli Fuller.

The first attested private owner of the central portion of Villa Sciarra was Alessandro Mignanelli, who in 1647 gave the villa to his daughter Margherita when she married Domenico Vaini. But the *canone* (rental fee) owed by the villa to the Abbot of the Abbey of SS. Clemente and Pancrazio points to earlier ownership by a monastic institution.[1] In any case, Domenico Vaini initiated the process by which such *vigne* became larger (see, for instance, Mirka Beneš on additions to the Villa Pamphilj, pp. 165-178). He acquired a little neighboring vineyard belonging to Ottavio Falletti. Then, in 1654, he agreed to lend his villa to his cousin Cardinal Antonio Barberini, who in 1653 had purchased the adjoining Villa Malvasia, but found it a bit small for his princely status (see p. 46). Thus, until his death in 1671, Cardinal Antonio enjoyed the extensive grounds of both the Vaini and Malvasia properties. At his demise, however, the Vaini section reverted to its legitimate owners.

Thereupon began a series of disputes between the Barberini and Vaini heirs over rights to water from the Acqua Paola and general neglect of the vineyards. These disputes finally ended in 1688 when Cardinal Carlo Barberini won a court suit that allowed him to buy the Vaini estate for 9000 scudi. Thus again united, the Malvasia and Vaini properties remained together until the division of 1886 described above. In the meantime, other neighboring *vigne* were acquired to enlarge the property – de Blanchis in 1674, a casino near S. Pietro in Montorio from Antonio Vaini in 1710, and the large Orto Crescenzi in the first half of the nineteenth century – thus bringing the borders of Villa Sciarra to the eastern edge of the modern Viale Glorioso (for more details, see Malvasia Chronology at the end of Chapter 5, pp. 54-55).

In its heyday in the eighteenth century, Villa Barberini-Sciarra was intensely cultivated with rows of vegetables, fruit trees, olive and almond trees. It also had stands of elm, willow, laurel, and cypress. The focal point of all this estate was, however, the principal casino, a sturdy house placed near the highest ridge of land, probably built about 1600 or perhaps slightly earlier.[2] The Papal Wall of 1642-44 barely circles this high land, buttressing the outer terraces of the property with mammoth fortifications. Specifically, the house lies just within the wall between the fifth and sixth bastions. The Casino Mignanelli-Vaini-Barberini-Sciarra-Wurts (if we include all its names, but from now on referred to as "Casa Barberini") was a solid structure with three floors.[fig. 28. 4] Its front, which faced northeast, featured a portico jutting out with three large arched openings, supporting a long balcony reached from the *primo piano*. From the portico a wide corridor led back to a courtyard with a fountain and pots for plants. The ground floor rooms were utilitarian (storage, office, etc.), and to the left side of the main block were stables, a cistern, and the formal enclosed *giardino segreto*. Up the staircase, the *primo piano* contained the main living areas, including a large *salone* and a chapel. Additional bedrooms occupied the top floor above.[3] Views from the upper windows were spectacular.

The war of 1849 inflicted severe damage on the Casa Barberini because its high location at the Papal Wall made it strategically important. A photograph by Stefano Lecchi and a drawing by P. De Cuppis, both dated July 1849,[4] show that much of the façade and the northwestern corner were blown away, indicating that damage was inflicted by both French and Italian shelling. Such destruction was caused by the French as they opened up breaches in the Papal Wall on June 20-21 at the sixth bas-

Fig. 28. 4. Casino Barberini Sciarra.
Photograph, K. A. Geffcken, 2004.

Fig. 28. 5. Map showing the breaches in the wall
between Bastions 6, 7, and 8. Trevelyan, opp. 210.

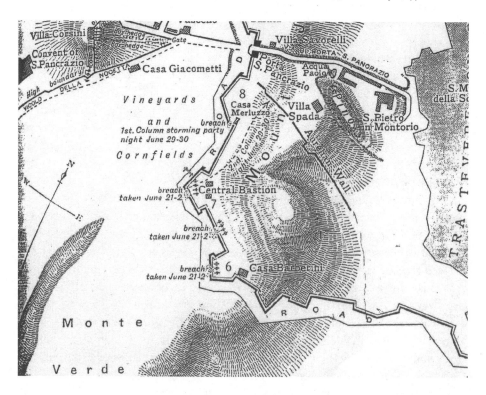

tion and in the stretch between the sixth and seventh bastions, and by Italians, as they tried to dislodge the enemy after the French had poured through the breaches [fig. 28. 5].

On June 21, the Italians had responded to these dangerous breaches by piling up mounds of bulrushes and undergrowth in the openings, but on the night of June 21-22, the French silently penetrated these obstructions and surprised the exhausted defenders. Although the Italians holding the Casa Barberini resisted, the French soon overpowered them. Nino Costa describes how on the morning of June 22 he climbed onto the roof of his family home next to S. Francesco a Ripa, from where he was appalled to spot the French now in control of Casa Barberini.[5] That same morning a detachment of Italians was sent to retake this strategically essential building. The French hid inside, let the Italians enter, and then suddenly emerged from hiding places, to bayonet them. The painter Girolamo Induno received almost twenty such wounds and was thrown down the steps. Amazingly, he survived, but Enrico Casati of Milan and Giacomo Venezian of Trieste, both of Giacomo Medici's legion, were less fortunate. A French sapper split open Casati's skull with an ax, and Venezian was so gravely wounded that he died ten days later, on July 2. Twenty-eight Italians are recorded as killed or mortally wounded on June 21-22, and Garibaldi was immediately forced to fortify his second line of defense, the Aurelian Wall. [6]

After the Italians surrendered and the French entered Rome, the Barberini Colonna di Sciarra family repaired the Casa, basing their reconstruction of floors, windows, and façade on documents of 1687, 1688, and on the plan drawn in 1794 by architect Antonio Taddei.[7] The grounds were also replanted, though they never became again quite the intensely cultivated *azienda agricola* of earlier times.

In his novel *Il Piacere* (written in 1888 and published in 1889), Gabriele d'Annunzio included a lush description of the Villa Sciarra on a May morning in 1887.[8] He chose the gardens as the scene of a duel between his hero Andrea Sperelli and Giannetto Rutolo. As Andrea and his two seconds drive up the Gianicolo, d'Annunzio describes the radiant city panorama below, bristling with campanili, columns, obelisks, and cupolas. Within the Villa Sciarra they first pass through half of it already "dishonored" (*disonorata*) by builders of new houses, and then they enter the core preserved as a park, riding down a driveway between laurels and banks of roses. D'Annunzio interweaves soft, lavish description of the villa with the hard, precise ritual of preparation for the duel. The trees sigh gently, the fountain murmurs, the white and yellow roses tremble, and a *merlo* whistles unseen in the trees. In this poetic setting, the custodian opens the ground floor of the Casa Barberini so that the duelers can ready themselves and the two doctors in attendance can lay out their instruments and disinfect the swords. Deadly serious, the duel is fought on beaten gravel to one side of the Casa. This tranquil spot and the tense sword fight with its blood and brilliant skill produce a startling and morbid contrast.

After the financial collapse of Maffeo Sciarra, the court (Tribunale di Roma) in 1896 awarded the villa to George Clark, and shortly later in 1897 to the Società di Credito e Industria Edilizia. From this Società, a retired American diplomat, George

Washington Wurts, bought the villa in 1902 for 300,000 lire. Wurts had been posted in Spain, Italy, and Russia. A passionate collector, he acquired, over the years, especially in Russia, an immense assortment of antiques, tapestries, paintings, silver, and other objets d'art. His second marriage to extremely rich Henrietta Tower, like him a Pennsylvanian, assured the couple of the wealth to support a princely style of living. [fig. 28. 6]

While in St. Petersburg in 1892, Wurts had decided to resign from the diplomatic corps and return to Rome, where he had spent fourteen years before his Russian posting. On reaching Rome, the Wurtses settled into an impressive apartment on the *piano nobile* of the Palazzo Antici Mattei, which they filled to overflowing with their growing collection. Ten years later, when they acquired the Villa Sciarra, their attention shifted to restoring and embellishing their new property. They added a wing to the right side of the house. Upstairs they created a two-story baronial dining hall by merging together rooms on the *primo piano* and the floor above. They added a tiny tower on the roof, and at some stage in the renovations, the arched openings in the façade were closed with wooden doors finished off with iron grills in the arches.

Most notable was the Wurtses' development of the park in a romantic nineteenth century style. D'Annunzio's description cited above suggests that Sciarra had already introduced a nineteenth century character into the gardens. But the Wurtses (George Wurts was probably the leader in all this planning) elaborated the design much more extensively, with winding paths, fountains, and *ninfei*, unexpected vistas, topiary pruning, and exotic plantings. The dominant objects, however, installed in the park were numerous statues, clearly from northern Italy as indicated by the presence of the Visconti crest here and there. This crest showing a snake either swallowing or regurgitating a *putto* linked the sculpture to some Visconti structure in Lombardy, but the exact property remained unknown until recently [fig. 28. 7]. By careful research, Amalia Pacía discovered the source: Villa Visconti at Brignano.[9] Her juxtaposition of drawings by Marc'Antonio dal Re (1726) with the present arrangement of the sculpture offers an enlightening and amazing contrast – formality and balance in the eighteenth century design, but no formality or balance in the Wurtses' arrangement. Instead, they scattered statues in the park, achieving a distancing effect [fig. 28.8]. The mood is romantic, suggestive perhaps of melancholy, like coming upon unexpected visitors, frozen in their spots. Today, this elegiac effect is sadly emphasized by the destruction, here and there, inflicted on the statues since the park became public.

In 1906 George Wurts began building a house for his custodian on the steep slope amid dense woodlands just above the curve of Via Dandolo (see below, p. 248). As the ground was prepared for foundations, antiquities emerged from the soil. Wurts promptly arranged for the archaeologist Paul Gauckler to supervise excavations in the area. From 1906 to 1910, Gauckler's team thus investigated the remains of the Syrian Sanctuary and the Grove of Furrina (see Chapter 29)[fig. 29. 1].

The Wurtses never made the villa their main residence. They opened it in the

Fig. 28. 6. George and Henrietta Tower Wurts. Photograph,
Archivio Fotografico Soprintendenza Speciale per il Polo
Museale Romano.

Fig. 28. 7. Fountain opposite the Casino with father and his own *putto* playing at the edge. Note the snakes (*biscioni*) either swallowing or regurgitating the sculptured *putti*. Photograph, N. W. Goldman, 2003.

Fig. 28. 8. Sculpture of Apollo chasing Daphne in front of the Casino. Photograph, K. A. Geffcken, 2004.

late spring, when they entertained there at teas and elaborate *feste*. Descriptions of these parties appear in Giorgio Nelson Page's *L'Americano di Roma* and in brief references in the diaries of Gorham Phillips Stevens. Page, whose family had a distant connection with Wurts (through Wurts's first wife), was commanded as a child to play the piano by an imperious Henrietta, whom he describes as covered with her famous pearls and socially inept. In his diary, Stevens begins noting the Wurtses' May parties in 1915, the first spring after the Academy's move to the new Main Building on the Janiculum. At that time Stevens was head of the School of Fine Arts of the Academy; later he would be once again Director, as he was when the School of Fine Arts at the American Academy was located at Villa Mirafiori. Besides his entries about May teas and receptions at Villa Sciarra, Stevens mentions taking occasional walks in the villa, sometimes to show it to visitors, sometimes to accompany Academy Fellows who needed to study the gardens or the swans and peacocks.[10]

In January 1928, George Wurts died, and Stevens recorded signing the book of condolences. As Mrs. Wurts quietly pondered the fate of her villa, rumors about its future circulated on the Janiculum. On March 13, 1930, Stevens reported that it would become a home for retired people. Then on March 19, 1930, he noted that Italian artists were trying to get it for young government artists. But in fact, on March 22, 1930, Mrs. Wurts donated the villa to the State of Italy in the person of Mussolini, with the proviso that it become a public park in perpetuity; she also gave funds for its upkeep. When it soon became clear that the City of Rome was better equipped to care for the property, ownership was transferred to the Comune di Roma.

In 1932, on the anniversary of Goethe's death, the Casa Barberini became home for the Istituto di Studi Germanici, which still occupies the building. At the dedication of the Institute, Mussolini and other dignitaries spoke, and the Director outlined his plans for the Institute to further cultural relations between Italians and Germans through sponsored lectures, conferences, and publications. The Institute, for instance, possesses a library, reportedly the best collection of Germanic materials in Italy, and it publishes a scholarly journal entitled *Studi Germanici*.

The Institute pamphlet describes its scope as dedicated to sponsoring research on the cultural, social, political, and economic life of countries of Germanic origin, not only Germany, but also Austria, German-speaking Switzerland, Denmark, Sweden, Norway, the Low Countries, and Iceland. The Casino Barberini has been renovated to accommodate offices, studios, and conference rooms. A large aula has been constructed for lectures in the former *cortile* at the rear of the *pianterreno* [fig. 28.9]. On the *primo piano*, some of the handsome Wurts furniture — sofas and a complete dining room set — has been restored and returned to its original location, in rooms used for conference entertaining. From these rooms, windows provide fine views of the garden, fountains, and sculpture.

Fig. 28. 9. Aula in the restored Casino Barberini occupying a space formerly a courtyard. Photograph, N. W. Goldman, 2003.

Fig. 28. 10. Library in the Institute for Germanic Studies. Librarian Bruno Berni on right. Photograph, N. W. Goldman, 2003.

Fig. 28. 11. Fountain of fauns inside the entrance nearest the Papal wall, described in the poem by Richard Wilbur. Photograph, N. W. Goldman, 2004.

Since 1977, the Institute has been especially active, with meetings, conferences, and exhibitions on classical and modern topics. Supporting the work of the Institute is its excellent library, located on the *pianterreno* and underground, containing about 80,000 volumes and 200 periodicals [fig. 2. 10]. Beginning with the collection of Max Koch, a German scholar from the University of Marburg and Breslau, a donation acquired in 1931, and enriched by successive acquisitions, the library is an adjunct to several fine collections in Rome, such as those of the German Archaeological Institute and the Hertziana. The Studi Germanici also cooperates with the Goethe Institute, the Swiss Institute, and the Austrian Institute.

Over the years, Academy Fellows and visitors have spent endless hours enjoying the Sciarra park. No one has expressed that appreciation better than Richard Wilbur who, during his year as an Academy Fellow (1954-55), wrote "A Baroque Wall-Fountain in the Villa Sciarra." [fig. 28. 11] This poem about the fountain of the fauns, just inside the upper entrance on Via Calandrelli near the Papal Wall, begins:

> Under the bronze crown
> Too big for the head of the stone cherub whose feet
> A serpent has begun to eat,
> Sweet water brims a cockle and braids down
>
> Past spattered mosses, breaks
> On the tipped edge of a second shell, and fills
> The massive third below. It spills
> In threads then from the scalloped rim, and makes
>
> A scrim or summery tent
>   For a faun-ménage and their familiar goose. (lines 1-10)

◈ REFERENCES

Ai Caduti per Roma MDCCCXLIX-MDCCCLXX (Rome, 1941).

Belli Barsali, Isa. *Ville di Roma: Lazio I* (Milan, 1970), 461.

Benocci, Carla. "Villa Sciarra: dal Mecenatismo Americano degli Anni Trenta all' Ipotesi Comunale di Musealizzazione," *Bollettino dei Musei Comunali di Roma.* n.s. 12 (1998), 123-47.

Callari, Luigi. *Le Ville di Roma* (Rome, 1934), 46-48.

Costa, Nino. Excerpts from *Quel Che Vidi e Quel Che Intesi* in *Scrittori Garibaldini*, ed. G. Trombatore (Turin, 1979), 1.5-31.

D'Annunzio, Gabriele. *Il Piacere*, ed. Federico Roncoroni (repr. Milan, 1995), 125-30.

Frutaz, A. P. *Le Piante di Roma* (Rome, 1962).

Gigli, Laura. *Guide Rionali di Roma: Rione XIII Trastevere. Part V* (Rome, 1987), 108-26.

Lanciani, Rodolfo. *Notes from Rome.* ed. A. L. Chubberley (British School at Rome, 1988), 174.

Mancini, Paolo. "Villa Sciarra," *Alma Roma* 25 (1984), 1-31.

Massari, Giuseppe. "La Flora di Villa Sciarra," in *Il Balcone di Roma*, eds. Renato Funiciello and Antonio Thiery (Rome, 1998), 38-52.

Pacía, Amalia. "George Washington Wurts (1843-1928)," in *Un Itinerario Artistico nella Russia dell'800*, eds. M. L. Casanova, A. Pacía, and F. Ciofi degli Atti (Rome, 1988), 5-9.

Pacía, Amalia and Renata Piccininni. *Villa Sciarra: Interpretazione Romana di una Villa Lombarda* (Rome, 1992).

Page, Giorgio Nelson. *L'Americano di Roma* (Milan, 1949).

Stevens, Gorham Phillips. Diaries 1911-1932 (unpublished notebooks in the Rare Book Room, Library of the American Academy in Rome).

Trevelyan, G. M. *Garibaldi's Defence of the Roman Republic* (London, 1919).

Wilbur, Richard. "A Baroque Wall-Fountain in the Villa Sciarra," from *Things of this World* (1956), reprinted in *New and Collected Poems* (San Diego, New York and London, 1988), 271-73. Also reprinted in *A Roman Collection*, ed. Miller Williams (Columbia and London, 1980), 69-70.

⬚ NOTES

1   The rental fees (*canoni*) due annually on the Villa Sciarra to the Abbey (in later years administered by the Congregation of the Propaganda Fide) were cancelled only in January 1906 (See Mancini 15, and 24, note 37). Callari (46) states that the original structure of the Casino Barberini-Sciarra belonged to the fifteenth century and that it rested on Roman remains, as discovered in renovations of 1906, but he does not provide any details.

2   See Note 1 above for Callari's statement that the house is earlier in at least part of its structure. The Casino Barberini-Sciarra is attested in the marriage contract between Margherita Mignanelli and Domenico Vaini (1647), (see Mancini 17-18, 22, note 12). On maps of Rome, it first definitely appears on the plan of Giovanni Battista Falda in 1667 (Frutaz III, plate 348). Earlier plans may possibly show it, but before the Papal Wall was included on maps, the designers indicated only generic *casali* scattered outside the Aurelian Wall. The best possibility may be a house on Giuseppe De Rossi's map of 1637, which shows a *casale* on a hill – maybe the Malvasia or the Barberini-Sciarra (Frutaz III, plate 333). In any case, Mancini suggests that similarities between the Malvasia and the Barberini-Sciarra houses point to construction of both in the same broad period. The Nolli map of 1748 shows a *vigna* outside the Papal Wall still with the name Mignanelli. As pointed out elsewhere (p. 48), the Nolli map in fact indicates Ottoboni still as owner of the Barberini-Malvasia property (Cardinal Pietro Ottoboni, owner 1710 to his death in 1740), but the estate had become once again Barberini property in 1746, when Cornelia Costanza Barberini and her husband Giulio Cesare Barberini Colonna di Sciarra bought it at auction. It is sometimes referred to as the San Cosimato Villa because its neighbor in its lower sections was the monastery of San Cosimato.

3   For plan and elevation dated 1794 by architect A. Taddei (in the Vatican Library), see Gigli 123.

4   Mancini 24, note 43, cites the reproduction of Lecchi's photograph in L. Vitali, *Il Risorgimento nella Fotografia* (Einaudi, Moncalieri, 1979), 19. Mancini reproduces the drawing by De Cuppis, p. 29, fig. 5.

5   For Costa's account of the events of the night of June 21-22 and of June 22, see *Scrittori Garibaldini* 26-27.

6   For Casati, see *Ai Caduti* 158, quoting V. Ottolini, *Cronaca della Compagnia Medici* (Milan, 1884). For Venezian, see *Ai Caduti* 193; near the Vascello on Via Aurelia Antica is a memorial tablet to Venezian with his bust. The Italian dead for June 21-22 can be gleaned from the list covering April 30 to August 11, 1849, in *Ai Caduti* 151-95.

7   See above, note 3, for this plan by Taddei.

8   *Il Piacere* 125-30. It is hard to resist the impression that d'Annunzio places a contest of male skill in a feminine setting. The duel was indeed fought over a woman, Donna Ippolita Albónico. It may just be coincidence that Maffeo Sciarra, founder of *La Tribuna*, was d'Annunzio's employer. Rodolfo Lanciani, in his letter to *The Athenaeum*, November 28, 1885, comments sadly on the sale of Villa Sciarra "to the same company which has destroyed the Villa Ludovisi" (Cubberley 174). Lanciani mentions that the Grand Dukes Sergius and Paul of Russia had recently resided in the Villa Sciarra.

9 Pacía and Piccininni *passim*, especially 20-42. The agent for sale of the Brignano sculpture was the antiquary firm of Sangiorgi, Rome.

10 On March 15, 1915, Stevens went with Fellow John C. Gregory to study peacocks for sculpture that Gregory was working on. On May 18, 1917, Stevens visited Wurts to request permission for Fellow Russell Cowles to draw the Sciarra swan. On July 21, 1918, Stevens visited the Sciarra with Edward Lawson, a Fellow in Landscape Architecture, who wished to study the gardens. For more on Stevens's references to the Villa and on the Fellows' work, see "The Villa Sciarra and the Wurtses," *Newsletter of the Classical Society of the American Academy in Rome* (2003), 13-17.

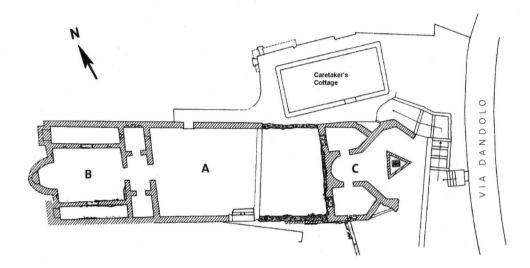

Fig. 29. 1. Plan of the Syrian Sanctuary, redrawn and modified by N. W. Goldman from plan by R. Meneghini in F. Catalli, "La Riva Destra del Tevere," in *Villa Doria Pamphilj*, ed. C. Benocci.

CHAPTER 29

THE SYRIAN SANCTUARY

Archer Martin

An archaeological site cut into the side of the hill at the bottom of the gardens of the Villa Sciarra, usually referred to as the Syrian Sanctuary, often arouses the curiosity of people traveling along Via Dandolo. It appears on the left about a third of the way up the hill as one rides by bus up from Viale Trastevere. It may be visited by appointment, when the guard, living in the small house on the site to the right as one enters, will open it. A short flight of steps leads to the platform of the site [fig. 29. 1]. The surrounding grove and spring deep in the hillside have historical and cultic associations reaching back to the Roman Republic. Scholars of ancient religion have investigated syncretistic currents evident there. Architects are intrigued by various structures discovered in the complex.

Three building phases have been identified on the site. The first is dated from the late first century B.C. or the first half of the first century A.D. A second phase indicates use from the late first century A.D. to the early fourth. A relatively short third phase, built in the first half of the fourth century, was destroyed by the end of that century.

The first two phases are known to a very limited extent. The early one includes various structures probably connected with drainage and water management. The second phase reuses some of the earlier structures and has the same orientation and probably similar functions. A long-standing hypothesis sees the *Lucus Furrinae* in these early structures: i.e. the sacred grove where historical references locate the death of C. Sempronius Gracchus in 121 B.C., a place with a spring sacred to a divinity obscure to the Romans already at the time of Varro. The goddess of this grove was worshipped in a festival called the Furrinalia or Fornalia on July 25. Her powers are disputed: in Hellenizing her, Plutarch calls this spot the grove of the Eumenides, while Cicero and Martianus Capella also give her underworld connections. Later inscriptions refer to the nymphs Furrinae.

Among the epigraphic and sculptural material found on the Janiculum relative to Jupiter Heliopolitanus and Syrian divinities in general, dating probably to the second and third centuries A. D., an inscription associates the Genius Forinarum with Jupiter Heliopolitanus. It is tempting to postulate that the site was indeed the *Lucus*

Fig. 29. 2. View from inside the walls of the Sanctuary looking toward the Caretaker's Cottage and Via Dandolo. Photograph, B. Goldman, 2004.

Furrinae, in which the new deities were installed by the mid-imperial period.

Only the last phase, however, has left any considerable structural remains, built on a different orientation from the underlying walls. It consists of three parts: A) a rectangular courtyard, which was the entry area with the main doorway on the south side [fig. 29. 2]; B) a basilical building on the west, consisting of an apsed central nave with side rooms, preceded by a sort of narthex with side rooms [fig. 29. 3]; and C) a curious structure to the east with a non-rectilinear plan. The third element is the most interesting feature in the architecture. It consists of an octagon entered through the sides from two rooms in front.

The earliest tentative excavation and research began in 1720, when the Villa Sciarra was the property of Cardinal Ottoboni. In 1803 a larger excavation was undertaken, but it was only in 1908 that a full scale excavation was undertaken. It was again excavated in 1981.

A variety of sculpture was found in the sanctuary, some of it reused. The main emphasis is clearly Romanized Syrian, although the sculptural remains show further syncretism, including Egyptian elements. The statue of the main cult, a sort recognizable iconographically as a seated Jupiter, can be identfied as Hadad (the main god of Heliopolis, identified with Jupiter). This statue was found in the niche in the apse of the basilical building at the far end of the complex. A skull was found buried under this niche. The other two divinities of the Syrian triad, Atargatis (called Dea Syria by

Fig. 29. 3. The apsed central nave with side rooms.
Photograph, B. Goldman, 2004.

the Romans) and Simios (identified with Mercury), were probably worshipped in the side rooms. There was also a cavity under the altar at the center of the octagon that contained some eggs and a bronze statuette of a male figure with a serpent wound around it [fig. 29. 4]. This kind of figure has been identified as Adonis, god of death and rebirth (also symbolized by the eggs), but it could also be Osiris, who is connected with the same themes.

Roman emperors, influenced by Eastern cults, had often allowed foreign deities to be imported into Rome, deities often identified with Roman gods and worshipped along with them. Within these walls on the slope of the Janiculum, one can see a structure where such syncretism was established on a site once sacred to a Roman goddess only dimly remembered.

Fig. 29. 4. Excavated male statue with serpent wrapped around it, variously identified, and titled *Idolo del Gianicolo* in the Museo Nazionale delle Terme. Photograph, with the permission of the *Ministero per i Beni e le Attività Culturali – Soprintendenza Archeologica di Roma.*

REFERENCES

Calzini Gysens, J. "Iuppiter Heliopolitanus" in *Lexicon Topographicum Urbis Romae* III, ed. E. M. Steinby (Rome, 1996), 138-143.

Calzini Gysens, J. "Lucus Furrinae" in *Lexicon Topographicum Urbis Romae* III , ed. E. M. Steinby (Rome, 1996), 193-194.

Gauckler, P. *Le Sanctuaire syrien du Janicule* (Paris, 1912).

Goodhue, N. *The Lucus Furrinae and the Syrian Sanctuary on the Janiculum* (Amsterdam, 1975).

Mele, M. ed., *L'area del santuario siriaco del Gianicolo* (Rome, 1982).

Fig. 30. 1. Façade of the so-called Casa di Michelangelo, Passeggiata del Gianicolo. Photograph, K. A. Geffcken, 2002.

Fig. 30. 2. The Campidoglio by Giuseppe Vasi (1754). The Via delle Tre Pile curves up on the right apparently touching the side wall of the little "Casa di Michelangelo." Plate 80 from *Delle Magnificenze di Roma Antica & Moderna*, Vol. 4.

CHAPTER 30

THE SIXTEENTH CENTURY FAÇADE OF THE JANICULUM RESERVOIR: 'THE (*COSIDETTA*) CASA DI MICHELANGELO'

Katherine A. Geffcken

As you enter the upper stretch of the Janiculum *passeggiata* just outside Porta San Pancrazio, you notice immediately on the left an elegant Renaissance façade, with doors and windows that never seem open [fig 30. 1]. This façade, in fact, masks an enormous water reservoir,[1] and its reconstruction on this site was celebrated, as an inscription shows, on April 21, 1941. A second inscription states that it comes from the so-called house of Michelangelo on Via delle Tre Pile on the Campidoglio.

To be precise, the façade belonged not to the street side of the original house, but once formed the back wall of the *cortile*, which a person entering the house glimpsed down a corridor. Only the lower half of the façade you see comes from the *cortile* – and even it has been modified to make it suitable as an outside entrance wall. The central, arched doorway was originally a niche with a fountain and the reclining statue of a river god, and the windows on either side were also niches holding sculpture. The two outer doors opened on stairways leading to an upper building level and to gardens above and behind, visible from the *cortile*. The two end niches stood at right angles to the back wall, finishing off the design of doors and niches at the beginning of the side walls. As you see the façade today, it is as if wings on each side were opened out flat. Many elements survive from the Renaissance wall: the brickwork, travertine borders, *peperino* engaged pilasters, and the wide stone seats.

The so-called house of Michelangelo was probably doomed not to survive because of its location on the steep northwest side of the Capitoline, below the Palazzo dei Conservatori. In 1592 a sharply rising passageway for carriages was cleared, alongside the broad *cordonata* (ascent with shallow steps) that leads up to Piazza del Campidoglio. At the top, just below the terracing of the Conservatori, this road made an abrupt turn to the right, as can be seen in views of the Campidoglio by Lievin Cruyl and Giovanni Battista Falda. Driving up and down this road was apparently so perilous that further work was done on it in 1692, at which time the end house, closest to the Conservatori, was probably removed. Without the support of this house, the "casa di Michelangelo" next door became unstable. Half of the roof of its *primo piano* had to be lowered, dreadfully marring the appearance of the street façade [fig. 30. 2]. In the eighteenth century the house belonged to the

Monastero di S. Lucia in Selci, and in 1812 Benedetto Pellegrini bought it.

In 1872, however, the Comune di Roma decided to make the Via delle Tre Pile even less dangerously precipitous, and so demolished the house (1873). But nearby lived an architect, Domenico Jannetti, who asked for permission to reconstruct the *cortile* back wall as the façade of a new, smaller building he would put up next to his *palazzo*. Thus the wall was saved, but Jannetti added the upper section, with three windows and four panels, matching the brick, travertine, and *peperino* so closely that the whole was harmonious.

The façade was, alas, not left undisturbed, when in 1929-30 the Comune decided yet again to improve the Tre Pile, as part of the clearing and reorganization of the entire area between Piazza Venezia and the Theater of Marcellus. Both Jannetti's own *palazzo* and his building next door with the sixteenth century façade were demolished. But once more, the façade was saved, stored away, and in 1941 reconstructed in its present location on the Janiculum. At this time, Jannetti's nineteenth century grills on doors and windows and his pots on the roofline were removed, and a balustrade was added along the top.

If you want to see where the so-called house of Michelangelo stood, note as you go up the Via delle Tre Pile the bit of ancient city wall, which was discovered when the house was demolished. The Palazzo dei Conservatori looms not far away, on the top of the Capitoline, and you can imagine traffic moving slowly up and rapidly down the dangerous road passing around the house that no longer stands at this spot [fig. 30. 3].

Whether Michelangelo ever lived in this building is doubtful. His known residence, near the Column of Trajan and S. Maria di Loreto, was taken down in 1871. How his name came to be associated with the house on the northwest slope of the Capitoline remains a mystery.[2]

Fig. 30. 3. The long white balustrade in middle distance marks the edge of the *cordonata* ascending up to the Piazza of the Campidoglio. Area of shadow shows the approximate spot on the Tre Pile where the so-called House of Michelangelo stood. Photograph, K. A. Geffcken, 2002.

◈ REFERENCES

Gigli, Laura. *Guide Rionali di Roma: Rione XIII Trastevere, Parte I*, 2nd ed. (Rome, 1980), 192.

Pernier, Adolfo. "Notizie Inedite sulla Casa detta di Michelangelo alle Pendici Occidentali del Campidoglio," *Capitolium* 17.1 (1942), 85-102. Pernier was in charge of setting up the façade on the Janiculum; his article includes *vedute* and photographs.

Piccininni, Renata. "Il Serbatoio del Gianicolo (Peschiera)," in *Il Trionfo dell'Acqua: Acque e Acquedotti a Roma, IV sec. a.C.-XX sec.* (Rome, 1986), 304-308, esp. 306 (photograph of interior of the reservoir).

Pietrangeli, Carlo. *Guide Rionali: Rione X Campitelli. Parte I* (Rome, 1975), 60, 62-63.

Ragionieri, Pina. *Michelangelo tra Firenze e Roma*, catalogue for the exhibition, Rome and Syracuse 2003 - 04 (Florence, 2003), 146-49.

For *vedute*, see: J.M. Wiesel, *Visioni di Roma* (Florence, n.d.), plate 47 (G. B. Falda 1658); Barbara Jatta and Joseph Connors, *Vedute Romane di Lievin Cruyl* (Rome, 1989), 43 (cat. N. 8), 54 (*veduta* dated 1665); A. M. Hind, *Giovanni Battista Piranesi* (London, 1922), n. 38 (*veduta* circa 1757). All the depictions tend to flatten the slope, not showing how steep it was.

◈ NOTES

1   Water pressure strong enough for the top of the Janiculum was long a problem. For instance, in his diary (July 9, 1913), Gorham Stevens notes, "The City refuses to send water to top of NB." [NB=New Building, the Main Building of the Academy, then under construction]. Again, in 1926, Stevens records many problems about water, at the Villa Chiaraviglio, at the Villa Richardson, and in garden areas. The large reservoir behind the Renaissance façade in the Janiculum park was constructed to meet some of these needs. It is part of the A.C.E.A. system (the Roman water authority), as signs on the gate to the right of the façade indicate, and it is actively maintained by A.C.E.A. personnel. The diary of Gorham Stevens, a Director of the Academy, is stored in archival material held at the Library of the American Academy.

2   Ms. Ragionieri provides interesting comments on the *vedute* of the so-called house of Michelangelo (Giuseppe Galli, Paul Letarouilly, and an anonymous artist of ca. 1850). She observes that Galli's lithograph (1825) carries the first reference to the house on Via delle Tre Pile as Michelangelo's, and she supports the identification of "la casa di Macel de'Corvi" near S. Maria di Loreto as Michelangelo's true Roman residence. But she is confused in identifying from which house the façade on the Janiculum comes (149).

◈ **ADDENDUM**

Meisha Hunter

Contrary to what one might expect to find behind the façade of the so-called "House of Michelangelo," there is no grand entrance hall or salone; there are no corridors. Immediately beyond the wooden doors of the reconstructed street-wall façade is the *Serbatoio di Gianicolo*, a two-story high rectangular utilitarian chamber, c. 40 x 20 meters, bisected by a deep concrete-paved balcony at grade level. The balcony is terminated in a simple metal railing overlooking a chamber below street level with a two-story blank wall opposite the entrance door. The deep open chamber is punctuated by large red, blue, and yellow distribution pipes, each measuring approximately a meter in diameter, carrying water in and out, as well as metal access stairs for servicing the pipes. The wall and pipes conceal a large *castellum* beyond, which is not publicly accessible. Located in the yard adjacent to the *Serbatoio* are the field offices and servicing areas for the A.C.E.A. (*Azienda Comunale Energia Elettrica ed Acque*, Rome's Municipal Enterprise for Electricity and Water).

The A.C.E.A. operates the *Serbatoio di Gianicolo* (constructed 1938-1941) from this location on the Passeggiata del Gianicolo. The *Serbatoio* is the primary distribution center for potable water within intra-mural Rome sourced from the Peschiera (1949, 1971) and Capore aqueducts (1979). The Peschiera aqueduct, whose construction was initiated under *Azienda Governatoriale Elettricità ed Acque* (Governmental Enterprise for Electricity and Water, precursor to A.C.E.A.) draws water from drainage tunnels in Monte Nuria, east of Rieti (60 km north of Rome) and reaches the City via two tunnels, dating from 1940/1949, and 1971, respectively, when the Capore aqueduct was brought on line.

As of 2005, the A.C.E.A. provides services to approximately 3,700,000 residents in the area of Central Latium-Rome, including the City of Rome as well as an additional 111 municipalities. It is responsible for managing all phases of potable and non-potable water collection, transportation, distribution, and purification. It should be noted that the water from the *Serbatoio del Gianicolo* is potable, whereas alternate sources of non-potable water are reserved for fountains and agricultural purposes (i.e.: Acqua Paola). In addition to Rome's historic aqueducts, the A.C.E.A. procures water from ten aqueduct sources (including the Peschiera, Capore, Acqua Marcia and Simbrivio [Simbruini]), maintains more than 6,000 kilometers of distribution pipes, includes three reservoir tanks with a storage capacity of 480,000 cubic meters, and hosts 70 purification plants at different locations throughout the city. All potable water for the Janiculum, including the water used for drinking and cooking at the American Academy, comes from this *Serbatoio*.

◈ **REFERENCES**

A.C.E.A. website http://web.aceaspa.it/acea/acea_eng/index.html

Aicher, Peter. "Aqueducts of Modern Rome and their Displays," *Guide to the Aqueducts of Ancient Rome* (Wauconda, IL, 1995), 169-70.

Coppa, Giorgio et al. "L'Acquedotto Paolo-Traiano," "Il Sistema Acquedottistico Peschiera-Capore," *Acque e acquedotti a Roma 1870-1984* (Rome, 1984), 128-33, 134-89.

Piccininni, R. "Il serbatoio del Gianicolo (Peschiera)," *Trionfo dell'Acqua* (Rome, 1986), 304-08.

Rinne, Katherine Wentworth. Serbatoio del Gianicolo. Object ID 0481. *Aqua Urbis Romae*. http://www.iath.virginia.edu/rome/first.html

N.B. We are indebted to Christiano Franceschini of the A.C.E.A. for his tour of the facilities and for his valuable information.

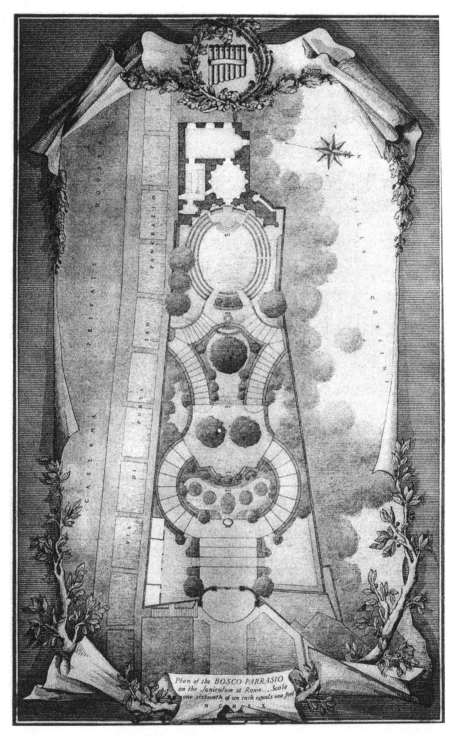

Fig. 31. 1. E. Lawson's drawing of the Bosco Parrasio. Photograph, Photographic Archive of the AAR, published in Lawson's "Bosco Parrasio, Rome," *Landscape Architecture* 19.3 (April, 1929), 171-74.

CHAPTER 31

BOSCO PARRASIO

Allan Ceen

> Bosco Parrasio is that place where the Arcadians gather
> to exercise in song and poetry, and to give of themselves
> in open proof of their talent.
>
> 1761, M. G. Morei,
> *Memorie istoriche dell'adunanza degli Arcadi*

Bosco Parrasio is a half-acre villa on the steeply sloping flank of the Janiculan hill. Its narrow area is confined between the ancient (third century) Aurelian city walls and the even more ancient trace of the Via Aurelia Vetus, the modern Via di Porta San Pancrazio. It is entered by a gate set in a concave wall, facing the first curve of Via Garibaldi. The gate gives access to an elaborate three-tiered garden with stairways whose design is remarkably similar to that of the contemporary Spanish steps. Upon reaching the top level one enters a small oval amphitheater which backs onto a curved wall with engaged columns. Its plan is beautifully illustrated in a 1920 drawing by the first Fellow of the American Academy in Rome in Landscape Architecture named Edward Lawson[1] [fig. 31. 1]. At the top of the drawing Lawson put the emblem of the Arcadians, which he describes as "a Syrinx, the Pipes of Pan, encircled by laurel [sacred to Apollo] and pine [sacred to Pan], emblematic of the pastoral chants of Theocritus and Virgil." But who were the Arcadians?

When the self-exiled Queen Christina of Sweden died in Rome in 1689, she left behind a circle of literati and artists many of whom became the founding members of the Accademia degli Arcadi the following year. Arcadia was a region in ancient Greece inhabited by a pastoral people. The members of the Academy saw themselves as simple shepherds meeting in sylvan locations: Bosco Parrasio (*Bosco* = woods) was a reference to a wooded site in Greek Arcadia sacred to Apollo, the god of poetry and pastoral pursuits (among other attributes). The stated purpose of the *Arcadi*, as they called themselves, was to "exterminate bad taste," and to cleanse Italian poetry from the "barbarisms" of current (seventeenth century) poets. Each member adopted a classical name such as Elpino, Palemone or Opico, by which they

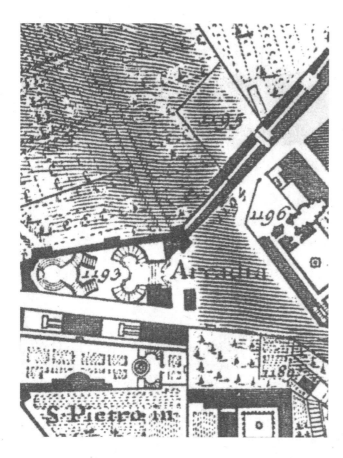

Fig. 31. 2. Enlarged section of the Nolli map of 1748 showing the Arcadia in the center (1193) with its curved staircases and theatrical setting at the top of the stairways.

were addressed by other members. Their chosen meeting place was always a garden, preferably with a little wood, which was intended to embody the bucolic character of their pursuits.

In October of 1690 Giovan Maria Crescimbeni presided over the first meeting of the *Arcadi* in a "small pleasing wood in the garden of the [Franciscan] Padri Minori Riformati Osservanti in S. Pietro in Montorio."[2] This garden, which was alongside the left flank of the church, was absorbed into the Via Garibaldi in the late nineteenth century. In the following years, the *Arcadi* were hosted in the gardens of one of their number, in seven different locations before finally acquiring their own site and building the Bosco Parrasio in 1725. It is worth following their peregrinations around the city:

1690-91	Mattei gardens near S. Pietro in Vincoli [no longer there]
1691	Riario gardens (Palazzo Corsini on Via della Lungara)
1693	Orti Farnesiani on the Palatine hill
1699	Salviati gardens (Palazzo Salviati on Via della Lungara)
1705	Giustiniani gardens outside Porta del Popolo [no longer there]
1707	Ginnasi gardens next to S. Sabina on the Aventine hill

From the early stages the *Arcadi* conducted their meetings in the gardens (listed above) seated around a *"fosso rotondo"* (a round hollow). Three such circular shapes can be identified on the 1748 Nolli map, in the gardens of the Mattei, the Farnese and the Ginnasi. The amphitheater in the Bosco Parrasio on the Janiculan Hill is oval, reflecting the con-

Fig. 31. 3. The Casino, curved back wall of the amphitheater at the top of the double staircase. Photograph, N.W. Goldman, 2006.

temporary Baroque taste for that shape over the circular form [fig. 31. 3].

At different times the *Arcadi* were a curious mixture of poets (Pietro Metastasio, Vittorio Alfieri, Goethe), architects (Carlo Fontana), scientists (Isaac Newton), playwrights (Carlo Goldoni), artists (Antonio Canova), and nobles aspiring to be intellectual. Pope Clement XI Albani was an Arcadian and took on the name of Almano. In 1724 an illustrious Arcadian, King John V of Portugal (reigned 1706-1750), known as "the Magnanimous," donated 4,000 crowns to the academy for the purpose of providing a permanent location for the meetings of the *Arcadi*. The garden and casino were then built on the design of Antonio Canevari.

By the early nineteenth century the villa had fallen into disrepair. It was restored by the architect Giovanni Azzurri, who completely remodeled the casino [fig. 31. 3]. The Bosco Parrasio is currently being restored (2005). The academy still exists, but does not meet in the Bosco Parrasio.[3]

NOTES

1   Edward Lawson, FAAR 1920. "Bosco Parrasio, Rome" in *Landscape Architecture*, 19.3 (April, 1929), 171-74.

2   G.M. Crescimbeni. *Storia dell'Accademia degli Arcadi* (Rome, 1712); as quoted by C. D'Onofrio. *Roma non vale un' abiura* (Rome, 1976), 270.

3   For a literary setting using the Bosco Parrasio, see K. A. Geffcken, "Crawford's *Cecilia*: Conversations on the Janiculum," in *Qui Miscuit Utile Dulci, Festschrift Essays for Paul Lachlan MacKendrick*, ed. G. Schmeling (Wauconda, Illinois, 1998), 185-99.

Fig. 32. 1. Eric Baade and his wife Isobel on a
riverboat cruise in Russia after his retirement.

CHAPTER 32

ROME 50 YEARS AGO

Eric Baade

N.B.: The late and greatly missed Eric Baade (1928-1998) was longtime Latin Master and Chair of Classics at the Brooks School, North Andover, Massachusetts. Through the years he and his wife Isobel maintained close contact with Rome [fig. 32. 1]. Besides his teaching in 1973-75 at St. Stephen's School, he and Isobel regularly spent the months of January and February at Pensione Fersen, just off Piazza Cucchi, helping the *Contessa* Olga Fersen with the running of her household. For a memorial essay on Eric Baade, see Corey Brennan's article in the *Society of Fellows News* (Spring 1999), 24. Those interested in the Monteverde of fifty years ago would enjoy two books of photographs published by the Associazione Culturale "Montedoro": *Come Eravamo* (1999) and *Ricordi Monteverdini* (2002) both issued by Palombi, Rome. (Katherine A. Geffcken)

In January of 1992, after a lecture at the Villa Aurelia, my wife Isobel and I, with Norma Goldman, were attempting, not very successfully, to cross the street at Porta San Pancrazio. When we happened to mention that forty years ago one could have strolled across without even a glance in either direction, Norma found this hard to believe. When we went on to tell more about the Rome of those days, she asked us to write down for her some of our reminiscences. We are glad to do this; but we want first to make it clear that these are not the sour reminiscences of a couple of elderly *laudatores temporis acti*. Rome has changed, but to those who love her she remains forever intensely lovable; and for every delight lost she manages to supply a new one.

I first saw Rome in 1950, as a member of the Academy Summer Session. I returned in 1953 as a member of the Cosa excavation staff, and again in 1955, to renew acquaintance with a beautiful and charming Scottish girl I had met in 1953. In 1956 we married and returned for a year, for I had won a Prix de Rome and could call myself FAAR 57.

We were just in time to see Rome as it was; the changes began in the mid-fifties and went on more and more rapidly. The oddest thing to remember now is that the Academy was at that time on the edge of the city. Where the blocks of shops and apartments west of Via Giacinto Carini now stand were meadow or farmland. The Ristorante Scarpone was "out in the country." On the northwest corner of

Giacinto Carini and Fratelli Bonnet was the Mei brothers' rustic trattoria, with a large garden. As you walk around Monteverde Vecchio you can easily distinguish the post-mid-fifties architecture from the rather Edwardian-looking buildings of the early part of the century and the Fascist or Futurist style, with its broad undecorated window-frames and its unfinished-looking columns, without capitals or entablatures. Everything else that you see was open country, with occasional farmhouses, some examples or fragments of which still appear among the modern constructions. So much was Rome felt to be bounded by its walls that on *Ferragosto* (the August 15th holiday), when it was the inflexible custom for everyone to leave the city and spend the day in the country, many Trasteverines came to picnic just outside Porta San Pancrazio or in the fields alongside the Via di San Pancrazio. In those days Rome within the walls was empty on 15 August: all shops and restaurants were closed, no buses or taxis ran, and the city seemed eerily abandoned by all humanity. Only the Vatican had businesses as usual, and there were opportunists with trucks who stuck bus numbers on their windshields and ferried pilgrims from the various railway stations to Piazza San Pietro. It was strange to see a crowd of nuns herded together in the back of a truck, trying to maintain their balance as it careened through the empty streets.

But when the people left the city by coming just outside Porta San Pancrazio, they were indeed in the country: it was not unusual to see flocks of sheep, accompanied by shepherds with pipes and whistles, crossing or even moving along Via Giacinto Carini. In the houses which did exist then, many people kept hens and occasionally a goat or two, so that academicians could be awakened by the crowing of cocks and soothed at their work by the comfortable sounds of rusticity, rather than by the roar of traffic. Even in the heart of the city, the dominant sounds were those of running water and human voices. The fountains flowed more abundantly, in those days before worries about erosion damage tamed them, and water from the fountains could be heard everywhere. (The *Fontanone*, Acqua Paola, however, did not flow at all, its aqueduct having been damaged in the war and not repaired until 1955.)

The human voices were those of the Romans, who used to sing a lot and spoke loudly and unselfconsciously to strangers. During the hour of the *passeggiata*, the sound of chattering and laughing became almost deafening. (The *passeggiata* was an evening stroll everyone took.)

There was, of course, little competition from traffic noises. There were many more bicycles and scooters than motorcycles and automobiles. The automobiles that did exist were not menacing. It was possible to make a considerable dent in a FIAT *Topolino* with nothing heavier than the toe of your shoe, so drivers tended to be very polite to pedestrians. The scooter was the real family vehicle. Antimo, one of the Academy staff, used to take his whole family for outings on his Vespa, his wife riding pillion and holding the baby, with the older girl wedged between her and her husband, while the little girl stood on the floorboard between Antimo's knees. The Vespa was barely visible in the midst of this globe of human bodies.

The voices that one heard offered a music rather different from the TV Italian one hears today. In 1950 only 18% of Italians spoke Italian, as opposed to more than 75% now. In Trastevere, which was then inhabited entirely by Trasteverini, one heard their language, which most of them called *Romanesco* — but which my friends, who mostly came from Rione Monti, called *Romanaccio*, insisting that the dialect which centered on what had been the *Subura* (*Suburra* in modern Italian) of ancient Rome was the true *Romanesco*. In any case, the dialects, and those who spoke them, remained, for the most part, in their own *rioni*: one would not in those days have seen a trattoria in Piazza Risorgimento advertising *"la mejo pastasciutta der monno."*

With so few internal combustion engines in use, the outlook from the Gianicolo was much different. The Castelli Romani were nearly always visible, not just very rarely, as now, and often looked near enough to reach out and touch. The hilltowns were sharply outlined by day, and at night one could see their lights twinkling. The Tiber, while not so clean as the air, was clean enough to swim in, and there were numerous swimming-clubs whose headquarters were barges anchored along the banks. One of these had the charming Virgilian name of the *"Rari Nantes."* If you were poor, as we were in those days, you could swim for free upriver at Acqua Acetosa, where cane brakes provided a place to change, and where you could leave your clothing without fear of thieves.

Visual pollution was also much less. In those pre-aerosol-and-felt-tip marker days, graffiti really were *graffiti,* messages scratched through the *rosso di Roma* coating of buildings to the white plaster or stucco beneath. Even when they were technically not graffiti but *dipinti*, they were done with pencil, charcoal or chalk, and hence were much smaller and neater than aerosol productions. Their spelling was worse, their wit perhaps a little sharper, than what one sees today. They were, though not so visible, everywhere. Long before graffiti became really common in the rest of the world, the Romans felt that they had the right, even the duty, to write messages in public places. I remember how, visiting Villa Borghese with my friends, I was hospitably invited to write my name on one of the busts of Italy's great men, and how mystified and offended my friends were when I refused. The top of the wall near the Forum of Augustus, where I used to meet my Monti friends, was covered with dated pencil messages telling us who couldn't come, or asking us to meet someone somewhere else.

Vandalism did not extend to the mutilation of fountains and statues: most of those in Villa Sciarra were still intact, for example. Nor had the wealthier vandals stripped the Via Appia Antica of its sculptures and inscriptions.

The streets and parks were clean and free of litter. This was not because the Romans were better than they are today about casually throwing things away as soon as they were through with them, indoors or out. My friend Giancarlo would casually drop his cigarette end (we all smoked in those days, if we could get our hands on a cigarette) on the marble floor of the family flat, and when I remonstrated, he simply said, "One of my sisters will sweep it up." The place of the sisters, on the street and in the parks, was taken by the elderly: old men and women who had this way of contributing some small amount to the family income. They used ordinary brooms made of twigs. Those too old or incapacitated to sweep the streets made a little money for the family by begging, a quite respectable occupation then. There were many beggars, neatly dressed and not at all importunate: they merely held out a hand to the passer-by, and rewarded with a blessing even the smallest contribution. This might be quite small: one-lira bills (about 1/6 cent) were still in circulation, and even when the aluminum coinage was introduced, anything above L. 100 was paper money. One always gave these beggars something, however poor one might be one-self. Not so to the Gypsies: Romans never gave to them. They were much less in evidence than they are today: there were a few in the *centro*, but always wasted-looking mothers with diseased-looking babies. It was a revelation to me the first time I saw a bunch of them going to "work" on a bus, laughing and gossiping, and with most of the babies standing on their own feet and looking quite robust.

But everyone gave to the elderly, and in fact age carried a great deal of respect. Teen-agers and young adults spent their free time with their parents and older relatives by preference. It was only when their company was not wanted at home that they spent any time hanging out together. And these groups, when they did exist, were entirely male. Girls went out only if chaperoned by a female relative. In fact it was considered hardly respectable for a girl who wasn't engaged-to-be-married to go out at all, even with a chaperon. It is not surprising that nominal, non-binding engagements were entered into fairly easily. What we called the "Morals Police" (actually Public Decency Police, I think) were on hand to inhibit public displays of affection, and to issue warnings to women whose tops were too low-cut or skirts too short (I never saw them warn a man). What would now be X-rated films were never shown in Rome, and pornography was never openly for sale.

Young middle-class social life was obviously somewhat restricted, but sometimes my friends would put on a dance. In those days, EUR consisted of a few buildings which had been put up for the ill-fated World's Fair of 1942 — the complex was generally known as the *Quarant'e Due* — gradually falling into disrepair. In one of these abandoned buildings, with a few holes in the floor, we held our dances. Music was provided by taking turns on the guitar and accordion, or by a portable wind-up phonograph. Refreshments were tea, made on a spirit stove, and lots of little cookies. All the aunts and grandmothers sat on folding chairs along the wall, watching the dancing. Those of us who were not *fidanzati* had to ask those who were for permission to dance with their girls, and occasionally a short interview with a chaperon would also be required.

It is amazing now to remember how cloistered the women were. The five female members of Giancarlo's family could not go out on the street unless one of the men, or one of the two grandmothers, accompanied them. Further, there was a lock on the telephone dial (only the two fathers had keys), so that it could be used only for incoming calls. Women of the servant class were better off, since they could go shopping unaccompanied.

Wineshops were very numerous, since the Castelli in those days were covered with small family vineyards, every one of which maintained a little shop, manned by one of the sons or brothers, in the city. These shops were all alike: dark, cool, rather vinegary-smelling. A large marble slab served as a rear wall, in which there were four spigots: one for sweet red wine, one for dry red wine, one for sweet white wine, and one for dry white wine. You had to bring your own bottle. The bottle was usually a *fiasco,* which held one glass less than two liters. The left-over glass was drunk at one of the two or three tiny tables provided. This sociable mid-morning drink gave the cooks and housemaids a kind of social life denied to housewives.

Rome was much better provided with public toilets forty years ago, but the vast majority were of course only for men. There were urinals everywhere — one in fact just outside the Porta San Pancrazio, across from the bar. They were all along the river, on both sides, near most of the gates in the walls, in the public parks, and at many street corners. Some were shielded by metal or concrete walls, but many had merely two small panels at the sides, not reaching the ground, and (if there were windows above) a bit of a roof. There were minimalist conveniences of this kind along the parapet of the roof of St. Peter's, over the treasury.

Once the men were home from work, the women could get out. True, there were large stag gatherings when the wives were left at home, but on a typical evening women would join their husbands. The wives I knew in the Monti would cook the dinner, wrap it up, and meet their husbands at a local pizzeria or trattoria, where they would eat their home-cooked food and drink the establishment's wine. The proprietors seemed to welcome this arrangement. No one, in fact, lived at home: they merely slept there. With no television, the entertainment was all outside the home. Just as today, there were few night clubs, and those rather dreary. Night life consisted in going to a restaurant and sitting over a meal until late at night, exchanging backchat with families at other tables and listening to the singers. These singers were usually very good, often the composers of their own songs, sometimes winners of national song contests. They were perhaps like our Vegas entertainers, but they were not attached to any particular place, and would move from one restaurant to another, collecting money from everyone when they had finished their songs, or perhaps getting a little extra for answering requests. Some would even improvise a sort of *stornello* on demand: I remember that I had one of these created in my honor the night before I left Rome in 1957.

The songs were not pan-European or international in style, but specifically Italian — or rather specifically Roman or Neapolitan. In neither case was the typical popular song a love song, unless it was addressed to the city herself. If falling in love with a woman was mentioned, it was usually to describe how treacherous she was, or how much pain the affair was causing one's poor old mother. Sung well, these songs were an emotional experience: it seemed rude just to go on eating in the presence of such emotion; so your food would get cold while you sat with a fork halfway to your mouth, in unbreakable eye-contact with someone who sang of his blasted hopes or his unbearable homesickness. Even during the few comic songs you hardly dared eat, since you were overcome with real or feigned laughter.

One reason no one lived at home was that there was not room. My friend 267

Giancarlo's middle-class family occupied a four-room-with-kitchen flat. In it lived Giancarlo, his father and mother, his father's mother and (in winter, when her home at Ostia was too cold) his mother's mother, his brother, his three sisters, the husband and son of one of the sisters, his father's brother, his wife, and their two sons. There was one cold-water tap, in the kitchen. There was a toilet in a little closet, which was flushed by bringing a bucket of water from the kitchen. The stove was exactly like the ones in the excavations of Pompeii, a masonry bench with iron tripods to raise the pots above the charcoal fire. Adjustments to temperature were made by Giancarlo's maternal grandmother, who fanned the charcoal rapidly or slowly with a turkey wing.

This family, though crowded, did have an apartment. Many quite respectable people did not. It is hard even for me, looking at the general affluence of Romans today, to believe how very poor many people were then. Most of them found shelter somewhere. The vaults that support the Baths of Caracalla housed a great many families; I remember the sad day when the police moved them all out and sealed the vaults with masonry, sending them, unwilling, to live in new public housing. There was even a family, complete with goat and chickens, living in the mouth of the Cloaca Maxima! These were *abusivi*, living unsanctioned by the government; but many ancient monuments were inhabited with government approval. A family lived in the tower at the Largo Argentina; four small families lived atop the huge podium of the Tomb of Romulus, and kept their livestock in the great tomb chamber.

The *abusivi* dwellings were without plumbing (unless we count the excellent drainage in the Cloaca); with so many urinals and fountains all over the city this was not really a problem. A young man used to come to the big wisteria fountain in Villa Sciarra every afternoon one summer. Modestly sheltering behind a hedge he would remove everything except his trousers. He would then carefully wash himself at the fountain, and then wash his clothes, which he would spread out in the sun to dry while he had his midday *riposo*.

Strangely enough, in those postwar days, when everyone had so much less money, there were few purse-snatchings, no muggings, no street people in the modern sense. Less strangely, there were also no drunks, at least beyond the level of hilarity and song. Because there was so little ready cash, nearly everything that could be was sold *sciolto*. In a grocery you bought jam from a big open tin: they scooped up whatever weight you wanted in a paper cone. Semi-dried blood was sold in the same way from a big heap of it in a glass case in the butcher shop. And at the tobacconist's, cigarettes were unwrapped and put into little bins, to be bought one or two at a time.

People did not think of themselves as poor, and there was a sense of community, of camaraderie, which made every part of the city feel like home. This is the Rome which is fixed in our hearts. When we show friends around now, we find it hard to see the city as it must appear to them. One of our college-age friends startled us by saying, "Rome? but it's so dirty, so crowded, so noisy, so much traffic!" For us, Rome remains as we first saw her, in the summers of 1950 and 1953, in a kind of honey-colored glow.

Fig. 32. 2 Piazzale Aurelio, Bar "G" and Trattoria, 1939.
Anonymous photographer, AAR postcard.

A Note on "Janiculum"

Katherine A. Geffcken

In *Aeneid* 8. 357-8. Vergil conveys the tradition that Father Janus established a citadel to which the name "Janiculum" was attached (cf. Ovid, *Fasti* 1. 245-6). But the noun "Janiculum" is far from simple. At first glance, it looks like the god's name (that is, *ianus*, a gate or archway) followed by the diminutive suffix. The hill, however, is not at all little. It is, in fact, the highest hill in Rome, the so-called "balcony of Rome." Paolo Liverani has suggested that linguistically the word "Janiculum" contains the same suffix as towns like Corniculum and Ocriculum. But evidence for an early settlement on the hill has not so far been found, nor is there any record of a temple or grove of Janus. Building on the remarkable work of Louise Adams Holland, Lawrence Richardson, jr. has argued that "Janiculum" was the name of the early fortified gate on the highest point of the Via Aurelia, approximately where now stands the Porta San Pancrazio. This proposal harmonizes with Festus's statement (Festus 93L) that the Janiculum was so named because through it the early Roman people crossed over into the Etruscan countryside. Placed then on the height overlooking Rome, this passageway had to be fortified because Rome was especially vulnerable to attack from Etruscan territory. If "Janiculum" originally designated a small gate and a citadel, when did it come to mean the whole hill, as we use the name today? And did the name, at least in adjectival form, extend into Trastevere, as "Janiculan district" in epigraphical evidence suggests? For full discussion, see:

Holland, Louise Adams. *Janus and the Bridge* (Rome, 1961), especially 224-33.
Ianiculum – Gianicolo: Storia, Topografia, Monumenti, Leggende dall' Antichità al Rinascimento. *Acta Instituti Romani Finlandia* 16, ed. E. M. Steinby (Rome, 1996), especially 3-12 (P. Liverani), and 13-27 (F. Coarelli).
Liverani, P. "Ianiculum," in *LTUR* 3, ed. E. M. Steinby (Rome, 1996), 89-90.
Richardson, L., jr. "The Janiculum and *Ianicula* in Ancient Rome," in *Homenaje a José Mª Blázquez* III, *ARYS* 2, eds J. Mangas and J. Alvar (Madrid, 1996), 293-300.
Richardson, L., jr. *A New Topographical Dictionary of Ancient Rome* (Baltimore and London, 1992), 205.

GLOSSARY

aditus entrance

Ai Caduti to the fallen (=the Dead)

allée a passage in a garden or park bordered by trees or shrubs

apparati temporary stage sets or celebratory arches

"Avanti" "Forward!"

belvedere a terrace or passage (often with a balustrade) offering a fine view

bersaglieri riflemen; sharpshooters (sing. *bersagliere*)

Cacciatori delle Alpi lit. hunters of the Alps, a volunteer unit of ca. 3,000 men commanded by Garibaldi in North Italy (campaign in the Alps, 1859)

cantina cellar, esp. wine cellar

casino a small house (*casa*), often a house in villa property; often, in modern Italian, a brothel

Castelli Romani lit. Roman castles, that is, the hilltowns near Rome

Cavalieri della morte Cavalrymen of death

Colonello Direttore Colonel Director

Comune di Roma the municipality of Rome

cortile courtyard, sometimes surrounded by a portico

dipinti paintings

edicola a sculpted frame enclosing a fresco or image in relief, often fixed to walls or corners of buildings

EUR=Esposizione Universale di Roma, now denoting a quarter south of Rome in which an international exhibition was planned for 1942, and though construction began in 1938, progress came to a halt in WWII

Ferragosto the August holiday on the 15th of August: Assumption of the Virgin Mary

fiasco failure; but in this volume, in its second meaning, a flask of wine

FIAT Topolino (*topolino* = a little mouse, esp. Mickey Mouse), a baby car, manufactured by FIAT

fidanzati sing: *fidanzato/a*, pl: *fidanzati/e*, lit. betrothed, but often just meaning steady boy/girl friend

Fontanone lit. big fountain, esp. the Acqua Paola Fountain

Garibaldini Garibaldi's soldiers and later units developing from the Garibaldi tradition

Giornata Lincea per celebrare le dimostrazioni astronomiche di Galileo Galilei "A daylong program sponsored by the Academy of the Lincei to celebrate the astronomical demonstrations of Galileo Galilei"

Grande Oriente d'Italia di Palazzo Giustiniani a Masonic group, headquartered 1896–1926 at Palazzo Giustiniani in downtown Rome

heroon a grave or temple or sacred area dedicated to a hero or divinity

"La mejo pastasciutta der monno" "the best *pastasciutta* of the world" (in *romanesco*)

Lancieri della Morte lancers of death – see above, *"cavalieri della morte"*

Mausoleo ossario gianicolense Janiculan ossuary mausoleum

mezzanino a floor of half height, often between ground floor and *piano nobile*

Monti see *Rione Monti*; *monte* mountain

Museo Garibaldino Museum of Garibaldi and the Garibaldini

Museo Storico dei Bersaglieri Historical Museum of the Bersaglieri

osteria inn or tavern

palazzo from *palatium* – a large, stately building (English "palace")

passeggiata driving or walking, or the place where one does a *passeggiata*

Passeggiata del Gianicolo road in the Janiculum Park, formerly part of the *Giardini Corsini*, the Corsini Gardens

piano nobile the most impressive floor in a palazzo or villa house, usually the *primo piano*

pianterreno ground floor

portone literally, big door. The main door or doors of a building

pozzo well

primo piano first floor = second floor USA

pineta pine grove

Quarant'e Due 40 and 2

Quattro Venti Four winds

Rari Nantes, from Vergil *Aen.* 1.118: "[men] few and far between, swimming" (ship-wrecked Trojans)

rione a section of a city. The Janiculum is part of Rione XIII: Trastevere

Rione Monti Rome's Rione I, a large area extending from the Imperial Fora east to S. Giovanni in Laterano

riposo rest

Risorgimento renaissance or revival: name of the period in which and process by which Italy was unified

Romanaccio pejorative name for the dialect of Rome (*-accio* = ugly)

Romanesco dialect of Rome

Rosso di Roma the red of Rome

sala room

salone lit. large room – a major living room

scarponi lit. big shoes

sciolto lit. undone or loosened – as in *vino sciolto*, open wine, sold by the liter, glass, etc.

scudi the *scudo* was an old Italian money unit, either gold or silver, varying in value according to the period and minting authority

secondo piano second floor = third floor USA

sotterraneo underground floor, basement

stemma coat of arms

stornello a three line ditty with the third line rhyming with the first

Subura in ancient Rome, the district between the Esquiline and Viminal Hills, a not respectable area

temenos an enclosed sacred area, often with a temple in the center

temporale a powerful thunder and lightning rainstorm

Trasteverini people of Trastevere

vascello ship

veduta, (pl.) *vedute* view, views, esp. the great series of prints in the seventeenth and eighteenth centuries by Falda, Piranesi, and Vasi

vigna, (pl.) *vigne* literally vineyard, but *vigne* usually included orchards and other plantings

villa country property, including land, house, and other buildings, gardens, and *vigne*

villeggiatura country holiday, summering in the country, country residence

vincolo a legal bond or tie, prohibiting the sale, alienation, export, or destruction of property or art or other objects

zona area, neighborhood (Eng. zone)

Earlier versions of many chapters in this book previously appeared in the annual *Newsletter of the Classical Society of the American Academy in Rome* (CSAAR). These have all been updated and/or revised.

"June 3, 1849, and Angelo Masina" (1988), 7-9 by Katherine A. Geffcken.

"The History of the Villa Aurelia" (1989), 8-12, by Lawrence Richardson, jr.

"Ruminations on Mrs. Heyland's Will" (1989), 12-14, by Elfriede Knauer.

"Morosini, & Casino Malvasia" (1989), 15-18, by Katherine A. Geffcken.

"The Aqueducts of Transtiberim and the AAR" (1990), 6-8, by Lawrence Richardson, jr.

"The Mills of the Janiculum" (1990), 9, by Malcolm Bell.

"June 26, 1849, Anita Garibaldi, and the Villa Spada" (1990), 15-18, by Katherine A. Geffcken.

"Rome 40 Years Ago" (1992), 12-15, by Eric Baade.

"Who were the Fratelli Bonnet?" (1993), 15-17, by Katherine A. Geffcken.

"The Botanical Garden of Rome on the Janiculum (1994), 17- 18 by Antonella Bucci.

"The Vascello: Part I" (1995), 19-21; Part II (1996), 15-19, by Katherine A. Geffcken.

"Renovating the Casa Rustica" (1996), 20-21, by Susan Wood.

"The Casino Riario-Corsini and the Fate of the Giardini Corsini" (1997), 17-21, by Katherine A. Geffcken.

"Burials on the Janiculum: the Cemetery of Santo Spirito" (1998), 17-21, by Katherine A. Geffcken.

"Scarpone" (1999), 12-17, by Katherine A. Geffcken.

"The Vicolo Cieco and Paolo Narducci" (2000), 14-16, by Katherine A. Geffcken.

"The Drummer Boys of 1849 and the Scalea del Tamburino" (2002), 13-14. by Katherine A. Geffcken.

"The Church of San Pancrazio," (2004), 8-12, by Katherine A. Geffcken.

An earlier version of Steven Bedford's article on the Main Building appeared first in *AMACADMY*, Summer 1991, "McKim, Mead & White and the New Academy Building," 3, 15.

Acknowledgements from Katherine A. Geffcken

For help in all ways, I am grateful to: Norma and Bernard Goldman; the Library staff of the American Academy in Rome, especially Christina Huemer and former librarian Antonella Bucci; William Barcham, Malcolm Bell, Joseph Connors, Nina Fersen, Domicella d'Incisa di Camerana, Wayne Linker, Sara MacVane, Helen Nagy, Suzanne Nicholson, Gearoid O'Broin, Antonio Ortolan, Pina Pasquantonio, Cristina Puglisi, Lawrence Richardson, jr, Patricia Waddy, Susan Wood; the staff of the Academy's Photographic Archive; the 2003 National Endowment for the Humanities Summer Seminar on the Risorgimento. Others who generously helped with specific information, I thank at the ends of chapters.

For support and encouragement, I am also grateful to: Charles and Mary Babcock, Sheila Dickison, Lisa Fentriss, Elaine Gazda, Judith Hallett, Elfriede (Kezia) Knauer, Anne Laidlaw, Gino and Stacy Mazzone, Anna Marguerite McCann, Helen North, and Michael C. J. Putnam.

Besides these listed above, many other colleagues have stimulated my interest in a building or a street by a question or a comment. I thank you all.

INDEX

Numbers in boldface indicate main entry; numbers in italics indicate illustration.